Anywhere
out of the world

MANCHESTER
1824

Manchester University Press

This life of ours is a hospital, in which all the patients are obsessed with a desire to change beds. One would prefer to suffer near the stove, and another thinks he would soon recover near the window.

I always have the feeling that I would be better anywhere except where I actually am, and the idea of a removal is one which I am constantly discussing with my Soul.

Charles Baudelaire, 'Anywhere Out of the World'

Anywhere out of the world

The work of Bruce Chatwin

JONATHAN CHATWIN

Manchester University Press

Published by Manchester University Press
Altrincham Street, Manchester M1 7JA, UK
www.manchesteruniversitypress.co.uk

British Library Cataloguing-in-Publication Data is available

Library of Congress Cataloging-in-Publication Data is available

ISBN 978 0 7190 9982 3 *paperback*

First published by Manchester University Press in hardback 2012

This paperback edition first published 2015

The publisher has no responsibility for the persistence or accuracy of URLs for any external or third-party internet websites referred to in this book, and does not guarantee that any content on such websites is, or will remain, accurate or appropriate.

Printed by Lightning Source

Contents

List of illustrations		*page*	vi
Acknowledgements			vii
List of abbreviations			ix
Introduction			1
1	Winding paths		15
2	The great unwriteable		31
3	At the end		51
4	Skin for skin		74
5	Those blue remembered hills		92
6	Transformations		113
7	The Harlequin		135
	Conclusion: A mythology for every man		155
	Appendix 1		161
	Appendix 2		162
	A Bruce Chatwin bibliography		163
	Bibliography		168
	Index		176

List of illustrations

Plates appear between pages 86–7

1 Nomad tent
2 Nomad woman, Sudan 1965
3 Nomad flocks, Sudan 1965
4 The Germans at Río Pico, Patagonia
5 Asado
6 Playing 'taba'
7 Patagonian bar
8 Abomey, Dahomey
9 Dahomey
10 West Africa
11 China, 1985
12 South Africa, 1984
13 Boat building
14 Wood surface
15 Graffiti
16 The chapel at Chora
17 Chapel view

Acknowledgements

One day in my childhood, I discovered, on the shelves of a bookcase at my home, a paperback copy of Bruce Chatwin's *The Songlines*. I was, as any nine-year-old would be, fascinated by the curious fact that I shared a surname with the author of this book, and also by the front cover image: an engraving – which I later discovered to be by William Blake – portraying a family of curly-haired Aborigines wandering through the desert. Though the contents remained inaccessible to me for another few years, that youthful moment established an interest in my fellow Chatwin which persisted throughout my childhood. When I was finally old enough to read and understand *The Songlines*, that interest developed into admiration, and a desire to read more by – and know more about – this fascinating writer. Such is the genesis of this book.

I owe a debt of gratitude to a number of people and institutions. I offer my thanks to the University of Exeter and the School of English for their support and, in particular, Robert Mack and Anthony Fothergill for their intellectual rigour and unfailing encouragement. Special thanks goes also to Bruce Woodcock at the University of Hull, who helped me get started in a number of ways.

For their commentary, insight and support, I must thank Gillon Aitken, Susannah Clapp, Robert Macfarlane and Nicholas Murray. For the use of his photographs of the chapel at Chora, many thanks to Peter Tomlinson. For their sage editorial advice, my thanks go to Jonathan Styles, Sebastian Hesse-Kastein and Claire Chatwin, as well, of course, to Matthew Frost at Manchester University Press. For her patience and support over months and years of writing, her editorial advice, her faith and her encouragement Sarah Donnelly has my sincere gratitude.

My work owes an inestimable debt to Nicholas Shakespeare. For his dedication in making accessible the details of Chatwin's complicated life, I offer my sincere thanks and admiration.

However, this work would simply not have been possible without the assistance and encouragement of Bruce's wife Elizabeth and his brother Hugh. For their magnificent support – too extensive to detail here – I offer my heartfelt thanks.

Finally, it should be noted that, despite the coincidence of that shared surname, I have no known family connection to Bruce or any of his relations.

Abbreviations

AOR   *Anatomy of Restlessness*
CCMM   Chatwin, Chatwin, Maclean and Murray, *Bruce Chatwin Remembered*
Footsteps   *In the Footsteps of Bruce Chatwin*
IP   *In Patagonia*
NA   *The Nomadic Alternative*
OTBH   *On the Black Hill*
P&N   *Photographs and Notebooks*
PR   *Patagonia Revisited*
TS   *The Songlines*
U   *Utz*
US   *Under the Sun: The Letters of Bruce Chatwin*
VO   *The Viceroy of Ouidah*
WAIDH *What Am I Doing Here*

Introduction

Ignatieff: Bruce, we're talking in a sunlit room of a farmhouse that looks over a banked meadow in which black sheep are grazing. There's a crackling fire in the grate, and we've just finished a delicious roast of lamb which Elizabeth prepared for us. The whole scene is a picture of home. For a wanderer, are you surprised at where you sit now? Is this home?
Chatwin: (*Long Pause.*) Terrible to say so, but it isn't. I don't know why, but it can never be. I couldn't explain why. It drives Elizabeth insane, but ... we have everything here, but I always wish I was somewhere else. (35–6)
Michael Ignatieff, 'Interview with Bruce Chatwin'

Diversion. Distraction. Fantasy. Change of fashion, food, love and landscape. We need them as the air we breathe. (100)
Bruce Chatwin, *Anatomy of Restlessness*

In December 1988, two days before the end of the year and less than a month before the end of his life, Bruce Chatwin dictated an encouraging letter to his friend and eventual biographer, Nicholas Shakespeare: 'So what's so awful about writing another book,' he queried. 'You can't escape your vocation' (*US* 524).

Writing did not always seem destined to be Bruce Chatwin's vocation; a sequence of false starts had to be navigated before he eventually settled down to his career. It became, however, the one steady element of a life defined by changes of direction; the only entanglement from which he never turned away.

Bruce's wife Elizabeth commented of his relationship with the craft:

Writing was for him incredibly compulsive. When we would be travelling, traipsing around somewhere and we'd go to say Venice, or somewhere in Northern Italy, or somewhere else, we'd get there and he'd arrange the room for his typewriter and then I would be sent off sightseeing ... If he spent more than about two days without being able to write he was getting twitchy. Because stuff was going around in his head the whole time. (2010)

This compulsion manifested itself in impressive productivity; in a career lasting less than twelve full years,[1] Chatwin produced six books, three of which – *The Songlines*, *Utz* and *What Am I Doing Here* – were put together whilst he struggled with serious illness. In addition, he wrote numerous features for newspapers and magazines, endless reviews, and not a few introductions to books he admired. Chatwin is often thought of as something of a dilettante, for whom literature was a secondary undertaking, subordinate to an exotic life as a traveller and socialite. The impression is utterly false; his commitment to writing was absolute. Chatwin's writing career was a litany of success. His first published work, *In Patagonia*, startled with its radical reconfiguration of the travelogue form, whilst *The Viceroy of Ouidah* consolidated an emergent reputation as an insightful chronicler of the extraordinary. His third book, *On the Black Hill*, received the Whitbread prize for best first novel, and, to a great degree, confirmed an arrival into the literary mainstream. However, it was *The Songlines*, an idiosyncratic hybrid work relating a deviating journey to investigate the Aboriginal concept of 'dreaming tracks', which truly brought Chatwin to public prominence. In July 1987 the novel reached number one in the *Sunday Times* bestseller list; it would remain in the top ten for the following nine months. Chatwin's followup to *The Songlines* seemed explicitly designed to contrast its predecessor in every way; *Utz* is a small novel concerning a sedentary Eastern European porcelain collector. It was, however, greeted with similar acclaim, and received a nomination for the Booker prize in 1988.[2]

In a 1987 review of *The Songlines* for the *New York Times*, Andrew Harvey captured the general sense of appreciation which swirled around the author: 'Nearly every writer of my generation in England has wanted, at some point, to be Bruce Chatwin; wanted, like him, to talk of Fez and Firdausi, Nigeria and Nuristan, with equal authority; wanted to be talked about, as he is, with raucous envy; wanted, above all, to have written his books … No writer has meant as much to my generation.'

However, over the course of his career and beyond, an attendant uncertainty emerged over the question of what *kind* of writer Chatwin was. 'So far the critics have been very complimentary,' he observed in a letter written a month after the publication of *In Patagonia*, 'but the FORM of the book seems to have puzzled them (as I suspect it did the publisher). There's a lot of talk of "unclassifiable prose", "a mosaic", "a tapestry", a "jigsaw", a "collage" etc.' (*US* 275). This incertitude became a familiar critical response as subsequent works emerged.

Unfortunately, however, the taxonomical queries generated by the formal ambiguity of Chatwin's writing have developed to become almost the only issues at stake in its contemporary analysis.[3] Are his books travelogues?, critics ask. Are they novels? Are they neither? And, if they are one — or if they are the other — what are the ethical and political implications of such denominations? This preoccupation has come at the expense of substantive discussion of the content and detail of Chatwin's literature. Nicholas Murray has observed the general failure of the critical establishment to 'listen carefully enough to what [Chatwin] actually said, to take seriously what he took seriously, to try to understand what made him write in the way he did' (2008). This book is an attempt to redress the balance. Intended as an overview of Chatwin's work and life as a writer, this volume seeks to address the content of his books, rather than semantic debates over their formal qualities.

Specifically, what follows will argue that, looking beyond the apparent formal diversity of Chatwin's work, one can discern in his oeuvre a significant and compelling thematic commonality. When they are examined in detail, and in the context of authorial biography, it becomes clear that all of Chatwin's books are preoccupied with a single issue: that of the affliction of restlessness, which became the 'question of questions' (*TS* 161) for Chatwin. 'All my life', he told his younger brother Hugh, 'I have searched for the nature of human restlessness' (H. Chatwin 2009).

Such an approach to Chatwin's work has been particularly supported by the insight offered by his literary archive, made available for the purposes of this study. The archive, which resides at the Bodleian Library in Oxford, and which was embargoed to the public until 2010, consists of diverse notebooks, typescripts and loose papers, all of which offer significant insight into Chatwin's working methods, his preoccupations, and his life. However, one resource contained within the archive particularly supports and extends a reading of Chatwin's work through the thematic prism of restlessness.

The Nomadic Alternative was Bruce Chatwin's first book, 'written in answer to a need to explain my own restlessness' (qtd. in Shakespeare 2000: 14), and formed an attempt to submit the notion to objective scrutiny. Chatwin struggled for years to complete a coherent draft; the manuscript he finally delivered was rejected by the commissioning publishers, Jonathan Cape. Chatwin claimed in *The Songlines* that, following its rejection by Cape, he had burnt the manuscript; in fact, he threw it into the wastepaper bin, from where his mother Margharita recovered it, commenting presciently: 'I'm sure he didn't mean to throw this away' (qtd. in *US* 378). As a result, a completed typescript of the work still exists in a foolscap folder amongst his archive in Oxford. In many ways this manuscript can, despite its manifest flaws, be seen as the *urtext* of Chatwin's oeuvre. It contains, in embryo, the philosophical conception of restlessness which he would continue to expound and expand throughout the rest of his work.

Restlessness is an undoubtedly nebulous concept. Not quite a medical actuality, yet an indisputable facet of the human condition, it is easy to understand, yet difficult to explain. Over the centuries, numerous writers and philosophers have attempted to unravel the motivation and meaning of the individual need for change; from the Gilgamesh epic to John Steinbeck and beyond, the subject has been a consistent focus of literary investigation. However, what follows does not propose to attempt to offer either a cultural history or generalised definition of restlessness. Rather, the work intends to examine Chatwin's treatment of the subject in his work, and to employ it as a unifying idea which can guide a holistic interpretation of his oeuvre.

Chatwin himself strategically avoided providing a totalising, consistent definition of restlessness; his preference, when required to offer elucidation of the term, was to fall back on the – often vague or cryptic – aphorisms of others, such as Baudelaire, who wrote of 'the great malady, horror of one's home' (qtd. in *NA* 2); Petrarch, who asked of his secretary: 'What is this strange madness, ... this mania to sleep each night in a different bed?' (qtd. in *NA* 2); and Pascal, whose observation that all of humankind's troubles stemmed from the individual's inability to stay quietly in one room was oft-cited by Chatwin.

The elision which Chatwin practised on this subject was partly born of the noted vagaries of the term – but was also calculated to ensure a degree of flexibility in his application of it. Taking Chatwin's work as a whole one can draw out a broad definition: restlessness is a condition which compels the individual to wish always to be elsewhere, and which leads to profound anxiety and dissatisfaction if the individual sufferer is forced to remain *in situ*. However, there is a complexity to both the substance and presentation of this broad theme in his oeuvre. What follows offers an account of the detail of Chatwin's approach in order to provide an overall perspective of his treatment of the subject.

Chatwin's oeuvre can, in the context of the current discussion, be initially divided into two interrelated categories: 'restlessness described' and 'restlessness explained'. The majority of Chatwin's work resides in the former category, offering a literary exploration of the affliction of restlessness through character description, authorial self-representation and metaphor.

In these descriptive works, restlessness is depicted as an individual affliction emerging from the frustrations of settlement. In Chatwin's first two books, this settlement takes the form of exile, with restlessness born specifically of a misguided longing for return to a lost homeland. *In Patagonia* presents a litany of characters afflicted by this desire. Typical is the Canary Islander from Tenerife whom the narrator encounters at Paso Roballos, and who is described as: '[h]omesick and dreaming of lost vigour' (112). He goes on to talk of 'the flowers, the trees, the farming methods and dances of his sunlit mountain in the sea' (112) whilst, in an observation which metaphorically encapsulates the impact of Patagonian life upon his pastoral dream, '[h]ailstones battered the currant bushes' (112) of his garden. Similarly, in *The Viceroy of Ouidah* the eponymous protagonist, Francisco Manoel da Silva, spends much of the novel daydreaming of a return to Brazil, stuck as he is on the west coast of Africa.

In *On the Black Hill* and *Utz*, however, it is a different manner of confinement that provokes restlessness: namely, the restrictive tyranny of domestic life. Thus, though the novel does imply a possible means of contented settlement, Lewis Jones, the restive brother of *On the Black Hill*, is depicted suffering the constraints of a life he did not choose, speculating upon an impossible existence away from his family farm and his brother:

> 'Sometimes, I lie awake and wonder what'd happen if him weren't there. If him'd gone off ... was dead even. Then I'd have had my own life, like? Had kids?'
> 'I know, I know,' she said, quietly. 'But our lives are not so simple'. (203)

Similarly, Chatwin describes Joachim Utz, the Czech porcelain collector of Chatwin's final novel, suffering the rigours of a restlessness which emerges from his wilful seclusion in his Prague apartment – and, more specifically, the burden of the possessions he has hoarded within it: 'By April ... he felt acute claustrophobia, from having spent the winter months in close proximity to the adoring Marta: to say nothing of the boredom, verging on fury, that came from living those months with lifeless porcelain' (88).

If it were the case that Chatwin's representation of restlessness relied purely on these literary foundations, any analysis of the subject would perhaps be both generalised and slight. However, the situation of these characters and the wider approach of the works they are drawn from must be viewed within the context of those other, fewer, texts that fall into the latter camp of 'restlessness explained' and which attempt to formulate an explanation for the individual frustrations and responses described. When looked at in conjunction with texts such as *The Nomadic Alternative*, that work's foster-child *The Songlines*,[4] and the numerous essays he wrote on the subject, it becomes apparent that the individual characters and situations of Chatwin's descriptive works can be read as representative of a specific framework of ideas. Both *The Nomadic Alternative* and *The Songlines* present a theory that, far from simply being a manifestation of personal dissatisfaction, restlessness emerges from a genetic predisposition towards travel and against settlement that developed in the protohistory of humankind:

> [I]n becoming human, man had acquired, together with his straight legs and striding walk, a migratory 'drive' or instinct to walk long distances through the seasons; that this 'drive' was inseparable from his central nervous system; and that, when warped in conditions of settlement, it found outlets in violence, greed, status-seeking or a mania for the new. (*AOR* 12)

In support of this theory, Chatwin invoked the lifestyle of differing groups of travelling tribespeople – 'nomads', as he generically termed them – whom he saw as exemplifying the natural state he identified. The manner of life of these nomads – ascetic, seasonal, peaceful and, of course, migratory – became totemic for Chatwin, representative of a 'Golden Age for which we preserve an instinctive nostalgia' (*AOR* 177). Much of his theoretical work on restlessness concentrates on proving this genetic heritage – and thus identifying the source of our restlessness. For, if once we were nomads, it is to be expected that settlement should frustrate us.

The effects of settlement are rendered more acute, Chatwin argues, in the condition commonly attendant upon it: civilisation, which he defines specifically as the condition of living in cities (*AOR* 75). Such a manner of living is inherently corrupting: 'Locked within their walls,' Chatwin writes of city-dwellers, referencing Diogenes, 'they committed every outrage against one another as if this were the sole object of their coming together' (*AOR* 85). On an individual level, civilised existence also encourages acquisition – it is, he writes, an inherently 'thing-oriented'

(*AOR* 171) state – which Chatwin sees as exacerbating the frustrating effects of settlement: 'Possessions disquieten their possessors' (156), Chatwin writes in *The Nomadic Alternative* – an assertion which will find its creative expression in *Utz*. The manner of living engendered by civilised settlement is simply untenable in Chatwin's view. The cure is to engineer an escape of some kind. The ideal manner of this escape becomes a central – and to some extent unresolved – point of debate traceable through Chatwin's work.

In presenting his argument, Chatwin employed a barrage of literary, philosophical, ethnographical, anthropological and religious texts, from Baudelaire to Pascal, from Robert Burton to Theodor Strehlow, constructing a vast, compelling roster of supporting literature for his notion of inherited instinct for travel, identified by Patrick Holland and Graham Huggan as 'a potpourri of materials that Chatwin, as determined bricoleur, can seize upon and utilize at will' in support of his 'highly idiosyncratic personal mythology' (169).

Such a definition is persuasive; his conception of humankind's peripatetic nature transcended the theoretical, and at times appeared to approach the level of a secular religion, with Chatwin offering up his expansive vision of a unifying genetic predisposition towards travel as a belief system to explain individual and cultural phenomena. As Nicholas Shakespeare wrote, 'The nearest thing he had to religion was his theory of restlessness' (2000: 450). This theological aspect of Chatwin's belief is evident in *In Patagonia*, where he tells the Persian, Ali, of his faith in the sacrament of walking: 'My God is the God of Walkers. If you walk hard enough you probably don't need any other God' (*IP* 43). He commented in a letter dating from the writing of *The Songlines* that: '[O]nce you enter the world of nomadism, you have to tackle Renan's dictum, "*Le désert est monothéiste*" – and from there the search for nomads becomes the search for God' (*US* 378).

Chatwin's grand mythology cannot fail to add an extra dimension to any exploration of the individual representations of restlessness in his creative work, encouraging a reading wherein the situations and characters of his books become allegorical of the author's philosophical ideas, situated in a scheme greater than the specifics of the text might indicate. That is not to imply that Chatwin's creative work acts purely as a vector for his philosophy, but rather that an awareness of the author's conception of restlessness adds a depth and complexity to any possible reading of that work.

However, as has been suggested, the arguments presented in *The Nomadic Alternative* and *The Songlines* do not posit any sort of successful totalising theory. Trading on the noted vagueness in Chatwin's work as to what 'restlessness' specifically means, these works fail – intentionally or otherwise – to offer a rationally convincing explanation of the subject, but rather provide insight into a personal belief system, with all the ambiguity, subjectivity and unreliability that implies. This book will not argue, then, that Chatwin's work offers a coherent analysis of the theme, but rather that the descriptive and explanatory elements of his work combine to create an appealing and romantic mythology of restlessness, offering empathetic portrayals of the restlessly afflicted supported by a poetic and often unstable theory that posits the affliction as resulting from a genetic call to travel. Chatwin's work transmutes the relatively prosaic and seemingly negative 'affliction' of restlessness into something grander and more appealing, in a similar manner to those Renaissance writers who constructed a romantic explanation of depression in the concept of melancholy.

The romantic appeal of Chatwin's concept of restlessness is compounded by the image presented, in his work and biography, of the author himself. In life, Chatwin clearly suffered from symptoms of the affliction that John Steinbeck referred to as the 'virus of restlessness' (1). He believed personally that this tendency had been instilled by his years as a 'war baby': 'From when I was born in 1940 until 1947, we really had no home', he told Melvyn Bragg. 'I seem to have been shunted up and down England on railway trains' (*The South Bank Show*).

Whether the genesis truly lay in his childhood or in other unarticulated neuroses, Chatwin certainly demonstrated a consistent tendency throughout his life towards sudden removal from both place and situation. His letters testify to his need for movement; his persistent fascination was always where to be next. In 1987, he wrote to his friend, the collector George Ortiz – who would provide a partial model for the character of Joachim Utz – apologising for having missed meeting him in Geneva: '[O]ur arrangements in July got a bit out of hand', he wrote. 'Now they are even worse: Prague, Budapest, Vienna, Rome, London, New York, Toronto – all in the space of a month. The Chatwin yo-yo is functioning again' (*US* 486).

Chatwin's restless tendencies are perhaps most evident in his lifelong search for the perfect dwelling; he spent many years scouting around Europe for a Mediterranean bolt-hole: 'I used to resist', comments Elizabeth, 'it became a sort of game because I didn't want to move. And then he started: "let's get a house in France, let's get a house in Italy, let's get a house in Greece, let's get a house in Spain'" (2007). Each prospective place he found, however, eventually palled for him: 'Everything was absolute paradise etc for about a month and then things were not quite what he wanted them to be' (*US* 257). Travel also played a crucial functional role in the author's literary career; like Mandelstam, the author believed 'Like dogma!' (Ignatieff 1987: 37) in the idea that rhythms of prose and of travel were inextricably linked, and his writerly need for change whilst composing was clearly a real part of the cause of Chatwin's restlessness; none of his books were begun and completed in the same location.

However, these facets of personality were transmuted and romanticised – consciously or otherwise – in both his work and its attendant publicity, creating an elevated literary persona that embodies the appeal of the 'affliction' of restlessness. This persona was built in part from biographical passages such as this, taken from an essay on Howard Hodgkin, which recounts a dinner party at Chatwin's apartment at which the artist was a guest: 'The result of that dinner party was a painting called *The Japanese Screen*,' wrote Chatwin, 'in which the screen itself appears as a rectangle of pointillist dots, the Welches as a pair of gunturrets, while I am the acid green smear on the left, turning away in disgust, away from my guests, away from my possessions, away from the "dandified" interior, and, possibly back to the Sahara' (*WAIDH* 76).[5]

The inclusion of such self-representative passages helped to build an image which finds perhaps its most resonant overall allegory in the portrait of Chatwin shot by Lord Snowdon in 1982. The picture shows the author, walking boots strung around his neck, his celebrated leather rucksack on his back, staring implacably off into the horizon. The image distills and reinforces the public impression of Chatwin: of a solitary and refined wanderer of style and erudition, strolling through the desert with nothing but a half-bottle of vintage champagne and an edition of Hemingway's *In Our Time* poking from his rucksack.

There is undoubtedly an element of performance in the constructed authorial persona conveyed in Chatwin's life and work. His first ambition was to be an actor; he was a precocious child performer, taking on numerous roles during his years at Marlborough, the Wiltshire public school which he attended from age thirteen, including that of the Mayor in Gogol's *The Government Inspector* and Mrs Candour in Sheridan's *The School for Scandal*. Such a background seems subliminally conveyed in Chatwin's work; there is an impression throughout his life – not just in his strategies of self-presentation, but also in the erudition which he cultivated – that he was playing a role. The writer W.G. Sebald remarked upon 'the art of transformation that came naturally to [Chatwin], a sense of being always on stage, an instinct for the gesture that would make an effect on the audience, for the bizarre and the scandalous, the terrible and the wonderful' (182). His father's decision that the eighteen-year-old Bruce was not to go to drama school – '[T]hat's absolutely fine, you can be an actor at any time of your life but, no, I'm not going to pay for you to go to RADA' (CCMM), he told his son – may have closed off a career which directly exploited those tendencies, but the impulse towards performance would remain with Chatwin throughout his life, and is manifest in his work.

However, the image can also be seen as continuing a tradition of the roving author as hero. In both personal and literary terms, Bruce Chatwin was following in the footsteps of the British travelling writers and explorers of the nineteenth and twentieth centuries – figures such as Charles Doughty, Richard Burton, Robert Byron, Wilfred Thesiger and T.E. Lawrence. Byron was an acknowledged influence: 'Anyone who reads around the travel books of the Thirties must, in the end, conclude that Robert Byron's *The Road to Oxiana* is the masterpiece' (*WAIDH* 286), he wrote in an introduction to the work, whilst Chatwin saw in Thesiger a man of similar convictions, commenting in a review of *Desert, Marsh and Mountain* on the author's belief 'that the heroic world of pastoral nomads is finer – morally and physically – than the life of settled civilisations' (*AOR* 110). The admiration went both ways; Thesiger remarked that, of recent works of travel literature, he had particularly 'enjoyed Bruce Chatwin's *In Patagonia*, though he found the late Chatwin, with whom he once had dinner at his agent's house, "the most talkative man I've ever met … He never stopped talking all the way through dinner. He was interesting but not fascinating"' (Asher 1994: 507). Yet perhaps the closest similarity to be found in this group of literary travellers is that between Chatwin and T.E. Lawrence.

Chatwin always professed to profoundly dislike Lawrence, saying 'I hate T.E. Lawrence. Well, I think I do. Incredibly unpleasant' (qtd. in Shakespeare 2000: 6). Yet there are striking biographical similarities shared by the two authors: both studied as archaeologists, though disliked the scholarly rigour demanded by the subject; both travelled as a means of personal escape; both shared the striking blonde hair and blue eyes which led to admiration both abroad and at home; both struggled with the burden of complicated sexuality; both died prematurely; and both were self-mythologisers.

Michael Asher highlights Lawrence's tendency towards self-mythology in his analysis of conflicting accounts of a journey undertaken to recover a number of Hittite seals from Syria. Writing to explain that this trip would, due to unforeseen circumstances, delay his return to Oxford and his studies, Lawrence's letter to Jesus College principal Sir John Rhys is, as Asher puts it, 'a masterpiece of English understatement and a display of stiff upper lip which would hardly have disgraced Lord Nelson. He told Rhys that he had had four attacks of malaria when he had "only reckoned on two", and had been "robbed and rather smashed up" only the previous week' (1998: 72). He also conveyed the impression that his journey had been undertaken alone and that he had travelled at all times in authentic dress. Asher refutes this claim and outlines Lawrence's exaggeration: 'He had not travelled alone all the time – at one point he had employed a guide, and for a major section of the journey he had travelled with a mounted escort ... [H]e had worn European dress throughout, including the pith-helmet which, as he himself said later, the Arabs regarded with superstitious hatred' (1998: 72).

Chatwin too was prone to conveying an impression of an intrepid independent traveller: 'I quit my job in the "art world",' he wrote in *The Songlines*, 'and went back to the dry places: alone, travelling light. The names of the tribes I travelled among are unimportant: Rguibat, Quashgai, Taimanni, Turkomen, Bororo, Tuareg – people whose journeys, unlike my own, had neither beginning nor end' (18). The image conveyed is self-consciously performative (if the names are unimportant, why tell us, other than to impress?), and substantially burnished. In reality, Chatwin rarely undertook long or severe journeys, often had company, and was frequently accompanied by large volumes of personal belongings, as Murray Bail observed, '[O]n his Indian trip it was like travelling with Garbo; he had dozens of suitcases and god knows what' (*Footsteps*). He wandered, comments Robyn Davidson, as 'a sort of nomad-de-luxe' (*Footsteps*).

Chatwin's tendency towards romantic self-presentation has led latterly to wildly disproportionate accusations of fraudulence – an unhappy result of the misfortune of his early death in an age which holds demystification as a profound moral virtue. He has been described as a 'virtuoso of mendacity' ('Yarn Spinner'), 'an absurd pseud and show-off' (Hensher) and 'a mix of Jay Gatsby and Princess Diana with a designer rucksack' whose 'constant preposterous reinvention' (Barley) obscured his work. However, whilst it is true that the contemporary preoccupation with Chatwin's mythologising tendencies has set up what Robert Macfarlane refers to as 'patterns of interference' which obstruct clear-sighted readings of his work, it is equally true that the romance of his self-presentation represents a primary influence upon the appeal and resonance of that work. The nomadic persona which Chatwin constructed is central to his literature, coming to act as both the personification of his theories of restlessness and a figure of aspiration designed to foster a spirit of communion with the reader, inviting the shared recognition of Rimbaud's dictum that 'La vraie vie est absente' (18).[6]

Whilst taking the theme of restlessness as its underpinning, the following study is not intended as an exclusive examination of that element of Chatwin's work. What follows is a chronological account of his literary output, which foregrounds a preoccupation with restlessness as its primary motivation, theme and interest. The work begins with *The Nomadic Alternative*, and continues to examine *In Patagonia* (1977), *The Viceroy of Ouidah* (1980), *On the Black Hill* (1982), *The Songlines* (1987) and *Utz* (1988). Each text will be discussed in turn, offering literary and biographical context, as well as addressing the formal strategies Chatwin employed in presenting his material. The topic of restlessness provides a binding narrative thread for the discussion.

Many readers will be aware that, since Chatwin's death, the number of works published in his name has nearly doubled. *What Am I Doing Here* (1989) was the first of these posthumous publications – though the compilation process was completed by the author himself during the latter stages of his illness. Since then, there has been another volume of uncollected writing, *Anatomy of Restlessness* (1996), two volumes of his photographs, *Photographs and Notebooks* (1993) and *Winding Paths* (1999), as well as a collection of his letters, titled *Under the Sun* (2010).[7] These works, though of individual significance and interest, are not treated separately in this volume; the insight they offer is rather incorporated into the commentary as relevant.

As has been noted, however, the following analysis will also draw on previously unseen archival material. Of the material stored at the Bodleian Library, this study has concentrated on those particular resources which pertain to the period of Chatwin's literary career. Of particular relevance are the celebrated Moleskine notebooks and the manuscript of *The*

NomadicAlternative, both of which offer invaluable insight into the literary approach and development of the author. In addition to this archival material, the volume also includes a number of previously unpublished black and white photos from Chatwin's collection, which, as yet, remains unarchived. Finally, a brief section following the conclusion outlines some of the key books which inspired Chatwin's writing; this list is drawn from both the archival sources detailed above, and also from Chatwin's library, which remains largely intact at his and Elizabeth's home.

As the title of the work implies, this book is primarily interested in the literature of Bruce Chatwin; for those seeking specific insight into the life, there exists an excellent biographical resource in Nicholas Shakespeare's *Bruce Chatwin* (1999), as well as Susannah Clapp's insightful memoir, *With Chatwin* (1997), and the published letters.

However, life and work were inextricable for Chatwin. In addition to the centralised authorial persona discussed above, the influence of Chatwin's life upon his work is manifest in a number of ways. The thematic content of his writing drew directly from the emotional preoccupations which pursued him from childhood through to his adult life. All of Chatwin's major themes – in addition to restlessness, the list includes such related topics as liminality, the psychology of exile, the innate goodness of man, the appeal of asceticism and the anxiety of the collector, amongst others – found their wellspring in the author's life. In addition to this philosophical influence, Chatwin's personal experience also fed directly into his books at the manifest level of plot and action; all of his work was rooted, to some degree, in his lived experience. 'I find it hard to get with the fictional process', he told his brother. 'Real life is so much more extraordinary' (CCMM). Finally, as shall be seen, his wider biographical experiences had a profound impact on the formal qualities of his work. Any study of the work clearly demands frequent cross-reference to the detail of the life.

Thus, before embarking upon a discussion of his writing, it is appropriate to detail the instructive years of Chatwin's early adulthood. This period was pivotal to his subsequent career as a writer, dictating the stylistic approach of his later work, as well as instilling long-standing interests which would come to crucially influence the content of his literature. However, the years before he began to write professionally also evidence the author's emergent tendency towards restlessness, as well as the corresponding development of his interest in the subject of nomadism – and the solutions and insights it appeared to offer.

NOTES

1 From the publication of *In Patagonia* in October 1977 until his death in January 1989.

2 It was beaten by Peter Carey's *Oscar and Lucinda*.

3 For more on this discussion see David Taylor (198–9), Barbara Korte's *English Travel Writing: From Pilgrimages to Postcolonial Explorations* (144–6), chapter one of Marie Williams' dissertation 'A Dystopian Modernity: Bruce Chatwin and the Subject in the Modern World', Manfred Pfister's 'Bruce Chatwin and the Postmodernization of the Travelogue', and Tim Youngs' 'Punctuating Travel: Paul Theroux and Bruce Chatwin'. *Tourists with Typewriters* by Patrick Holland and Graham Huggan also touches on the issue of genre; see 167–70.

4 *The Songlines* does, of course, manifest many of the qualities of the descriptive work; the detail of his overall approach in this work is outlined in Chapter Six.

5 A striking irony of this passage is that Chatwin is employing an aesthetic metaphor to depict his own disgust with aestheticism.

6 'True life is elsewhere.'

7 Additionally, Bruce Chatwin and Paul Theroux compiled an account of a joint speech given to the Royal Geographical Society in November 1979, which was published in 1985 in the UK as *Patagonia Revisited*.

I

Winding paths

> The quest for knowledge or any creative endeavour is a hunt through a
> dark night of uncertainty. The quarry is the solution to a problem. But the
> quarry is fleet of foot and never tires, and the hunter tires and is mortal. (4)
> Bruce Chatwin, *The Nomadic Alternative*

It was originally intended that, having completed his studies at
Marlborough, Bruce Chatwin would follow the well-worn path of Old
Marlburians and progress to an Oxbridge college. He had planned to try
for a place studying Classics at Merton in Oxford; however, as National
Service gradually ended in the late 1950s, competition for university
places increased, and Chatwin was informed that he might perhaps have
to wait for two years before going up. His youthful gaze thus turned to
other horizons: Africa was considered, as was architecture – 'the family
business' (H. Chatwin CCMM) – and, of course, a stage career. Ultimately, however, Chatwin elected to begin his career at a theatre of a
different sort: Sotheby's auctioneers in London.

Having secured an introduction through a school friend of his father's,
Chatwin began at the auction house in late 1958. He was hired as a porter,
a post which, despite its lowly title, was considered 'usual and fashion-
able' (Maclean CCMM) at that time. In particular, it provided the potential for being noticed: 'Setting recruits to work as porters was the no-cost
training scheme that [the firm] had devised to uncover talent', (96) writes
Robert Lacey.

Various accounts exist as to Chatwin's first distinguishing moment at
the auction house; he told Susannah Clapp of an encounter with the
collector Sir Robert Abdy, who, unrecognised by the young Chatwin,
asked for his opinion of a Picasso gouache. Chatwin asserted – correctly,
as it would turn out – that the picture was a fake. Abdy subsequently
'spread the word about the talented youth, and eased his way within

the firm' (Clapp 1998: 82). In his essay 'The Bey' he tells of a similar encounter with the 'Grand Chamberlain du Cour du Roi des Albanis' (*WAIDH* 358). Whether there was in fact such a specific moment of recognition, or whether Chatwin rather gradually distinguished himself through his well-attested talents of appraisal, is unclear. What is beyond doubt, however, is that Chatwin's progress within the auction house was rapid. Under the mentorship of Sotheby's chairman, Peter Wilson, Chatwin was promoted first to a post as a junior cataloguer in the Antiquities department – with responsibility for the composition of brief and enticing descriptions of the objects to be sold – and then to assume overall responsibility for both Antiquities and the newly created department of Impressionists, or 'Imps' as it became known.

He was fortunate in joining Sotheby's at a time of extraordinary growth. His arrival was coincidental with the now legendary Goldschmidt sale of seven impressionist masterpieces in October 1958. The auction – attended by 1,400 people, including Somerset Maugham, Margot Fonteyn and Kirk Douglas, and masterminded by Peter Wilson – lasted just 21 minutes and generated £781,000. It was the highest-grossing fine-art auction in history. Robert Lacey, in his history of Sotheby's, describes the atmosphere on New Bond Street in the decade which followed the Goldschmidt sale: 'Beautiful objects fetched beautiful prices. Sellers were happy. Buyers could not wait for the next sale, and breathless newspaper articles extolled the whole process. For Peter Wilson and his bright young men, the auction business seemed the perfect combination of taste, excitement, and money' (156). Chatwin, the archetypal provincial youngster, was at the very centre of this glamorous and exotic world as Katherine Maclean, Peter Wilson's personal assistant, attests:

> [T]his not so callow youth found himself precipitated into drawing rooms all over Europe and America, meeting the rich and famous, taking them all with a slice of spice, a bit of a joke, and enjoying their manipulations and getting a lot of business. ... He'd flown all over the world, he'd been entertained in the best restaurants, he'd been in the best salons and the best drawing rooms, and he was very fêted. (CCMM)

Few would anticipate that such a lifestyle, and such a career, would pall. However, in June of 1966, to the surprise and shock of his colleagues and family, Chatwin announced that he was leaving the firm. In an article written for the *New York Times Book Review* nearly twenty years later, Chatwin located the impetus for this precipitate departure in an epiphanic realisation which had struck during a trip to the Sudan in early 1965.

This journey to Africa had been suggested by his doctor after Chatwin had suffered an anxiety-induced loss of vision,[1] '[a]pparently the result of over-doing it in America' (*US* 63), he wrote to a friend at the time.[2] Whilst there, he began to suffer misgivings over his involvement in the art world:

> I went to the Sudan. On camel and foot I trekked through the Red Sea hills and found some unrecorded cave paintings. My nomad guide was a hadendoa, one of Kipling's 'fuzzy-wuzzies'. He carried a sword, a purse and a pot of scented goat's grease for anointing his hair. He made me feel overburdened and inadequate; and by the time I returned to England a mood of fierce iconoclasm had set in.
>
> Not that I turned into a picture slasher. But I did understand why the Prophets banned the worship of images. (*AOR* 11–12)

This account of the young auctioneer turning away from craven materialism towards a life as a writer and modern nomad fits appealingly within the grander constructed narrative of Chatwin's life, and his trip can rightly be viewed as a significant motivator of his emergent interest in the subject of restlessness. However, contemporaneous accounts also testify to the influence of more prosaic factors; in particular, the questionable business dealings of Sotheby's in the months following Chatwin's trip to the Sudan.

In the summer of 1965, Chatwin was informed by Sotheby's that he was to be made a director of the firm. Katherine Maclean, recalls the handling of this promotion: 'Come the late sixties, Sotheby's had to restructure its financial basis in some way, and it had done very well over the last ten years, and it was decided to reward about half a dozen of these young men with directorships. They were all told this good news; unfortunately in such a way they all believed themselves to be the sole choice for this great distinction, and so slightly had their noses put out of joint to find that other colleagues were in the same *soi-disant* distinguished field' (CCMM). Such were the numbers of new directors that it became standing room only at board meetings from that point on.

Chatwin was aggrieved at the management of this affair, which alone would seem an understandable cause of disillusion. In later life, however, he would privately identify a darker scandal concerning Sotheby's. Chatwin accused his superiors of implicating him in the fraudulent dispersal of a privately held collection of ethnographic artefacts – the Pitt-Rivers collection: 'On 27 August 1988, six months before he died, Chatwin focussed his rage against John Hewett, John and Puntzel Hunt in Ireland, and the Sotheby's chairman, Peter Wilson: Chatwin claimed that he left Sotheby's because he was being forced to sell the Pitt-Rivers collection "fraudulently" to American and other collectors' (US 80).[3]

Such were the contemporaneous events which framed Chatwin's announcement that he was leaving Sotheby's. He departed the auction house for a four-year degree course in Archeology at Edinburgh University. In the intervening years since leaving Marlborough, Chatwin had come to regret not taking up his proposed place at Oxford, and his decampment to Edinburgh was intended to rectify this lack of formal eduction. In September of 1966, Chatwin wrote to Michael Cannon: 'You may not have heard that I have LEFT Sotheby's to read a degree in archaeology at Edinburgh. Change is the only thing worth living for. Never sit your life out at a desk. Ulcers and heart condition follow' (US 85).

Chatwin was a committed undergraduate at Edinburgh, engaging with the degree course with enthusiasm, despite occasional bouts of self-doubt. The course was intensive, with Bruce having to write 'at least one paper a week ... He was writing all the time' (E. Chatwin 2010). However, Chatwin came to find much of the course itself too dry for his taste, characterising it later as 'a dismal discipline – a story of technical glories interrupted by catastrophe' (AOR 12).

Nor was any redemption offered by location; both Bruce and Elizabeth found living conditions in Edinburgh – 'that grim northern city' (AOR 12) – challenging. In a review of James Pope-Hennessy's biography of Robert Louis Stevenson, Chatwin would later write of the city as a 'place of absolute contrast and paradox. ... The rational squares and terraces of the New Town confront the daunting skyline of the Old. Slums still abut the houses of the rich. ... On fine summer days nowhere is lighter and more airy; for most of the year there are icy blasts or a clammy sea fog, the haar of the east coast of Scotland' (AOR 133).

Despite the challenges of curriculum and location, however, Elizabeth asserts that Chatwin would have finished his degree course, were it not for the restrictions placed upon him by his professor, Stuart Piggott. As with Peter Wilson at Sotheby's, Bruce had charmed the man in charge, and, as with Wilson, Piggott was unwilling to let his protégé leave, as Elizabeth recalls:

> He could have completed and would have been happy to have completed in three years, because they'd lost this very nice professor who did the Dark Ages and never replaced him. So Bruce was going to be stuck doing Roman Britain forever; I mean, he was bored already after two [years].

But Stuart wanted him there. I was on a train with David Talbot Rice[4] ...
and he said 'Why doesn't Bruce finish at the end of this year?', and I said
'He'd love to, but Stuart won't let him'. (2010)

In November 1968, Elizabeth drove to Edinburgh to help Bruce effect
his escape: '[H]e just didn't go back. He didn't tell anyone that he wasn't
going back. I went up to get him for Thanksgiving and loaded him into
the car with some stuff and so on, and then he never went back at all'
(2007).

Later in his career, and more confident in his autodidact identity,
Chatwin, eliding practical motivations, framed his departure from Edinburgh in grand terms, as an inspired crisis of confidence similar to that
experienced in the Sudanese desert. Alluding to youthful visits to Shakespeare's tomb at Holy Trinity Church in Stratford-upon-Avon, Chatwin
described his epiphany:

> [L]ong before I could read, Aunt Gracie had taught me to recite the lines
> engraved on the tomb-slab:
> *Bleste be ye man yt spares thes stones*
> *And curst be he yt moves my bones.*
> ... One day, while excavating a Bronze-Age burial, I was about to brush
> the earth off a skeleton, and the old line came back to haunt me:
> *And curst be he yt moves my bones.*
> For the second time I quit. (*AOR* 7–12)

Chatwin's tendency to romanticise the manner and motivation behind
relatively prosaic life-decisions results partly from his writerly tendency
to form narrative from incoherence and ambiguity. However, it can
perhaps be argued that Chatwin's grand moral stance against both archeology and the art world belies the fact that, in reality, the reasons for
leaving both situations were more persuasive than compelling. Chatwin
could have remained at Sotheby's; he was young and successful, a director
at just 26, despite the compromising manner in which his promotion had
been effected. Even the dispersal of the Pitt-Rivers collection, whilst
undoubtedly questionable in ethics and motive, was not terribly out of
keeping with the general tenor of auction house life. Colleagues such
as Marcus Linell and David Nash chose to remain at the firm, despite
the compromises, and made a career of Sotheby's. Equally, many
undergraduates have survived dull degree courses and unappealing living
conditions whilst at university.

Whatever the practical objections of the time, or the romantic
explanations posited later, it seems apparent, viewing Chatwin's life from

the present juncture, that these departures were at least partly the consequence of his 'inbuilt restlessness' (*Footsteps*). His life would be marked
by this tendency towards sudden changes of direction: from Sotheby's to
Edinburgh; from Edinburgh to freelancing and the *Sunday Times*; from
the *Sunday Times* to Patagonia. Chatwin rarely stayed in one place or at
one undertaking for very long, suffering persistently from the persuasive
voice of conviction which Baudelaire described so effectively: 'I say,
Soul, poor shivering Soul, how would you like to go and live in Lisbon?
It must be pretty warm there, and you would soon be as spry as a lizard'
(191). It is perhaps unsurprising that his specific interest in nomads and
the solutions that their means of life seemed to offer emerged as this
tendency began to influence his life more practically. These early experiences of restless departure crucially influenced the thematic material of
Chatwin's future creative work, inspiring him to seek an explanation for,
and justification of, the persistently felt desire for change.

His time at Sotheby's and Edinburgh had done more than simply
encourage his emergent interest in the question of restlessness, however.
Both had provided an invaluable practical apprenticeship for a future
writer. His time as a cataloguer at Sotheby's provided particular training
in the skill of ascertaining provenance and of paring down description:
'He wouldn't have had that discipline without being at Sotheby's, that's
the thing, of observation', comments Elizabeth (2007). It also schooled
him in the techniques and virtues of thorough background investigation;
Elizabeth recalls his 'endless research' (*US* 1) at the British Museum and
Musée de l'Homme in Paris. He told Colin Thubron of the influence
of these experiences: 'The technique of art detective-work – treasure
hunting – is the way in which I research a story'.

Edinburgh brought a degree of academic rigour to his working
practice, and extended his existing abilities in inferring meaning from
inanimate objects and presenting it succinctly to the reader. This skill is
a hallmark of Chatwin's prose style; his works are dotted with brief and
enticing descriptions of conversations overheard, landscapes glimpsed,
interactions captured, objects conjured. He compared himself at the time
of writing *In Patagonia* with the photographer Henri Cartier-Bresson,
but perhaps the more compelling analogy would be with the skilled
caption writer, who is able to articulate the moment captured: 'As a
writer, as a collector, Chatwin scanned all he encountered, distilling an
essence' commented Robyn Ravlich ('Chatwinesque').

On a more general level, his time at Sotheby's and Edinburgh provided him with a thorough schooling in the subjects which would foster his key themes: art and aesthetics, anthropology, archeology and history. It gave him an idiosyncratic but overarching insight into the evolution of human culture and society, from the earliest nomadic peoples to the most revolutionary modern artists, fostering a remarkable knowledge base. In a letter to Deborah Devonshire (*US* 412), Patrick Leigh Fermor referred to Chatwin's astonishing breadth of reference, citing the Oliver Goldsmith couplet:

And still they gazed, and still the wonder grew,
That one small head could carry all he knew. (52)

The polymathy that impressed Leigh Fermor – a man tough to outclass intellectually – was established by Chatwin's years at Sotheby's and Edinburgh.

His apprenticeship was not yet complete, however. He was to experience another, equally instructive, failure before turning more directly towards the creative work for which he would become celebrated. This final stage of Chatwin's circuitous route to becoming a professional writer was initiated by a commission he had received in early 1968 – whilst still at Edinburgh – to co-curate an exhibition for the Asia Society in New York entitled '*Animal Style' Art from East to West.*

This invitation resulted more from his experience at Sotheby's and connections in the art world (in particular his friend, the scholar and collector of Islamic and Indian art, Cary Welch) than his qualifications as an archaeologist – the undergraduate is vaguely described in the foreword to the exhibition's catalogue as 'connected to the University of Edinburgh' (Washburn 7). However, in addition to sourcing many of the items for the event, Chatwin was also expected to produce an essay on the Animal Style for inclusion in the catalogue. With no other immediate prospects on the horizon, Chatwin settled in at the Gloucestershire farmhouse he and Elizabeth had bought in 1966 and dedicated himself to this task. The resulting piece – titled, like his later, full-length work, 'The Nomadic Alternative' – is significant to the present discussion as it marks Chatwin's first written engagement with the topic which was becoming his obsession – that of the nomadic life, and the possible insights it offered into the affliction of restlessness.

Chatwin would later comment that his goal in the '*Animal Style*' essay was to demonstrate 'that the people one most wanted to know about were not those who left trace in the archeological record, but those who were invisible in it' ('Chatwinesque'). His particular interest in this notion was another specific bequest from his time at Edinburgh, where, during his studies, the conspicuous absence of nomads from history had begun to fascinate Chatwin: 'In the Cairo Museum you could find statues of pharaohs by the million', he wrote in the late essay 'I Always Wanted To Go To Patagonia', '[b]ut where was the face of Moses' (*AOR* 12). It was not part of Chatwin's remit to rectify this omission, but, ignoring his brief to write a straightforward and academically robust introduction to the phenomenon of the Animal Style,[5] he instead set enthusiastically about this task, composing a short-form cultural history of nomads.

The essay begins by contrasting the degraded nature of settled civilisation with the possibility of a life 'in harmony with "nature", unhampered with possessions, free from the grinding bonds of technology, sinless, promiscuous, anarchic, and sometimes vegetarian' (*AOR* 85), and continues on to present a synoptic outline of the virtues of nomadism, setting up the binary opposition between nomad and civilisation that would come to be a defining facet of the full-length version of *The Nomadic Alternative*. 'Nomad and citizen belonged to exclusive systems and both knew it', Chatwin writes (*AOR* 88), prefiguring Deleuze and Guattari's notion of the philosophical division presented in *A Thousand Plateaus*.

At times 'The Nomadic Alternative' feels like an impressive undergraduate exam response, crammed with arcane knowledge; in the space of two paragraphs, Chatwin cites Aristeas of Proconnessus, the Spartan poet Alcman, Herodotus, Aeschylus, Simias and Hesiod. His tendency towards the airy presentation of impressive facts and citations would later become a hallmark of his shorter writing (and occasionally his longer prose), but whereas, in his later work, such referencing appears for deliberate literary effect, here – as in the full length *The Nomadic Alternative* – it feels at least partly designed to paper over the academic flaws in his argument.

There is little discussion of the actual Animal Style itself until the final paragraphs, as if Chatwin realised that mention of the *raison d'être* for the essay was something of a necessity. Even at this stage, Chatwin's central assertion – that shamanism formed an overarching influence on the Animal Style – emerged more from the writer's interest in the figure of the shaman through history than from any widespread academic consensus. The central argument – that through the collective psychological state attained by shamanistic ritual, the artistic homogeneity of the Animal Style (an aesthetic phenomenon common to many, often extremely geographically diverse, groups of people) can be explained – is more romantic than anthropologically provable. Chatwin describes in the essay the similarity between shamanistic visions and the Animal Style itself: 'Animals are depicted from both sides at once, their heads abutted to form a frontal mask. The so-called X-ray style is common and shows a schematised view of the animal's skeleton. ... The similarities between hallucinatory experience and nomadic art cannot be explained away as pure chance' (*AOR* 98).

Chatwin here presents a grand, romantic hypothesis that, although of obvious interest and appeal, was not quite what the organisers had anticipated. He had attempted to conform to their expectations through – for almost the only time in his published work – the use of footnotes. This one concession to academic rigour, however, did little to persuade the organisers of the exhibition that the essay was a suitable, or even desirable, contribution to the catalogue: 'We came from different angles', one of the organisers, Emma Bunker, told Nicholas Shakespeare. 'I came from a strictly academic background and I had not really travelled the world as he had. I expected him to have more footnotes. He was bored with academic nonsense. "Those frilly-shirted fools," he said' (qtd. in Shakespeare 2000: 216). In the introductory essay to the catalogue the Director of the Asia House exhibition, Gordon Bailey Washburn, reflected on the methodological differences between the curators:

> During all of this pursuit of answers to one of the world's most difficult historic problems, it is not to be wondered if our trio of scholars were inclined to differences of opinions. And it must not be supposed that unanimity of opinion was either expected or achieved. Mr. Chatwin, an anthropologist at heart, is inclined to find shamanism the most likely inspiration for the Animal Style in its various ramifications – seeing in it the natural explanation for the style's apparent encirclement of the globe ...
>
> Mrs. Bunker and Dr. Farkas are less interested in an unprovable hypothesis and more concerned with the exacting research that traces the movements of ancient peoples and their styles of ornament across the vast face of Asia and the smaller one of Europe. They belong to that very small band of specialists, an international group of scholars, whose largely invisible research may in the end restore to us some of the many lost pages of ancient history. (Washburn 7)

Despite the implied criticism of his colleagues – he is conspicuously excluded from the referenced 'international group of scholars' – the wider reception of 'The Nomadic Alternative' was not entirely negative; in an essay for *Artibus Asiae*, Karl Jettmar commented: 'Chatwin has the most difficult task in this book. He has had to give us justification of the decision to arrange such a bold exhibition. As an anthropologist he does his best' (258). However, the experience had encouraged Chatwin's emergent tendency – initiated by his unhappy time at Edinburgh – to define himself against the academic world; in a letter written to James Ivory as preparations for the exhibition began, Chatwin described himself as an 'intrepid English amateur who has dared plant his unwary feet on the hallowed ground of American scholarship' (*US* 148). In the aftermath of the publication of his essay, Chatwin's ambivalence towards academia hardened into hostility, and he began increasingly to identify himself as an autodidact.

Correspondingly, his writerly ambitions gravitated away from the academic. His next project, embarked upon in the immediate aftermath of his essay submission, was to be a generalised full-length examination of restlessness and nomadism which developed on the ideas he had put forward in 'The Nomadic Alternative'. He envisaged the result as 'a wildly ambitious and intolerant work, a kind of "Anatomy of Restlessness" that would enlarge on Pascal's dictum about the man sitting quietly in a room' (*AOR* 12).

Chatwin's chosen analogy demonstrates just how ambitious his vision was in constructing what would become the unpublished *The Nomadic Alternative*, consciously alluding to the gargantuan *The Anatomy of Melancholy* by the Renaissance scholar Robert Burton (1577–1640). Burton, who like Chatwin grew up in the provincial West Midlands, spent almost the entirety of his adult life in intellectual seclusion at Christ Church College, Oxford – one biographer stated of his dedication to the literary life that 'To describe Burton as "bookish" can only be called ridiculous understatement' (Bamborough). Rarely leaving the city, Burton passed much of his life engaged in work on his *Anatomy*, a colossal work of scholarship, which grew with each edition until his death in 1640, eventually numbering more than 500,000 words.

In addition to its overwhelming length, *The Anatomy of Melancholy* is notable for an idiosyncratic approach to its subject matter; ostensibly set up as an investigation into the affliction of melancholy, the work in fact presents a wide and miscellaneous 'compendium of science, philosophy, poetry, history, and divinity which contains examples of numerous literary genres yet remains *sui generis*, the singular expression of its

author's humane knowledge' (Fox 1). The diversity of the text was a
reflection of Burton's own generalist tendencies; writing in the *de facto*
introduction to the text, the author references his 'great desire (not able
to attain to a superficial skill in any) to have some smattering in all, to be
aliquis in omnibus, nullus in singulis,[6] which Plato commends … "as fit to
be imprinted in all curious wits, not to be a slave of one science, or dwell
altogether in one subject, as most do, but to rove abroad, *centum puer
artium,*[7] to have an oar in every man's boat, to taste of every dish, and sip
of every cup"' (22).

That Chatwin would choose to compare his undertaking with Burton's
grand project is telling both of his ambition to create something overarching, and his increasing antipathy, following his recent experiences
with the Asia Society in New York, towards academic convention. Both
of these impulses are manifest in the extant synopsis for *The Nomadic
Alternative*, which takes the form of a letter composed to Tom Maschler,
chairman of the publishing house Jonathan Cape.

Maschler's interest in Chatwin had been piqued when literary agent
Deborah Rogers sent on the '*Animal Style*' introduction:

> I was introduced to Bruce's work by an article he had written about
> nomads, sent to me by his agent Deborah Rogers. With her usual perspi-
> cacity she thought she had discovered a new and special writer. In my
> experience of all the literary agents in England, Deborah is the most likely
> to be right when it comes to quality. (86)

Cape was a high-profile publisher at that point in the late 1960s; Maschler
describes the house, with only a small amount of trademark self-promo-
tion,[8] as 'the greatest literary publishing house in England' (64) over the
period of the 1960s to 1980s. Certainly, Cape was remarkably influential
in the post-war period; during his time at the publishing house, Maschler
introduced Thomas Pynchon, Gabriel García Márquez and Joseph Heller
to the British market, published Salman Rushdie, Ian McEwan and Doris
Lessing, and had, at the time of meeting Bruce Chatwin, just orches-
trated one of the literary sensations of the 1960s with the publication of
Desmond Morris' *The Naked Ape*.

Adding to the appeal of Jonathan Cape was its history as one of the
pre-eminent publishers of travel writing in the golden age, as Paul Fussell
recounts: '[Cape] was acute in sensing the postwar demand for travel
books of all kinds – Lady Warren's *Through Algeria and Tunisia on a Motor
Cycle* was on the 1922 list – and signing up some of the brightest stars,

like Robert Byron, Peter Fleming, and Beverley Nichols' (60). To the young Chatwin, the idea of becoming attached to the same publishing house as Robert Byron must have appealed enormously, as must the fact that Cape had later published Ernest Hemingway – whose *In Our Time* would have profound influence upon the prose style of Chatwin's later work.

The synopsis which Maschler received in February of 1969 asserts that *The Nomadic Alternative* is not intended to 'provide a history of nomads. It would take years to write. In any case,' Chatwin goes on, 'I want the book to be *general rather than specialist* in tone' (*US* 131–2, emphasis added), addressing the correspondingly non-specific question: 'Why do men wander rather than sit still?' (*US* 132). Chatwin goes on to admit – in tellingly confessional parentheses – that he has a personal interest in attempting to resolve this question:

> [T]he mutual antagonism of citizen and nomad is only one half of the theme. The other is much nearer home – ESCAPISM (a good personal reason for writing the book). Why do I become restless after a month in a single place, unbearable after two? (I am, I admit, a bad case). Some travel for business. But there is no economic reason for me to go, and every reason to stay put. My motives, then, are materially irrational. What is this neurotic restlessness, the gadfly that tormented the Greeks? Wandering may settle some of my natural curiosity and my urge to explore, but then I am tugged back by a longing for home. I have a compulsion to wander and a compulsion to return – a homing instinct like a migrating bird. (*US* 132)

The work is thus set up as an idiosyncratic, personal and generalist exploration of the subject of restlessness. Yet, troublingly, as the synopsis continues, a sense is simultaneously conveyed of Chatwin's ardent desire to be taken seriously: the constant citation of obscure historical sources; his occasional bracketed references; sentences such as 'Looking at some of today's studies of animal and human behaviour, one can detect two trends...' (*US* 133); all belie a longing for intellectual approbation. This implied crisis of identity, first glimpsed in the synopsis, and absolutely manifest in the work itself, engendered the work's failure. An attempted conflation of the personal and scholarly, *The Nomadic Alternative* would fail to satisfy on either level.

Though evident in retrospect, these issues were at the time either not apparent or thought to be resolvable by Cape. On the back of his proposal, Chatwin signed his contract in May of 1969, receiving a two-hundred-pound advance. Tom Maschler's hopes for the nomad book

were high: 'I do just want to put into writing that I am convinced it will
be an important book. Important in the way *The Naked Ape* was important ... I very much look forward to the first chapters of the book just as
soon as you can manage them' (*US* 140).

A month after signing his contract, Chatwin embarked upon a research
trip to Afghanistan with his friend Peter Levi, a poet and Jesuit priest.
Levi, who had organised the trip, was travelling to investigate the influence upon Afghanistan of the Greek invasions of Inner Asia in around
245 BC.[9] This was to be Chatwin's third trip to the country and, whilst
Levi explored Greek and Afghan history, he sought out material for his
book on nomads.

Levi was later to turn the story of the journey they undertook around
Afghanistan into a book, *The Light Garden of the Angel King*, and this now
almost forgotten travelogue offers one of the only published first-hand
representations of Chatwin the traveller. The glimpses the reader catches
of the young Bruce – introduced, even at this stage of his career, as 'a
specialist in the study of nomadic peoples' (86) – testify to his humour
as a travelling companion, as well as his occasional tendencies towards
self-aggrandisement. Levi was, however, clearly enamoured of his fellow
traveller:

> [I]t will be obvious from every page of this book that I was extremely
> fortunate in the travelling companion I did have. Most of our best obser-
> vations and all the best jokes were his; and it was he who was interested
> in nomads, he who told me to read Basho, he who had done all the right
> homework in my subjects as well as his own, who knew the names of
> flowers and who understood Islamic art history. These are luxuries; but
> he was even stronger in the bread and butter virtues without which we
> would have been doomed, for a journey like this one ought to be inde-
> fatigable, extremely patient, open-minded, friendly, and talented with the
> right kind of gifts both of conversation and of silence. (15)

Levi and Chatwin travelled widely, visiting many of the architectural
and archaeological treasures of Afghanistan, including the tomb of Babur
in Kabul (from which Levi took the title of his book), the Buddhas of
Bamiyan – now destroyed after the Taliban, in a fever of iconoclastic
fury, spent several weeks shelling and dynamiting the statues to rubble in
2001 – and the Minarets of Ghor and Ghazni. Chatwin wrote to Elizabeth
after this last expedition in full Robert Byron mode, having successfully
photographed the Mausoleum of Gohar Shad, 'being the first (I believe)
person to do so except for a Russian lady from Tashkent, and this is the

monument that D[erek][10] has been longing to get at for years but was refused permission. I simply got myself up in a turban and fitted a jeep with Afghans, presented bottles of coca cola to the soldiers and drove by. Whoopee!' (*US* 144).

Despite the irreverent tone of his letters, however, there can be little doubt as to the profound personal significance of this journey to the young writer. Levi, who had already established some reputation as a poet, became, after Peter Wilson and Stuart Piggott, the newest mentor for Chatwin, who was struggling to make the transition from interested amateur to authority on nomadic peoples. Levi offered him a personal model of a creative writer, a very different beast to those in the worlds of commercial art and academia who had previously mentored him. Chatwin admired the apparent freedom the older poet seemed to represent: 'He wanted from me a way of life that was largely in his imagination. He thought my life was some kind of solution: I travelled about and I was a writer. That interested him for the first time while we were in Afghanistan. We talked about the problems of writing, about Russian poets like Osip Mandelstam. What I didn't know or notice was that Bruce was changing *himself*. You write in order to change yourself in my view. He was trying to remake his life and become a writer' (qtd. in Shakespeare 2000: 222). On 21 July 1969, Bruce wrote to his wife from Afghanistan: 'I have realised several things on this trip. You know – they are very good for me. They act as purgatives', he wrote by way of signing off, adding 'I am going to be a serious, and *systematic* writer' (*US* 145).

Upon his return to England, Chatwin faced the realities of this transformation. The journal that he kept over this period testifies to some of the frustrations he encountered in the early stages of writing *The Nomadic Alternative*:

December 15
Worked during the morning with interruptions on the book. Fluency is elusive. Reached an impasse with the first chapter. I think I have bitten off far more than I can chew.

December 16
I have finally rearranged the first chapter and hope for God's sake that, third time lucky, it is final.

December 18
Spent the morning clearing and organizing my study, and the latter part of the afternoon fiddling with the book. Less unhappy now than I was.
(Box 34)

Chatwin would struggle with this process for nearly five years. Each time he seemed to near the point of completion, his subject receded into the distance. Around this time, Chatwin wrote to Peter Levi: 'I have written two chapters of my book. Then I decided they were boring. So they will have to be rewritten. If only I didn't have an argument to follow. Arguments are fatal. One always forgets what they're about' (*US* 147). Nearly three years later, he wrote to his parents with similar anxieties over the thesis of the book:

> Of course I've completely unscrambled it. In fact I'm completely rewriting it. It'll be about half as long and instead of six whopping chapters with an argument linking them all in a continuous flow (which not even I could understand let alone the poor reader), we now have about thirty chapters, each one I hope intelligible by itself. (*US* 218)

By April of 1974, Chatwin's proposed resolutions to the problem of structure were becoming increasingly complex: '[T]oday I have had a ? brilliant (tomorrow it will be poor) idea for one of my chapters. I am going to write my hunter's chapter in the manner of Turgenev's sketches. My first chapter is called *Diogenes and Alexandra* being the least and the most' (*US* 231). The extant version of *The Nomadic Alternative* is testimony to the fact that, despite dedicating years of his life to the problem, Chatwin never succeeded in resolving the challenges that he described in his letters.

NOTES

1 That Chatwin should suffer a failure of vision is, as David Taylor observed, significant for a writer and aesthete who prided himself on his 'eye'. See Taylor 196.

2 Chatwin would tell Colin Thubron that his loss of sight was also attended by 'sores on my palms – rather like the stigmata!' (Thubron).

3 Chatwin's rancorous opinion of Wilson is evident is his late story, 'The Duke of M——', in which the narrator visits the eponymous duke – an acquaintance from his days at Sotheby's – at his villa in Madrid. Whilst there, conversation turns to the auction house: '"I've left Sotheby's," I said to the Duke of M——. "I'm glad to hear it," he smiled. "We had a most disagreeable experience with a man from there. Wilson, I think his name was. He called to ask if he could see my collection. Of course, after *our* agreeable experience, I invited him to lunch. But he started to tell me the price my Gaudis would fetch at auction. I had to show him the door"' (*WAIDH* 357).

4 David Talbot Rice 1903–1972. British art historian and Watson Gordon

Chair of Fine Art at Edinburgh University. He visited Mount Athos with Robert Byron in 1926.

5 The so-called Animal Style is a loose title given to an artistic practice that dates back to the early Iron Age and applies to portable artefacts inscribed with animalistic images.

6 'To be somebody in everything, nobody in anything.'

7 'The servant of a hundred arts.'

8 In one of the images from his memoir *Publisher*, Maschler is shown wearing a T-shirt emblazoned with the slogan 'The world's greatest publisher is only sixty'.

9 For more on their experiences, see Ure 170–4.

10 Their friend, the artist Derek Hill.

2

The great unwriteable

In the mid-nineteenth century, pioneers in Texas were surprised to see illiterate Comanche warriors taking Bibles and other books during their raids on outlying farms and settlements. In true nomadic style, the Comanches had discovered that paper made an excellent padding for their bison-hide war shields and would absorb a bullet if you packed it in thick and tight enough. The early Texas cattleman Charles Goodnight found a Comanche war shield stuffed with a complete history of ancient Rome (its rise, efflorescence and fall to nomadic barbarians from the north). (177) Richard Grant, *Ghost Riders: Travels with American Nomads*

The Nomadic Alternative exists as a loose manuscript of 268 typed, double-spaced pages, stored in a separate green folder with the rest of Chatwin's literary archive at the Bodleian library in Oxford. Whilst the existence of this alternate work has been widely known since the publication of Nicholas Shakespeare's biography in 1999, the form and content of *The Nomadic Alternative* has remained largely mysterious. There have been various calls for the estate to publish the manuscript, but, for reasons which will become evident, the work is not suitable for unexpurgated publication; the original decision by Jonathan Cape to reject the manuscript remains the correct one.

The analysis undertaken in this chapter does not intend either to glory in the obvious flaws of the text or, indeed, to laud it as a lost masterwork. Rather the desire is to outline, as cogently as is possible, Chatwin's general argument in *The Nomadic Alternative*, whilst simultaneously subjecting it to the critical analysis appropriate to a work which never reached the public domain. The account presented is thus unavoidably partial, given the constrictions of space, and the dense and digressive nature of the text. It is not intended as the definitive analysis of *The Nomadic Alternative*, but rather to offer illumination to the general reader, to provide ideas and material for a continuing critical discussion of the work, and, within the context of this volume, to establish an awareness and understanding of the foundational theories of restlessness which Chatwin would go on to explore and expand in his later published work. As such, the chapter pursues a linear analysis of the argument of *The Nomadic Alternative*, and presents fuller citations than would necessarily be the case in the discussion of a publicly available text.

The Nomadic Alternative is organised into five main chapters, preceded by a long and digressive introduction, which begins inauspiciously by railing against the very act of writing itself: 'The best travellers are illiterate', Chatwin writes. 'Narratives of travel are pale compensations for the journey itself, and merely proclaim the traveller's inadequacy as a traveller. The best travellers do not pause to record their second-rate impressions, to be read third-hand. Their experience is primal. Their minds are uncongealed by the written word' (1). Chatwin goes on to describe his project in *The Nomadic Alternative* as 'a provisional account of an ill-advised and ill-prepared expedition to discover the source of The Journey itself' (1), designed to interrogate the rhetorical question:

> *Where* does happiness lie? Why is Here so unbearable? Why is There so inviting? But why is There more unbearable than Here? 'What is this strange madness', Petrarch complained of his young secretary, 'this mania to sleep each night in a different bed?' (2)

He depicts the human species as afflicted by a 'malady' raging 'with the regularity of an undulant fever' (2). 'Few are secure', Chatwin writes, 'from the fury of this infection, this compulsion that beckons us towards the unknown' (2). It is, he asserts, quoting Steinbeck, the 'virus of restlessness' (2), and his undertaking in *The Nomadic Alternative* is to provide an explanation as to its cause.

The introduction begins this undertaking by proposing an alternative history of the human species. Chatwin sets up this subversion by first outlining what he clearly considers to be the consensus view, which he terms 'anti-primitivist'; namely, the notion that the development of our species has followed a linear progression from a violent and mobile pre-history of hunting and gathering towards the redemptive light of civilisation. This position asserts that '[t]hrough ingenuity and their capacity for self-improvement, men dragged themselves from a mire of taboos and ignorance and began to enjoy the rewards of settlement, instead of roaming the earth in a ceaseless struggle to keep alive' (6). The philosophy contends, however, that we have inherited an unfortunate predisposition from our savage forebears. In order to reconcile the notion of linear progression with the anomalous violence of the modern world, contemporary anti-primitivists such as Konrad Lorenz have concluded, influenced by Nietzsche, that we carry with us an innate aggressive instinct, instilled by the structure of early social groups, which mirrored the 'hierarchy of dominance' (9) evident in some animal species. This instinct became problematic in societal terms when the inhibiting factors which control violence in groups of competing animals were overridden by our technological advancements: 'The professional carnivores, wolves or lions, know instinctively when to stop fighting ... But, armed with an artificial weapon or fang of his own making, the semi-vegetarian human beast fails to recognize the white flags of truce. He skirmishes and gores till the rival lies dead at his feet' (10).

Chatwin reverses this anti-primitivist assessment of our ancestry, asserting instead that the wandering hunter-gatherers from whom we supposedly inherited our tendency towards aggressive behaviour in fact embodied the 'dream of every idealist thinker – the *non-violent* Society of Equals' (22; emphasis added). Existing in a state of 'Adamic nakedness', these small tribes 'pass through their lands on a perpetual migration. They never store food for more than a day or two, and decline to possess anything they cannot carry' (22). The argument of *The Nomadic Alternative* here appeals consciously to the account of human history proposed in the work of Jean-Jacques Rousseau, who, in his ordination of the 'noble savage' similarly romanticised the harmonious lifestyle of our ancestors: '[N]othing is more peaceable than man in his primitive state', Rousseau wrote in his *Discourse on Inequality*, 'placed by nature at an equal distance from the stupidity of brutes and the fatal enlightenment of civilized man, limited equally by reason and instinct to defending himself against evils which threaten him' (115).

Chatwin asserts that the internecine violence of the modern world identified by the anti-primitivists is in fact the consequence of our abandonment of this model means of mobile existence: 'Pinned to one place he verbalizes or enacts his sexual fantasies', Chatwin writes of the settler. 'Violent solutions to complicated problems attract him; for diabolic energy is less insupportable than torpor' (3). Settled society erupts into violence not because of an innate *aggressive* instinct, but rather because it suppresses a predisposition for movement evident from our ancestry. We are hardwired for a life on the move; or, as Chatwin put it in his proposal letter to Tom Maschler: 'Wandering is a human characteristic genetically inherited from the vegetarian primates' (*US* 133). This is the central assertion that *The Nomadic Alternative* sets out to demonstrate in an attempt to answer for our proposed innate restlessness.

It does so initially by scrutinising the apparent biological evidence for this instinct, assessing the tools for movement that we share with the animal world. Chatwin writes that 'the wanderer of every age has sensed his affinity with the migrant bird' (24), and, whilst accepting that our biological apparatus for travel is not identical to that of migrating animals, Chatwin asserts that we are allied by our ability to orient chronologically, through the influence of the body clock, which manages our circadian rhythm, but also, he argues, hitches itself to greater spans of time: 'Some glands perform on a weekly basis; the menstruation cycle of a woman synchronizes itself to the waxing and waning of the moon; and these smaller units of biological time aggregate to form an annual cycle – that of the revolution of the earth about the sun' (27).

Chatwin concedes, however, that this innate chronological sense is merely one element of the apparatus which the migrating animal utilises to orient itself, and that the human species does not appear to share the crucial 'inborn direction finder to steer with' (28). Instead, he asserts that our nomadic forebears developed a technology which allowed them to triangulate location and move through landscape safely – language: 'The simplest societies orientate themselves to their land and its resources by naming everything there, subjecting its content – useful and useless – to a classification of Linnaean complexity. Beyond their territory lies the Unknown – a frightening place because it is *unnamed*' (30).

Chatwin argues that, in pursuing this project of ascribing linguistic labels to the surrounding world, the human species undertakes an act of psychological creation: 'Man invents the Universe in his mind and then joyfully recognizes his own creation as a place for him to live' (32). This notion that the world is a linguistic formation is extended beyond pure semantics, however, for, in Chatwin's conception, language does not merely mediate our relationship with our environment; rather, part of its function is to orchestrate the 'biologically timed events of the life-cycle' (33).

Our genetic predispositions, it is argued, have become enshrined in language through our ability to construct metaphor and have been subsequently codified into myths, which are, Chatwin asserts, 'human instincts verbalized' (34). These myths express the correct way of living in accordance with surroundings and genetic instruction – essentially telling us what to do and when – and remain as stable elements of cultural life, unless the 'original contract' articulating the correct way of life is challenged by a failure of observation: 'As he failed to synchronize the events of his life to the given sequence, he became progressively disoriented in time and space. And with this derangement new myths surfaced in his consciousness which recorded his anxiety or feelings of guilt for failing to enact the ideal paradigm' (35–6).

Chatwin has already asserted that, in renouncing our peripatetic existence in favour of settled civilisation, we have abandoned an ideal lifestyle. Our cultural preoccupation with stories and myths of travel has emerged, it is argued, as a consequence of this abandonment:

> THE IDEA OF THE JOURNEY is, along with the Creation and Oedipus stories, one of the most persistent of all human myths. And for a band of wandering hunters – perhaps twenty five of them, perhaps fifty – walking unprotected through the wilderness, matching their footfalls to the progress of the seasons – from the water-hole to sources of food or on visits to their neighbour, savouring alternate phases of plenty or want, suffering the trials of youth and the debilities of age, life was quite literally a journey – and, in the light of palaeozoology, a dangerous and heroic one for all. Through life our ancestors *walked* through a sequence of initiations or new beginnings and correctly timed their appointment with death.
>
> But once they settled down and barricaded themselves from the horrors of the bush, they began to compare their settlement with the dangerous but exciting mobility of former times. Settled home brought no new freedom from anxiety, but introduced fresh sources of anxiety. And it remained for them to reenact symbolically the Myth of the Archetypal Journey, that of the Hero and his Road of Trials. Deprived of an actual journey the mind invented one. The animal compulsion to migrate through life emerges in man as the Idea of Life's Journey. And this is what my exegesis has been about. (36)

The basic structure of the archetype[1] that emerges is as follows:

> A young man, bursting with vigour and often credited with superhuman audacity in childhood, leaves home on a long journey. After a sequence of adventures in remote and fabulous lands, he faces the Jaws of Death. A fire-breathing monster menaces with fangs and claws ... and jealously hoarding a treasure, threatens the inhabitants of the land with total destruction unless they cringe before it and appease its bloodthirstiness with sacrificial victims. The hero fights and kills the monster, rewards himself with the treasure and a bride, returns home to the jubilant acclamations of his proud parents and people, and they all live happily ever after. (36–7)

Chatwin goes on to compare this archetype to two compelling narratives of Western civilisation: the story of *Beowulf* and the biography of Ernesto Guevara. Stories such as these are appealing to us, in Chatwin's formulation, because they allow us to follow in narrative form a journey which we would have physically undertaken in former times. This cathartic effect is also a central attraction of religion, Chatwin asserts, which he describes as 'a travel guide for settlers' (45). The pilgrimage is – like the myths described – a codified version of the journeys that were once a material fact of human existence. These cultural preoccupations are thus seen to demonstrate Chatwin's central assertion that we are hardwired for a life on the move.

Chatwin's discussion of the cultural and religious manifestation of our travelling instinct concludes this first section of *The Nomadic Alternative*. All of what follows will broadly expand upon the basic case that Chatwin has set out, with frequent digressions and contradictions, in the introduction analysed above: namely that our restlessness emerges from the suppression through settlement of an innate instinct for movement, inherited from our ancestors, shared with migratory animals, and evident in our cultural preoccupation with ritualised travel.

In the first chapter proper of *The Nomadic Alternative*, titled 'The Pyramid', Chatwin moves on from these generalised assertions concerning his proposed instinct for travel and expands upon his earlier discussion of the innately violent nature of settled civilisation. This section of the work outlines an argument against the excesses of settlement, metaphorically embodied, in Chatwin's conception, in the absurdity of monumental architecture which, the author asserts, reveals:

> [T]he cold rationality of the lunatic. Before the Nuremberg rallies, Hitler communed with himself in a subterranean cell inspired by the burial chamber of the Great Pyramid.
> All monumental architecture is abusive, bought in blood, the token of past and future suffering. ...
> The harmonious proportions of the Parthenon did not reflect some inner harmony in the minds of the builders, but merely announced that an age of turmoil and demagoguery had begun. (48)

Monumental architecture of the sort described is not intended to inspire those who live in the shadow of it, but rather to oppress them into a state-centred mindset where the individual simply becomes the unwitting tool of civilisation. The monuments are 'the unfailing marks of autocracy, of the supposed need to subdue the individual to the needs of the state' (48).

Eventually, however, this collective belief falters, engendering the fall of the great civilisation:

> There comes a point when human individualism says NO. People realize they have been tricked by false promises and fake explanations of human nature and the purpose of human existence. The government presses them to work harder to maintain a way of life that has become meaningless. Fewer and fewer people pay more and more taxes, once the advantages of no fixed address become obvious. Devotion to the machine is, in human terms, futile, as more people adopt a Taoist attitude to the future of material improvement. (62)

Stylistically, 'The Pyramid' suffers from the weight of Chatwin's condemnatory argument; the thesis of *The Nomadic Alternative* demands that civilisation is presented as an irredeemably negative phenomenon which cannot hope to endure. Consequently, the language (reminiscent of some of the more severe passages of the later novel *The Viceroy of Ouidah*) is emotive and oppressive: 'One Pyramid text describes metaphorically a Pharaoh's cannibal bloodlust. He eats men, strangles them, draws out their entrails, swallows his enemies for breakfast, smashes their backbones for the spinal marrow, and sinks his royal fangs into their lungs and palpitating hearts' (50). Like the constructions described, the prose is monumental and overbearing.

Chatwin's aim is to make explicit the contrast between the violent instability of the civilised world and the eternal contentment of the nomads who form the subject of the subsequent chapter, and his histrionic language is employed in support of that endeavour. One can compare the following passage:

> In America too the Aztecs constructed Pyramids of hewn stone that mirrored the petrification of the social hierarchy. Here were scenes of senseless carnage – the glinting of obsidian daggers, iridescent plumage, quivering hearts severed from the bodies of sacrificial victims and blood running into the interstices of turquoise mosaics. (50)

with the opening of the following chapter, entitled 'The Nomadic Alternative', in order to clearly demonstrate Chatwin's aim:

> Each spring the nomads of South West Asia brindle the hills with their herds. Thin lines of animals – sheep and goats, horses and camels – follow the unfurling of the leaves on their journey from winter pastures to the mountains. The nomads are lean and sinewy, burnished by the sun and wind. They do not pause to talk to strangers and scowl at villagers. They

fix their hawk-like eyes on their animals, watching for the first signs of
sickness ... The snow streaked flanks of the mountains are calling him.
Beyond lie the green uplands of summer.
The women suckle silent babies in the folds of their dresses. Their lithe
bodies ebb and flow to the pitching of the saddles, their kohl-dark eyes
glued to the road ahead. Showers of gold glisten on their breasts, and they
have bought fresh printed calico dresses for the spring migration, brilliantly
coloured to match the spring flowers that lacquer the ground. (67)

The implication of the contrast is explicit: civilisation is a violent aberration, whereas nomadic life, securely hitched to the rhythms of the
unchanging natural world, represents a model existence. The nomads are
in tune with their surroundings; the dresses of the nomad women match
the spring flowers, whilst the men are allied with the animal world, 'lean
and sinewy' with 'hawk-like eyes'.[2]

The generalising idealisation of this introductory passage is a hallmark
of the chapter which follows. Specific, sustained anthropological detail
is absent, with the reader instead offered anecdotal and romantic fragments of insight into nomadic life. Outlining both the general manner
of pastoral nomadism and the evolutionary and cultural forces which
shaped it, 'The Nomadic Alternative' attempts to persuade the reader of
the sustaining 'rightness' of that way of life.

Chatwin's introduction invokes the timeless qualities of nomadic
existence, and the contrast it forms to transient civilisation: 'Empires
have been smashed and great cities blown up', he writes, 'but life in the
black tents continues without significant change since the days when
Abraham the nomad sheikh guided his flocks on his annual migration'
(68). This manner of living, in Chatwin's assessment, finds its motivation in a fundamental predisposition for movement; nomadism is not
just a practical manner of pursuing pasture and keeping animals fed
and watered, but a moral state emerging from a horror of settlement:
'The idea of flight is ingrained in the nomad. His will to move forward
averts the appalling consequences of sitting still and offers the promise
of better things ahead' (69). Chatwin allies this idea to a philosophical
notion which both echoes his earlier assertions regarding the archetypal journey myth, and simultaneously prefigures a recurring trope
in his future creative work: the attainment of the 'golden land': 'Each
tribe possessed its Promised Land – a place where the greenery does not
wither in the summer and the milk flows and the flowers give honey to
the bees. But that place lives on the north face of a mountain range, and

the migration path to this annual Paradise passes through a Valley of the Shadow of Death' (69).

There is a constant tension in this chapter – echoed in Chatwin's work generally – between the desire to idealise nomads and the specific manner of nomadic life, which is complex and diverse. The chapter is characterised by periodic interludes which belie Chatwin's awareness of the need to be analytical. He notes that 'The word "nomad" lies open to malicious misinterpretation' (71), an observation that would seem to invite further discussion of what a nomad is, exactly, both generally and within his work. And, indeed, such is the case to some degree in the subsequent paragraphs; we learn of the etymology of the word 'nomad', and of broad differences between nomadic groups: 'The timing of nomadic movements varies from climate to climate' (72), Chatwin writes, before going on to discuss the migrations of the Reindeer Tungus in Siberia. However, Chatwin quickly slips back into the philosophising and generalisation necessitated by the vagaries of his argument: 'Nomads see life as a sequence of linked horizontal planes. The end of the road is the end of joy and sorrow and lies within the traveller himself; for the annual migration enacts the human life cycle in miniature' (74). Such alternation characterises the chapter.

Chatwin passes on from this brief attempt to define his terms to discuss the general virtues of the nomadic social system, and the contrast it forms to that of the civilised world. He asserts the nomad's independence of the system of acquisition: 'Things hamper movement', he writes. 'Precious possessions tether their owner to a place. The nomad whittles them down as he asserts his independence of the economic system he has learned to despise ... Nomad life is an education in asceticism' (76).[3] This antimaterialist inclination is fostered in part by the nature of nomadic living accommodation; a tent does not encourage the acquisition of bulky or precious objects.

The attitude reflected in this approach to possessions manifests itself in the nomads' general manner of living. Nomad life is predicated upon a communal culture: 'All food is shared equally and once a passing stranger shows himself a friend, hospitality is automatic, his life and property sacrosanct. The owner of a tent is honour-bound to share his "bread and salt" with a visitor' (81).

On the rare occasions that conflict breaks out amongst nomad groups, Chatwin argues that the social response is proportionate. The nomads, he asserts, exercise a tradition of brutal but swift justice, but refrain from committing atrocities on the scale of settled peoples, as Charles Doughty observed: 'Their justice is such, that in the opinion of the next governed countries, the Arabs of the wilderness are the justest of mortals ... The nomad justice is mild where the Hebrew law, in this smelling of the settled countries, is crude' (79–80). Chatwin points out that, to the nomad, '[t]he exquisite refinements of the torture chamber, that combination of blood, cracked ribs and mechanics, are unknown' (81). Nomadic life relies on a system of self-policing in order to maintain social harmony: 'The notion of equivalence informs his criminal code – "An eye for an eye and a tooth for a tooth". A nomad never runs to the law. He is his own court and executioner and heaven help him if he makes a mistake. He identifies the criminal, personally pays him out for the crime. And he takes full responsibility for so doing' (81).

Such is the situation within nomad society. However, Chatwin observes, nomadic interactions with outside groups – in particular those of the civilised world – are more antagonistic. Raids against the city are common: 'The obese upper echelons of the city are the nomad's favourite target and he wills to pull down its hierarchies. Professional herding encourages him to think that all citizens are mindless animals, fit for the abattoir, to be milked, coralled and butchered at all times' (85). Out of the tradition these raids established emerged the modern tenets of guerrilla warfare, Chatwin argues.

From this point, the chapter drifts away somewhat from the practicalities of nomad life, and embarks instead upon an historical account of nomadism's emergence 'on the slopes of the Fertile Crescent – that great arc of hills and mountains extending from Palestine to South West Persia' (94). This cultural history continues the chapter's project of idealisation, and reinforces the philosophical division already posited between the nomad and the settler.

For Chatwin, the development of agriculture – and the settlement attendant upon it – marks the genesis of restlessness: '[I]t substituted longer hours of back-breaking work for the excitements of the chase and deprived the hunter of his infinite capacity for leisured discourse. Monotony and inertia replaced his need for struggle and the unpredictable danger, and forced him to look elsewhere for stimulants' (97). Chatwin sees this moment as metaphorically allied with the Fall; it represents a move away from a state of existence that was peaceable and idyllic. The biblical metaphor encapsulates the thrust of the chapter: 'Eden was a place and an idea', Chatwin writes. 'The idea, if not the place, survives. It was a happy hunting ground where men were equal and every fish, fowl, beast, herb and fruit was free for the taking. When Man presumed to plant his own garden, he fell. And God took his revenge' (97–8).

The 'Nomadic Alternative' chapter seeks to offer an account of nomad life which demonstrates its inherent 'rightness', and to set it in positive contrast to the development and manner of civilised life. However, in the chapter subsequent to 'The Nomadic Alternative' – titled 'Hunting – The Art of the Minimum' – Chatwin outlines a means of existence which cleaves even more closely to the ideal state he identified in the introduction to *The Nomadic Alternative*. A notebook of Chatwin's contains the assertion that: 'If you're going to idealize the Noble Savage – as I do – the problem is to pick the right savage' (Box 6). Chatwin believed that in '[t]he hunters and gatherers who live at the minimal level of material culture in bands of twenty-five to fifty, bound up within a kinship structure of five hundred or so all speaking the same dialect … to be distinguished from all others by their complete freedom of movement', he had discovered exactly the 'right sort of savage' (*NA* 134).

In *The Nomadic Alternative*, Chatwin fixes upon the example of the Yaghan of Tierra del Fuego as prime representatives of this ideal. Historical precedent did not offer Chatwin much support in his choice of the Yaghan. Charles Darwin had visited Tierra del Fuego in December 1832 and had been profoundly unimpressed by the aboriginals he encountered, commenting that the Fuegian language 'scarcely deserves to be called articulate. Captain Cook has compared it to a man clearing his throat, but certainly no European ever cleared his throat with so many hoarse, guttural, and clicking sounds' (1989: 173), adding in a letter that 'the cries of domestic animals are far more intelligible' (1897: 227). Darwin's impression was compounded by his preconceived notion that the standard of intelligence and civilisation dwindled the closer one got to the poles; Tierra del Fuego, the final stop before the Antarctic, was, then, prime territory for the discovery of the most limited of beings. For Darwin, thus, the Yaghan of Tierra del Fuego represented the most primitive state of man; his assessment was 'anti-primitivism' of the most profound sort.

Chatwin saw Darwin's assessment as a grave injustice, and in 'Hunting – The Art of the Minimum' he sought to rehabilitate the reputation of the Yaghan, positing them as representatives of the finest ascetic existence:

> The Yaghan had invested in freedom of movement, not in things. Therein lay their sense of well-being. Those who abandon a settled existence may feel the flickerings of such liberty, but this is a poor substitute for the

liberty of those innocent of the alternative. The Yaghan – in common with other hunting and gathering peoples – knew that settlement entails hoarding, and hoarding the genesis of a hierarchy. Settlement robs men of the risks that give a sense of accomplishment to the processes of life ... As an act of policy they had remained in the State that Rousseau recognized as being best for man. This was *not* the State of Nature, extolled by the Romantics, a condition we would now describe as sub-human passivity. This state demands man fully formed, fully equipped with an intelligent brain, fully satisfying his material and intellectual needs, each for himself within the framework of a society of equals. (128)

The Yaghan provided the prime example for Chatwin of the ideal state of human society: existing on just enough to get by, constantly moving about their territory and never coveting what the other man has, having reached 'the golden mean between the indolence of the primitive state and the petulant activity of our own pride, [which] must have been the happiest epoch and the most lasting' (Rousseau 115).

As was outlined in the analysis of the introduction to *The Nomadic Alternative*, Chatwin believed that the suppression of the ideal means of life represented by these 'noble savages' manifested itself culturally in an enduring and universal preoccupation with the journey. Chatwin returns to this assertion in the subsequent chapter – titled 'Wanderers' – citing, at length, a diverse range of social groups for whom travel has become a codified element of their existence.

In particular, Chatwin focusses upon those who travel according to the instruction of theological ritual. Religious doctrine has frequently emphasised the significance of the ritualised journey:

[P]rofessional mystics, who answer a call to leave the chains of settlement, have always realized that the brief release of carnivals, pilgrimages and religious festivals might be prolonged indefinitely. The spiritual athletes either take to the perpetual pilgrimage of the road and walk their way to enlightenment; or they experiment with narcotic vehicles or harsh disciplinary exercises to resurrect the rewards and hardships of a wandering life. (178)

The author goes on to outline multiple religious philosophies that emphasise the spiritual significance of the journey; from Sufism, whose followers speak of themselves as '"travellers on the Way" – migrants along a spiritual *Il-Rah* that leads to Heaven' (179), through Hinduism ('The appalling discomfort of India, the pullulating populations, the inequality of rich and poor and the visible presence of death reinforced the illusion that the body was a cage for the soul' (182)), to Buddhism, Taoism and Christianity: 'The Early Mediaeval Church inaugurated the perpetual pilgrimage as a therapeutic cure for the sins of settlement' (203).

Chatwin does also briefly reference secular travellers and anti-urbanists, notably the Cynics and their 'ascetic counterparts in Palestine, the Essenes' (199), as well as mentioning the later traditions of the anarchist and the wandering scholar, who 'drifted from school to school in search of a better education or more interesting thesis' (207) and who was known as a 'vagus'. He conspicuously avoids, however, any mention of the romantic tradition[4] of the traveller, which would appear an equally relevant example of our cultural preoccupation with the journey. The absence perhaps reflects the fact that, fundamentally, Chatwin was conscious on some level that the romantic tradition of wandering was a more plausible explanation for the endemic restlessness which he perceived in the modern world than that which he was attempting to construct from our evolutionary history.

In the final chapter of *The Nomadic Alternative* – titled 'A Journey Is Walking Itself Out in Us' – Chatwin changes approach, and attempts to draw his argument together through the development of a unified theory of existence which asserts not only that the lifestyle of our travelling forebears prescribes our instinct for movement, but also that it has imposed upon us an instinctive blueprint for how best to structure the course of our existence.

Chatwin argues that the professional traveller comes to coordinate 'annual activities to his biological clock' (221), in tune with the passage of the seasons which 'organically affects our bodies and in turn the way we behave' (220). This argument will be familiar to the reader from the earlier analysis of Chatwin's introduction, in which he describes the 'circannian' rhythms that we are subject to as a species. In this chapter, however, Chatwin moves beyond his earlier position to assert that these smaller units of prescribed activity aggregate to form a plan for the whole of life. Echoing Shakespeare, he proposes that this blueprint sets out seven separate ages:

> The annual death and rebirth implicit within the cycle of the seasons repeats again and again in miniature the events of that larger unit of time, The Seven Ages of Man ... In the course of each of these ages, the glands of the body perform a fixed sequence of functions which should coincide with a fixed sequence of messages that surface in the brain, telling the individual how to behave. (224)

This series of initiations begins, of course, with birth, followed closely by the second stage of weaning, which, Chatwin argues, is 'the most important initiation of all. For if it is incorrectly timed all successive stages will be displaced' (234). Subsequent to weaning, the next important stage that Chatwin identifies is that of puberty, which the author asserts as particularly important to the young male, offering a chance to prove that he is 'now a man, fit to mate with a woman and defend her' (242). The initiate is obliged to demonstrate his virility; traditionally, Chatwin argues, this test would have come with an encounter with one of man's early predators: 'The male initiate introduces himself to the Devil ... Young manhood thrives in the jaws of death, and if they fail to snap, the man is less than a man' (242). In contemporary tribal communities, however, the test has become sublimated into a puberty ritual, often constituting 'the splitting of the urethra or skinning of the groin' (242).

The next stage in Chatwin's seven natural ages comes with marriage: 'One man and one woman join themselves into an economic and sexual partnership, which should last the rest of their lives. Neither can afford to remain single. If they did, the man would go without his share of vegetables, and the woman be deprived of her share of the meat' (244).

The fifth stage comes when a man reaches full maturity, and becomes a tribal elder, an acknowledged repository of wisdom to whom 'young hunters attach themselves ... in the hope that this wisdom will rub off on them' (245). In the sixth stage, this authority begins to wane: 'The leader finds that his eldest son has supplanted him in influence, and he must reconcile himself to his reduced status. During the period of decline the ageing man prepares himself for death' (244).

Death itself is, of course, the seventh and final stage. Chatwin sees the promise of heaven as implicit in the end of a correctly lived life: 'Their subject has lived his myths on time and has recovered the Peaceable Kingdom, where even a hungry lion is a friend. Extinction of the body is of no further interest to him or to anybody' (245).

In settling into a sedentary existence, the human species has become disconnected from the natural forces which control this life cycle, and it is this disconnection, Chatwin argues, that has led to the 'violence, neuroses and repressions' (226) evident in the civilised world. If we are to emerge from this state, which Chatwin describes as a 'suspended adolescence' (226), then we must learn the lessons inherent in the life of the professional travellers so idealised elsewhere in *The Nomadic Alternative*, and to whom Chatwin returns in order to posit a definition of basic human society:

> A human society is a small unit of men and women, paired off into sexual and economic partnerships.
>
> They do not settle in one fixed place, but migrate along the tracks of a given stretch of territory, to exploit its animal and vegetable resources as they come in season, without taking active steps to store surplus or propagate their food supply.
>
> They deliberately calculate for alternate seasons of plenty and want, and their bodies allow for at least one unenjoyable period of enforced torpor in the year.
>
> They divide the human life cycle horizontally into distinct phases, or units of biological time, which synchronize with glandular changes of the body; and they actively ensure that the members live out all the possibilities contained within each phase. (246)

At this point of *The Nomadic Alternative* the basic arguments of the work have fallen away, lost to a thesis that has snowballed as it has progressed. As the assertions have become grander, and the theory more all-encompassing, so the prose has become less coherent. By the final passages of the book, the initial aim of this overwhelming work seems forgotten, and incoherence appears to have taken firm hold:

> The question is, 'Do you belong to MAN or the MACHINE?' With each day more and more reply, 'We belong to MAN, and there's nothing wrong with him.' There is no possibility for creating a New Man. To tamper with his genetics will not produce a New Man, but an adjunct of the machine, and ally of the Devil. Man is an infant beside the Iguana and his career a fleeting moment of evolutionary time. Yet he is an old man. His nature does not significantly change. And he is kicking hard, greeting the brutality of the machine with the sullen hostility of the pariah. The driving forces of history are the ways of the wandering savage. (268)

Chatwin's agent, Deborah Rogers, was the first to read the draft of *The Nomadic Alternative* upon its submission in November 1972: 'I remember the heart sinking' (qtd. in *US* 223), she told Nicholas Shakespeare. By this point, the manuscript had been endlessly worked over and revised for almost three years and the completion of the book had become for Chatwin a test of character and identity: he described the undertaking in a letter to his parents as the most important thing he had ever attempted.

Deborah Rogers dutifully sent on the manuscript to Tom Maschler, who made it through only 50 pages: 'I found them stilted, even boring' (86), he comments in his memoir. Maschler told Chatwin of the decision that the manuscript was not publishable face to face: 'He came to my office and I knew it would be a particularly difficult meeting. Obviously I had to be frank and equally obviously he was exceedingly disappointed' (86). Maschler hoped that he had managed to dissuade Chatwin from pursuing the project further.

He had not. Chatwin would continue to fruitlessly revise *The Nomadic Alternative* until his trip to Patagonia in late 1974 provided the necessary distraction of a new project.[5] It had turned out to be the 'great unwriteable' (*US* 204), as Chatwin had predicted to Joan Leigh Fermor in 1971 and the decision not to publish profoundly knocked his confidence: 'I do think he felt it was a failure' (2010), comments Elizabeth.

The overall failure was one of approach. Chatwin wished to use *The Nomadic Alternative* as a vehicle for his own personally held theory of restlessness. This chapter has traced, as linearly as is possible given the frequent incoherence of the text, the thrust of this theory, detailing Chatwin's assertion that the human species inherited from the vegetarian primates an inbuilt instinct to travel; that this instinct is evident in the lifestyle of nomads and – in particular – hunter-gatherers, both contemporary and historical, as well as our cultural preoccupation with travel; and that it is in the suppression of this instinct that the cause of the restlessness Chatwin saw as endemic to the modern world can be found. This argument is quite clearly a personal philosophy, rather than an anthropologically provable hypothesis, and hence Chatwin had adopted the authorial stance, in researching and writing the book, of the interested amateur or generalist, rather than the academic expert.

Yet Chatwin was not content to write a work which fully embraced its status as personal reflection. He wanted his theory to be taken seriously by the reader, and bolted on to it an overwhelming body of disparate research intended to convince the reader of the rightness of his idiosyncratic perspective. In adopting these elements of academic convention in an effort to invoke the reader's credulity, the work simultaneously invites the reader's scrutiny – under which Chatwin's thesis is found sadly wanting. The work comes resultantly to occupy 'a nebulous no-man's land between scientific theory and autobiography' (Box 31), satisfying on neither level.

There are ancillary failures as well, which are all too obvious from the above analysis: the contortions of the argument, the hectoring prose style, the incoherent digressions are all problems that would have affected the work even had the wider issue of approach been resolved. Yet all are ultimately rendered irrelevant by the fundamental incompatibility between the argument Chatwin wished to present and the form in which he chose to present it.

It thus may appear from the analysis undertaken that *The Nomadic Alternative* is unworthy of serious attention, marked as it is by such methodological failings. Yet the text is absolutely fundamental to both the understanding of Chatwin's core belief system and the appreciation of his development as a professional writer.

Even at a simply stylistic level, the influence of *The Nomadic Alternative* upon Chatwin's approach to his later work is clear. Nicholas Murray has written of Chatwin as a 'highly accomplished prose stylist. His spare, swift, economical prose is a rebuke to the prolixity and purple that have so often trammelled the travel writing genre. He was incapable of writing a slipshod or uninteresting sentence and the relative brevity of his books was the necessary outcome of an art that did not waste itself' (1993: 12). One need only glance at a typical sentence to note the contrast between Chatwin's published work, so elegantly and accurately analysed by Murray, and the prose style of *The Nomadic Alternative*:

> Commitment to the logical consequences of civilization demands limitless faith in vertical progress. But this inevitably reaches the point of diminishing returns. There civilization falters and may collapse into putrefaction unless men are prepared to learn some lessons from their pre-civilized past. Civilizations rarely – if ever – fall prey to an invader, for decomposition is internal. (62)

The stylistic approach throughout *The Nomadic Alternative* is of a writer not in full command of his prose or his subject. In its pedagogic tone; its baggy, unclear syntax; its long and ill-defined chapters – the work is the antithesis of Chatwin's later texts. For better or worse (and some – including Patrick Leigh Fermor – have argued that Chatwin's prose was *too* controlled), every word that Chatwin would write in the future would be set down with the memory of *The Nomadic Alternative* pressing on his mind.

The influence of *The Nomadic Alternative* was not merely stylistic, however. Its most lasting legacy is located in the framework of ideas which the text bequeathed to Chatwin's later work. His fascination with the archetype of travel would directly influence *In Patagonia*, which employed the quest as a structuring foundation. His interest in the virtues of asceticism and the perils of materialism emerges in *Utz*. The integrity of a life hitched to the changing seasons and in tune with the natural world would emerge as a central theme of *On the Black Hill*, and his belief in the violent aberration of settled existence would influence the brutal depiction of Francisco da Silva in *The Viceroy of Ouidah*.

More generally, each of Chatwin's subsequent texts would bear the overall influence of his continuing obsession with the topic of restlessness, which the failure of his nomad book had merely encouraged. The intellectual conversation begun in *The Nomadic Alternative* would continue in his work, sublimated, up to and beyond its summational expression in *The Songlines*, which Chatwin would patch together, over a decade later, from the raw material contained within the manuscript of his 'Anatomy of Restlessness'.

With its own, author-written, creation myth; its formally inventive central notebooks sections; and its 'vision of the Songlines stretching across the continents and ages' back to the First Man who, 'opening his mouth in defiance of the terrors that surrounded him, shouted the opening stanza of the World Song, "I AM!"' (282), Chatwin's Australian novel successfully married form and content in a manner which starkly contrasts the mismatch evident in *The Nomadic Alternative*. Whilst that work had insisted through its formal approach upon its credibility, *The Songlines* eschewed academic convention altogether, with Chatwin fully embracing the idiosyncrasy of his theory. It was a remarkable, alchemical achievement; Chatwin had managed to fashion, from a work rightly considered unpublishable, a sprightly, engaging narrative which set out what he had intended to say in 1969, and which subsequently reached the top of the *Sunday Times* bestseller list; it was 'as if he had blasted oxygen through it', comments Nicholas Shakespeare (2010).

That revelation was more than ten years into the future, however. In the immediate term, Chatwin's creeping realisation of the impossibility of salvaging *The Nomadic Alternative* led to a redirection of his creative energies: 'The failure was a liberation', wrote Susannah Clapp (1998: 26). His letters over the course of the early 1970s constantly hint at the emergence of creative endeavours: there are endless proposals to James Ivory for prospective movie scripts; whilst in Niger, Chatwin wrote to his wife of a story he had embarked upon: 'I have started writing a long story – may even be a short novel. You know how I have an incurable fascination for French hotel/bordel keepers of a certain age in an ex-colonial situation. Well I've been in on a most amazing series of encounters with one in Tahoua. Even held the fort while she had a *crise cardiaque* after sleeping with a Togolese bandleader (*L'Equipe Za-Za Bam-Bam et Ses Suprèmes Togolaises*). Much better than writing a travel piece because one can lie' (*US* 209).[6]

These impulses were subsequently fostered by a post offered to him at the *Sunday Times* in its heyday, during the editorial reign of Harold Evans. Chatwin was recruited by Francis Wyndham as an arts adviser, and Wyndham became the latest, and most lasting, of Chatwin's mentors, and would be the first to read all of his subsequent manuscripts: 'Bruce had huge respect for Francis', comments Elizabeth (2010). His pieces for the *Times* covered a broad range of topics, and included profiles of André Malraux, Ernst Jünger (whose influence on *On the Black Hill* is explicit), the couturier Madame Vionnet, and Nadezhda Mandelstam. His assignments gave him the opportunity to develop his writing skills on pieces with a deadline, a word count and, perhaps most significantly, a tangible subject. Reading these articles in conjunction with *The Nomadic Alternative*, it becomes clear that his *Sunday Times* assignments perfectly suited his faculties as a writer. Concepts – it had become evident – were not his strength; rather, his talent lay in his noted ability to observe and distill his observation into narrative form. As Jorge Ramon-Torres Zavaleta observed: 'He was a person who noticed things, and in noticing them, invented them' (*Footsteps*).

In particular, he noticed people and their stories, and it was this skill – activated by his *Sunday Times* apprenticeship – which would form the basis of his future success: 'He had this amazing talent because I used to watch it', comments Elizabeth. 'He'd meet someone he'd never met before, didn't know anything about them and within five minutes he'd discovered what their main passion was, and then they were off and they always thought he was their friend for life. There were a lot of them' (2007).

Chatwin would subsequently turn to writing about the individuals who suffered from the affliction of restlessness he had attempted to deconstruct in *The Nomadic Alternative*, from the exiled migrants of *In Patagonia* to the anxiously confined Joachim Utz in his final novel. Though the theories he had developed in *The Nomadic Alternative* remained central to his world view, in the future these assertions would be framed within a narrative centrally concerned with the human implications of those theories. Chatwin moved away from the pseudo-academic objectivity of *The Nomadic Alternative*, towards an approach rooted in the individual, in the specific stories of those that he encountered. Nicholas Shakespeare

recounts in his biography a conversation between the Argentinean journalist Uki Goni and Chatwin in which Goni asks: 'Your fascination is
people?' to which Chatwin responds understatedly: 'Yes, in the end. It
took rather a long time to discover that' (qtd. in Shakespeare 2000: 291).

NOTES

1 Though, as is typical in *The Nomadic Alternative*, Chatwin does not cite any
secondary material in his discussion of cultural archetypes, the notion owes a
debt to a number of sources, most particularly Sir James Frazer's *The Golden
Bough* and Lord Raglan's *The Hero: A Study in Tradition, Myth, and Drama*.

2 This passage is also notable for its stylistic similarity to Chatwin's later
creative work. It is one of the few sections in *The Nomadic Alternative* where
the reader glimpses the prose qualities for which he would become celebrated; a reflection, perhaps, of the romantic attraction that he felt to the
way of life he describes.

3 However, characteristically, Chatwin seems to contradict himself later in
the chapter, writing that: 'The nomad "wanders for gain", full-bloodedly
committed to increased growth and shamelessly materialistic' (79).

4 For an analysis of the subject along these lines, see Rebecca Solnit, *Wanderlust: A History of Walking*.

5 The manuscript under consideration in this chapter is that submitted to Cape
in 1972.

6 This would become the short story 'Milk'.

3

At the end

[I]t may seem only a cruel kindness to whisper into the ear of the emigrant
the warning – 'That which thou goes forth to seek thou shalt not find.'
It is not said, be it remembered, that he will not find happiness, which,
like the rain and sunshine, although in more moderate measure, comes
alike to all men; it is only said that the particular form of happiness to
which he looks forward will never be his. (59)
W.H. Hudson, *Idle Days in Patagonia*

[T]his is no more a travelogue than Turgenev's *Sportsman's Sketches* is a book
about shooting woodcock. (11)
Bruce Chatwin, *Introduction to A Visit to Don Otavio*

In December of 1977, Bruce Chatwin wrote to his agent, Deborah
Rogers, with some suggestions for the forthcoming American edition
of *In Patagonia*. Having been disappointed with the blurb supplied by
Jonathan Cape for its British edition, which Chatwin deemed 'down-
right misleading' (*US* 277), the author offered 'to do a bit of explaining'
(277). 'Lots of other things have been said about Patagonia', he wrote.
'I saw and did lots of other things in Patagonia, but cut them out for
a specific [reason]' (277). Chatwin goes on to outline his intentions in
writing *In Patagonia*. 'The book', Chatwin wrote, 'is the narrative of an
actual journey and a symbolic one' (277).

The actual journey was undertaken by the author in late 1974 and early
1975. The prospective subject of the South American peninsula had long
been a preoccupation for Chatwin, as Elizabeth attests: '[H]e had always
talked about Patagonia', she observes; 'it was something in the back of
his head all the time' (2007). Famously, on assignment for the *Sunday
Times* in the early 1970s, he had visited the designer Eileen Gray at her
apartment in the rue Bonaparte in Paris; she had a large gouache map of
Patagonia hanging on the wall of her salon and told Chatwin that she had

always wanted to visit the peninsula. Unable, at 93, to make the journey herself, she requested that Chatwin go on her behalf. His departure was made in no less romantic fashion. He abruptly set off alone for South America from New York, having travelled there with Elizabeth for her father's funeral. This sudden leave-taking generated a Chatwin myth – that of the telegram to his superiors at the *Sunday Times*. 'Gone to Patagonia', it was claimed to have read, though Nicholas Shakespeare found little evidence to suggest that it was anything more than a fable. Patrick Meanor, in his volume on Chatwin, concluded similarly: 'Two former editors of the *Sunday Times Magazine* claim to know nothing about any such telegram principally because Chatwin was never a member of their editorial staff; he was a freelance contributor who was paid a healthy retainer of £2,000 a year and would not have needed to announce his departure to any editor' (13).[1] The story was perhaps inspired by Eric Newby's telegram to his friend Hugh Carless, detailed in *A Short Walk in the Hindu Kush*: 'CAN YOU TRAVEL NURISTAN JUNE?' (17), it read. Newby had just left his job for a life of literary travel: 'It had taken me ten years to discover what everyone connected with it had been telling me all along,' Newby wrote, 'that the Fashion Industry was not for me' (17).

Chatwin had recently come to a similar realisation. Not only had he finally accepted that *The Nomadic Alternative* was unsalvageable, he had also become disillusioned with the *Sunday Times*. His journey to Patagonia thus partly resulted from a familiar desire for escape. However, he travelled also in the pursuit of a story, 'something I have always wanted to write up' (*US* 234), which would ultimately come to provide a conduit for the tangible expression of those experiences he had unsuccessfully attempted to deconstruct in *The Nomadic Alternative*.

This was the implication of his reference to a 'symbolic voyage'. From his travels in Patagonia, Chatwin would craft a narrative offering the reader 'a meditation on restlessness and exile' (qtd. in Shakespeare 2000: 311). The material contained within the book would be specifically oriented around this artistic goal: '*All* the stories and characters were chosen because they illustrate some particular aspect of wandering and/or exile' (*US* 277–8), he explained.

That in 1977 few critics and readers picked up on the underlying philosophical schematic of *In Patagonia* was not solely (or even predominantly) the fault of Jonathan Cape's blurb, however; Chatwin himself acknowledged that there had been 'certain things I flatly refused to say in the text for fear of sounding pretentious' (*US* 277), and, indeed, there is no authorial statement or textual preface which signals Chatwin's holistic intentions. Conscious of the didacticism of *The Nomadic Alternative*, he scrupulously avoided the impulse to tell, preferring instead to show.

Examined from the current critical juncture, however, the work's sense of continuity with *The Nomadic Alternative* is manifest; Chatwin set the stories of the individuals he met, and the historical anecdotes he uncovered, in the service of the subject of human restlessness which he had wrestled with for the past five years. 'The anatomy of restlessness is a very intangible subject', he wrote in an outline for *In Patagonia*. 'If you air it *in vacuo*, you spread into sweeping generalities and cannot make the theme cohere. I propose to use this journey through Patagonia as a vehicle on which to pin a series of notes towards a theory of the Journey itself' (Box 41).

In the increasingly numerous reports of Patagonia published during the course of the nineteenth century, one characteristic of the landscape was particularly emphasised – its emptiness. Charles Darwin, who visited the region aboard the Beagle in the 1830s, wrote in the journal of researches which emerged from his voyage that the plains of Patagonia 'are characterised only by negative possessions; without habitations, without water, without trees, without mountains, they support merely a few dwarf plants' (1989: 374). Later travellers to Patagonia, including Lady Florence Dixie and W.H. Hudson, echoed this sentiment, encouraging a view of the peninsula as an unpopulated wilderness.[2]

The environmental factors which had prevented any populous settlement in Patagonia had also ensured that the peninsula remained tantalisingly untainted by the institutions attendant on civilisation. Though nominally – and uncertainly – divided between Argentina and Chile, Patagonia was, in reality, beyond the influence of any governance. The peninsula, it appeared from the accounts which emerged, remained entirely free from the strictures of the civic world.

Consequently, the peninsula began to develop a perversely attractive reputation amongst those who wished to escape the impositions of their own society and, over the course of the latter nineteenth century, Patagonia experienced a small but significant influx of immigrants.[3] The motivations of these immigrants differed: some were fleeing religious or cultural repression, some sought an escape from poverty or the tyranny of landowners, whilst others had less tangible reasons for their journeying. To some degree, however, all were attracted by the notion of the landscape as a blank space, 'a kind of tabula rasa for a new life' (Blanton 100), which offered the possibility of living, to some degree, 'out of the world'.

The most well known of these migrant groups is, of course, the Welsh. Welsh emigration had begun in earnest in the early decades of the nineteenth century, a response to increasing hegemonic pressure from across the border. The pioneering emigrants of this period tended to relocate to the United States; however, the increasing population density of the American east coast in the early nineteenth century ensured that, upon arrival, the migrants were rapidly assimilated into English-speaking culture. Those who left Wales had usually done so because of strong nationalist views; the melting pot of American life held no appeal. It thus soon became clear to those orchestrating the Welsh emigration movement that an environment was needed free of external influence, a blank space upon which a true New Wales could be founded. In searching for such a land, a number of alternative options were considered by the emigration committee, including Oregon, Australia, New Zealand, Brazil, Uruguay, and Vancouver Island. However, as a result of its established reputation, as well as the promising overtures of the Argentine government, Patagonia emerged in the mid-nineteenth century as the preferred choice.

In order to encourage participants in this grand social experiment, the organising committee – led by the Reverend Michael Jones of Bala – produced and distributed a handbook which enthused as to the possibilities of a new life in the south. This document, which was nominally based on the findings of a research party who had returned from the peninsula in 1863, offered a substantially burnished vision of a country similar in landscape and climate to the Welsh borders, but outside the jurisdiction of a distant governing authority, with a fertile landscape of: '"tall strong forests" along the riverside, with the surrounding land being "green and splendid". Among these "luscious pastures", "herds of animals" pastured. No mention was made of the tendency of the Chubut to periodic flooding, as was reported by Fitzroy' (Williams 1975: 26). The weather, too, was presented in deeply favourable terms; the area was blessed by '"the most healthy and pleasant climates in the world", it was climactically a temperate land being "neither too hot, nor too cold"' (Williams 1975: 26). Despite the clear propagandism of this handbook, a number of the disenfranchised did sign up for the Patagonian project, and on 24 May 1865, 163 Welsh settlers sailed from Liverpool for Patagonia on the converted tea-clipper *Mimosa*.

They were unprepared for what greeted them upon their arrival at Port Madryn two months later. The fervent religiosity of the Welsh emigrants had led them to draw parallels between their own plight and that of the Israelites in the wilderness. The land to which they were sailing held almost impossible promise for the seafarers aboard the *Mimosa*; Patagonia was so little known that, coupled with the influence of the literature distributed by the emigration committee, it was easy for them to believe that they were sailing for the promised land, as God's blessed people. They must have realised on the very moment of their landing that such a belief was utterly misguided. Patagonia looked nothing like the promised land – or indeed Wales; there was little but thornscrub and sand to greet them upon their arrival. Life was desperately difficult for the first months and years; crops failed, washed out by floods or killed off by drought, and, even when a surplus was achieved, little possibility for trade existed. Six years after the first wave of immigration, the Patagonian explorer George Chaworth Musters noted that '[t]he visionary scheme of a Welsh Utopia, in pursuit of which these unfortunate emigrants settled themselves, ought not to be encouraged, likely as it is to end in the starvation of the victims to it' (244). He even recorded an account of the settlers eating grass, so desperate was their plight.

The story of Welsh emigration to Patagonia can be seen as analogous of the wider experience of those who left homes in the West for a life upon this remote peninsula. The disparity between the ambitions imposed upon the landscape, and the realities frequently encountered by the migrants upon their arrival cultivated a specific psychology. Patagonia became a land, in Andrew Palmer's words, 'populated by immigrants who both love the place and wish they could leave' (16), and who were subject to the torments of experience metaphorically depicted by W.H. Hudson:

> And now at his journey's end comes reality to lay rude hands on him with rough shaking. Meanwhile, before he has quite recovered from the shock, that red flag on which his dreamy eyes have been so long fixed stays not, but travels on and on to disappear at last like a sunset cloud in the distant horizon. (60)

The unique psychology of this gradual turning of hope into disillusion – which, whilst not universal, clearly became a prevalent experience amongst migrant communities in Patagonia – would offer the ideal metaphorical representation of Chatwin's dearly held ideas around restlessness, and it was upon the experiences of the 'dreamers and adventurers whose

dreams had failed them' (Shakespeare 2000: 290) that he focussed both
during his time exploring the peninsula and when subsequently honing
his material.

In an early section of *In Patagonia*, the narrator goes to visit a Patagonian
poet:

> The poet lived along a lonely stretch of river, in overgrown orchards of
> apricots, alone in a two-roomed hut. He had been a teacher of literature in
> Buenos Aires. He came down to Patagonia forty years back and stayed. (37)

As 'The Maestro' expounds on the bewitching nature of the peninsula,
the narrator observes the rain drumming 'on the tin roof' and comments
of the poet: 'For the next two hours he was my Patagonia' (37).

This aside testifies to the fact that the stories of those individuals
encountered in his geographical and historical exploration of Patagonia
constituted the substance of the peninsula for Chatwin. *In Patagonia*
relentlessly focusses on the individual story, eschewing the conventions of narratorial reflection or environmental description. On the few
occasions that the narrator offers a commentary on the landscape which
surrounds him, he emphasises the monotony of the scene as a contrast
to the vibrance of those characters he encounters. On his journey south-
ward from Bahia Blanca, for example, the narrator 'sleepily' observes 'the
rags of silver cloud spinning across the sky, and the sea of grey-green
thornscrub lying off in sweeps and rising in terraces and the white dust
streaming off the saltpans, and, on the horizon, land and sky dissolving
into an absence of colour' (17).

The tendency for separate elements of the Patagonian landscape to
amorphise remarked upon in this description presents a notable coun-
terpoint to the earlier depiction of the distinct and vibrant features of
Sonny Urquhart, to whom the reader has been introduced in the previous
chapter: 'Sonny Urquhart was a hard stringy man with blond hair swept
back and parted in the centre. He had moles on his face and a big Adam's
apple. The back of his neck was criss-crossed with lines from working
hatless in the sun. His eyes were watery blue, and rather bloodshot'
(15). This example offers an analogous demonstration of the contrasting
narratorial approach to landscape and character throughout the book.

That character is foregrounded in *In Patagonia* is a consequence of
the thematic thrust identified above; this is to be a book about the individual experience of restlessness, rather than a genre-typical account of

a journey around Patagonia. Chatwin foregrounds this theme, and its concentration in the personal, in the very first paragraph of *In Patagonia* set on South American soil:

> The history of Buenos Aires is written in its telephone directory. Pompey Romanov, Emilio Rommel, Crespina D.Z. de Rose, Ladislao Radziwil, and Elizabeta Marta Callman de Rothschild – five names taken at random from among the R's – told a story of exile, disillusion and anxiety behind lace curtains. (5)

Exile, disillusion and anxiety are to be the keynote emotions of those characters whom Chatwin depicts in *In Patagonia*, engendered by the rigours of life encountered by the migrants: the weather, the politics, the remoteness, the sterility. Even the emptiness which was an original attraction of the land becomes a cause of disillusion: 'In Argentina there was nothing – sheep and cows and human sheep and cows' (80), comments the Russian nurse at Río Pico. This sense of disillusion frequently manifests itself in a restless longing to escape to the distant homeland of parents or grandparents. Chatwin writes of the Scottish couple he encounters at the 'Estancia Lochinver':

> One year, when the price of wool was up, he and his wife went to Scotland. They stayed in first-class hotels and were a week on Lewis. There he became familiar with the things his mother spoke of – gulls, herring boats, heather, peat – and he had felt the call.
> Now he wanted to leave Patagonia and retire to Lewis. (90)

Chatwin repeatedly relates similar biographies; of families who, relentlessly confronted with the realities of Patagonian life, are searching for escape.

Few of those whom Chatwin describes seem destined to effect such an escape, however; it would, of course, undermine the authorial scheme if the characters of *In Patagonia* were able to cure their restlessness by locating a happy homeland. Such plans as those of the Scottish couple are inevitably frustrated: 'He did not know how to get out. The price of wool was falling and the Peronistas were after the land' (90). Chatwin wrote in his notebook of the anxieties and challenges of the situation: 'Imagine the horror of being stuck in your father's creation – *stuck*. And on an estancia in Patagonia you really are stuck' (Box 35). Often the Patagonians the narrator encounters appear trapped by a perverse and unquantifiable connection to the peninsula;[4] the poet comments of Patagonia: 'She is a hard mistress. She casts her spell. An enchantress! She folds you in her arms and never lets go' (37). As Chatwin observed in a notebook aside: 'Departure is, as they say in Patagonia, conditional' (Box 35).

As a consequence of their confinement, many undertake to live within consolatory fantasies of their European nationality, restlessly looking backwards. They travel imaginatively, rather than physically, in an attempt to recapture what has been lost. Upon the narrator's visit to the Swiss soprano, for example, an almost Proustian return to Geneva is described: 'She took up a coloured photograph of her city and began to recall the names of quays, streets, parks, fountains and avenues', Chatwin writes. 'Together we strolled around pre-war Geneva' (82).

The desire to reclaim lost national identity is also often expressed materially, however, with many of Chatwin's exiles attempting the construction of *physical* interpretations of their homeland, in their dress, their rituals of religion and culture and even their architecture: 'Apart from its metal roof nothing distinguished it from the houses of a South German village', Chatwin writes of the German dwelling at Río Pico, 'the half-timbering infilled with white plaster, the grey shutters, the wicket fence, the scrubbed floors, painted panelling, the chandelier of antler tines and lithographs of the Rhineland' (84). Often these constructions lapse into stereotypes, a tendency perhaps best exemplified by the character of Jim Ponsonby, who attempts in his dress to convey the impression of an English country gentleman. Chatwin describes 'the Norfolk jacket in brown herring-bone tweed, the hardwood buttons, the open-necked khaki shirt, the worsted trousers, tortoise-shell bifocals and spit-and-polished shoes' (40).

Separated by time and distance, however, these physical adoptions from ancestral homelands often mask a profound disconnection. Jim Ponsonby's grasp of the geography of his mother country is found to be profoundly lacking, asserting Gloucestershire to be 'In the North, what?' (40), whilst a Welsh family the narrator encounters in Bethesda, who have maintained the trappings of Welsh farming life with a 'Welsh sheepdog' and 'Welsh dresser with postcards from Wales on it' (30) are similarly disorientated:

> Their grandfather came from Caernarvon but she couldn't say where that was. Caernarvon wasn't marked on her map of Wales.
>
> 'You can't expect much,' she said, 'when it's printed on a tea-towel.'
>
> I pointed out where Caernarvon should be. She had always wanted to know. (30)

In Chatwin's conception, Patagonian life seems to offer confirmation of Salman Rushdie's observation that, should migrants attempt to recapture the culture they have lost, they 'must ... do so in the knowledge – which gives rise to profound uncertainties – that our physical alienation from [our homeland] almost inevitably means that we will not be capable of reclaiming precisely the thing that was lost; that we will, in short, create fictions' (10). However, in Rushdie's formulation these fictional recreations are imaginary; in Patagonia, the migrant population have gone so far as to construct their own physical interpretations.

The future consequence of this disconnection from their homeland and its traditions is cultural disintegration; the very phenomenon that many of the Patagonian migrants had originally travelled to avoid. Chatwin presents a steady stream of both metaphoric and actual representations of this slow dissolution; the Draigoch guest house in Gaimán, now owned by Italians who 'played Neapolitan songs on the juke box late into the night' (29); the grandson who 'called his grandmother "Granny" but otherwise ... did not speak English or Welsh' (29); even the introduction of pizza into the litany of the traditional Welsh tea.

As the bonds of culture and language begin to break down, the society itself fragments, with a new generation lacking the sense of investment common to their forebears. Many begin to look to a new life abroad: 'She spoke Welsh and sang in Welsh', Chatwin writes of the Genoese wife of Ivor Davies. 'But, as an Italian, she couldn't make the boys Welsh. They were bored with the community and wanted to go to the States' (35). Faced with similar problems and frustrations, Chatwin implies, the children and grandchildren of those European migrants to Patagonia he describes have adopted the strategy of their ancestors, seeking a new environment which will provide an apparent solution to their anxieties; a development which an elderly Patagonian interviewed by John Pilkington reflects upon:

> Just look at us: runaways, dreamers – hopeless romantics, every one! Our immigrants left their homes and countries to throw their fate to the wind, and now their grandchildren are doing the same. If a Patagonian has a choice, you see, he'll always go for the unknown. (166–7)

In this specific migrant experience, which recurs as a subject throughout *In Patagonia*, Bruce Chatwin found a neat allegory for his philosophy of restlessness. The narratorial encounters with such characters as those discussed above provide the thematic heart of *In Patagonia*; they come to embody literally the abstract questions he posed in the introduction to *The Nomadic Alternative*: '*Where* does happiness lie? Why is Here so unbearable? Why is There so inviting? But why is There more unbearable than Here?' (2).

However, the text of *In Patagonia* is constituted by more than simply these specific accounts of the migrant experience. Chatwin expounds in the course of his narrative upon a number of diverse and apparently unrelated topics, including the proposed establishment of a Patagonian kingdom, the mysterious fate of Butch Cassidy, and the Anarchist rebellion of Antonio Soto, amongst others. The disparate subject matter of these stories and anecdotes would seem to contradict the proposed thematic integrity of the text.

Yet cohesion is leant to these seemingly disparate anecdotes – and hence to *In Patagonia* itself – by the repeated invocation in the course of these stories of the subject of restlessness. Butch Cassidy writes to a 'Dear Friend' in the United States that his home country was 'too small' for him and that he was 'restless' and 'wanted to see more of the world'[5] (55); 'the restlessness' (118) is the cause of John Davies' exotic death; the 'story of the Anarchists is the tail end of the same old quarrel: of Abel, the wanderer, with Cain, the hoarder of property' (158), whilst in Puerto Deseado, the narrator talks 'late into the night' with the resident ornithologist of the Estación de Biología Marina, 'arguing whether or not we, too, have journeys mapped out in our central nervous systems; it seemed the only way to account for our insane restlessness' (114). Chatwin is not expounding an argument here, as he was in *The Nomadic Alternative*; the critical assertion of thematic continuity does not imply the didacticism of a thesis. Rather, the subject of restlessness becomes a kind of leitmotif, helping to bind the vast range of material presented by Chatwin, lending coherence to a work which would otherwise have fulfilled Susannah Clapp's initial assessment of the unworked manuscript as a 'collage-like collection of impressions, memories, histories and stories about Patagonia ... mostly functioning more or less autonomously' (1998: 27).

Thus far, the analysis presented has concentrated on the representation of the various Patagonian characters – both contemporary and historical – encountered by the narrator of *In Patagonia* during his travels around the peninsula, as is appropriate for a discussion of a text which so obviously cedes primacy to the stories of these characters. The narrator himself – who guides the reader from person to person – seems by comparison of lesser interest or critical significance, essentially sidelined, as he is, by the author, who, after a brief section of biographical introduction, eschews any lengthy description of the narrator's emotions or actions: 'I'm not interested in the traveller', Chatwin told an interviewer for Australian radio. 'I'm interested in what the traveller sees' (qtd. in Shakespeare 2000: 292). However, Chatwin's claim, though frequently referenced critically as a truism, is not strictly accurate. Whilst there can be little dispute that the Patagonians themselves form the central narrative interest of *In Patagonia*, the '"I" named Bruce' (Shakespeare 2000: 417) functions prominently in the text both structurally and thematically.

This role and influence is set up in the opening pages to the text, where the reader is provided with a biographical introduction which outlines the narrator's emergent curiosity in the peninsula. In part, this preoccupation is motivated by the same desire for escape as those migrants he will go on to describe; the peninsula figured imaginatively in the narrator's childhood as a safe harbour, the reader infers, away from the dangers of the civilised world. The narrator relates the nightmares, endured during the post-war years of his childhood, that the world teetered on the brink of nuclear holocaust. Having watched the civil defence lecturer 'ring the cities of Europe to show the zones of total and partial destruction' (*IP* 3) he 'started an Emigration Committee and made plans to settle in some far corner of the earth. We pored over atlases. We learned the direction of the prevailing winds and the likely patterns of fallout. The war would come in the Northern Hemisphere, so we looked to the Southern. We ruled out Pacific Islands for islands are traps. We ruled out Australia and New Zealand, and we fixed on Patagonia as the safest place on earth' (3–4). As Chatwin observed as he toured the Patagonian wilderness: 'Who would want to bomb Patagonia?' (Box 35).[6]

The young narrator imagined his retreat, the reader learns, as 'a low timber house with a shingled roof, caulked against storms, with blazing log fires inside and the walls lined with the best books, somewhere to live while the rest of the world blew up' (4). Notably the log cabin he encounters on his journey is far from this aesthete's retreat: '"In winter it's terrible," she said. "I covered the wall with *materia plastica* but it blew away. The house is rotten, Señor, old and rotten. I would sell it tomorrow. I would have a concrete house which the wind cannot enter"' (53). As for those Patagonian immigrants who failed to discover the paradise they sought, so the narrator's childhood dreams of a refuge turn out to be fundamentally illusory.

Alongside this profound childhood motivation, which neatly prefigures the general thematic preoccupation with the subject of restlessness, these opening pages also introduce another, apparently whimsical, explanation for the narrator's journey to the peninsula, which appears initially to be merely a structural conceit:

> In my Grandmother's dining-room there was a glass-fronted cabinet and in the cabinet a piece of skin. It was a small piece only, but thick and leathery, with strands of coarse, reddish hair. (1)

This piece of skin – thought to be from a Brontosaurus, but which was in fact taken from the preserved carcass of a mylodon, or giant sloth – had been sent to Chatwin's paternal grandmother by her sailor cousin, Charles Milward, who had settled in Punta Arenas after wrecking the ship under his command, and who will come to figure as a central recurring character in *In Patagonia*. Milward had played a role (later discovered by the narrator to have been somewhat disreputable) in the excavation of the preserved mylodon, which had been discovered at Last Hope Sound, near Puerto Natales in Chilean Patagonia, and had sent the skin as a wedding present for his cousin. It was subsequently placed in the cabinet of family treasures.

Nicholas Shakespeare sees this cabinet – which Chatwin referred to as the 'Cabinet of Curiosities' – as roughly analogous for the author to the wardrobe in C.S. Lewis' *The Chronicles of Narnia*: 'He reached through it into a fantastical world of lions, unicorns and ice queens where he would make his home' (2000: 27). Of the piece of mylodon hide sequestered within this cabinet, the narrator observes: 'Never in my life have I wanted anything as I wanted that piece of skin' (*IP* 2). However, upon the occasion of his grandmother's death the skin was disposed of, disappointing the young narrator, but offering the ideal motivation for an adult journey to Patagonia, which is undertaken in order to replace the lost piece of hide.

In a presentation to the Royal Geographical Society, Chatwin admitted that this premise was set up as a conceit supplying the impetus for a modern imitation of the 'oldest kind of traveller's tale', in which 'the narrator leaves home and goes to a far country in search of a legendary beast' (*PR* 17). Chatwin discussed his intentions in using the form with Melvyn Bragg on *The South Bank Show*: 'You find it in the Gilgamesh epic, in Gawain, in Beowulf', he observed. 'My story was so ridiculous that I wanted to use it as a spoof of all those things.' Chatwin's account of a journey to Last Hope Sound to retrieve a piece of the lost mylodon skin can thus be read as a postmodern quest: digressive, essentially pointless, and ultimately motivated by personal wish engendered by a domestic remembrance rather than necessity or glory. The narrator frequently disappears up blind alleys, chasing, at any opportunity, an offbeat anecdote or interesting character. When the narrator arrives in Last Hope Sound, the ultimate destination of his unfocussed journey, he at first discovers nothing but preserved mylodon droppings, observing deprecatingly: "'Well,' I thought, "if there's no skin, at least there's a load of shit'" (*IP* 249). Subsequently, however, having eventually discovered some remaining skin, the narrator observes that he has 'accomplished the object of this ridiculous journey' (249).

It is understood from this ending that Chatwin's *In Patagonia* is intended as a playful interpretation of the quest form, rather than any sincere emulation. Certainly, when compared to the generalised synopsis of the traditional quest put forward by Chatwin in *The Nomadic Alternative*, and cited at length in the previous chapter, it is clear that the narrative of the Patagonian travelogue is not intended to fit the prescribed format of such a specific journey. The voyage undertaken by the narrator in search of the mylodon skin is essentially anti-climactic and, indeed, does not form a coherent and resolved conclusion to the narrative, which drifts existentially onward for another ten pages after the discovery of the cave at Last Hope Sound. Yet to so fully abandon the sincerity inherent in the classical form of the quest seems perverse, particularly given the metaphorical weight such archetypes are leant in *The Nomadic Alternative*, which had argued that this literary form offered key evidence of humankind's inherited instinct towards travel.

In fact, far from being a superfluous conceit, Chatwin's employment of the structuring device of the quest can be seen to further the expounded theme of the affliction of restlessness and the inevitable disappointments attendant upon it. Examined within the context of the narrative of those Patagonian lives which Chatwin presents, the seemingly whimsical formal approach takes on a more tragic quality, implying an inevitably anti-climactic conclusion to any quest undertaken, whether to locate a piece of sloth skin, or to secure a happy existence in a new land.

The spirit of this quest is echoed in the narrative of the searches undertaken to discover Trapalanda, the mythical Golden City of South America whose 'buildings were of dressed stone, the doors studded with jewels; the ploughshares were of silver, and the furniture of the humblest dwelling of silver and gold' (110). Appropriately, the city was rumoured to have been founded by the Spanish explorers of the early sixteenth century – in particular Simon de Alcazaba in 1534 and Francisco de Camargo in 1539 – who had failed to return, as Carl Skottsberg recorded: 'The shipwreck of Camarga [sic] in the Magellan Straights in 1540, as well as the unhappy result of Sarmiento's colonizing enterprise in 1584, gave birth to all sorts of stories. It was said that survivors of these disasters had wandered into the interior of Patagonia, where they had found immense treasures and established a settlement, which by-and-by had developed into a flourishing city, mentioned in the tales as "la Ciudad de los Césares," the Town of the Emperors' (151).

In Patagonia extends this specific South American mythical metropolis to become metaphorical of the wider historical fascination of those who travel in the hope of locating a utopia:

> Few travellers have ever set eyes on the City. Nor is there any one opinion about its true location: the island of Patmos, the forests of Guyana, the Gobi Desert or the north face of Mount Meru are among the suggestions. All these are desolate places. The names of the City are equally various: Uttarakuru, Avalon, The New Jerusalem, The Isles of the Blessed. (111)

The city is, of course, an illusion, and the imaginative conception of the quest, in both its formal manifestation and citations within the text itself, becomes analogous of Chatwin's conception of the human condition: namely, that we are bound to search for an illusory 'golden city' which is inevitably elusive, but which draws us on restlessly, like Gatsby's green light, W.H. Hudson's red flag or, more prosaically, the gold mine, closed fifty years before, sought after by the young Patagonian miner: 'In the morning, he said he'd be heading on south. Man, he'd be alright. It was simply a question of finding the right mine' (72).

Whilst popular and critical commentary has rarely devoted specific attention to this notion of restlessness as the thematic glue which holds the fragmentary narrative of *In Patagonia* together,[7] critics have frequently commented upon the obvious partiality which resulted from this authorial desire for thematic integrity. Whilst very little of the book was pure invention, Chatwin did indisputably aim at presenting 'his Patagonia, rather than Patagonia' (Borm 25), shaping the characterisation and narrative line in order to accentuate his central interest in the subject of restlessness. Some, such as the British writer John Pilkington, who travelled to Patagonia fifteen years after Chatwin, have seen his authorial approach as manipulative:

I believe Bruce Chatwin knew very well, as he wandered through Patagonia in early 1975, that he was not going to give its residents a fair hearing. Indeed, having met them superficially he may have been afraid to delve too deeply, suspecting that underneath they might be rather dull. To liven up the narrative of *In Patagonia* he focused his attention on an array of larger-than-life characters – Patagonians, to be sure, but extraordinary ones – and where details were missing he made them up. (86)

Earlier in the text, Pilkington, who recorded his journey in the little-read travelogue *An Englishman in Patagonia*, cites his encounter with one of Chatwin's subjects – an Arab bar keeper from Perito Moreno – as evidence of authorial partiality: 'When Bruce Chatwin passed through Perito Moreno in 1975, he wrote that De Fuad kept a sprig of mint on the bar to remind him of a home he'd never seen. I saw no mint and found him not the slightest bit interested in his ancestral origins' (64).

Criticism has also been levelled at the notedly reserved approach of the author towards his narrator, which was another corresponding result of Chatwin's partiality in favour of an approach which foregrounded his thematic interests. Despite the significant literary role played by the narrator – outlined above – the figure does not at any point transcend this role; he remains a device rather than a convincing character, as Manfred Pfister observes: 'He is a pose rather than a subject; his is a brilliant self-stylization rather than the self-reflective depth and emotional richness of subjectivity' (263). The degree to which the narrative figure is refined is evident by comparison with Chatwin's contemporaneous notebooks. Though themselves reserved, they contain the reactions which are absent from the finished text. Of Rio Gallegos, he writes: 'What a dreadful place. … Hope to be out and away tomorrow because I don't think I can hope to stand this place a day longer' (Box 35), whilst his frustration with the Argentinean diet frequently recurs as a subject: 'Feeling very hard done by. At least sun is shining. It rained earlier. Difficulties of Patagonia. Want a salad. Cannot face any more meat' (Box 35). On the infrequent occasions that the narrator expresses such an emotion in the text of *In Patagonia*, it is inevitably aestheticised, emphasising the refinement of his taste: 'I sat and thought of fish. I thought of *portugaises* and Maine lobsters and *loup-de-mer* and bluefish. I even thought of cod' (113).

Just as Chatwin removes narrative emotion, he too divests the narrator of any orienting role, stripping away fripperies which distract from his authorial undertaking. Paul Theroux comments of this approach:

I used to look for links between the chapters, and between two conversations, or pieces of geography. Why hadn't he put them in?
'Why do you think it matters?' he said to me.
'Because it's interesting,' I said, and thought, *It's less coy, too.* 'And
because I think when you're writing a travel book you have to come clean.'
This made Bruce laugh, and then he said something that I have always
taken to be a pronouncement that was very near to being his motto. He
said – he screeched – 'I don't believe in coming clean!' (2000: 388)

David Taylor – in an essay which is generally critical of Chatwin –
observes similarly:

[P]racticalities of travel go largely unreported, as do arrangements for
meetings and interviews. Despite the air of urgency and authority in the
passages of intellectual speculation – historical, literary, anthropological
– there is no serious engagement with academic data, no apparent comprehension of the professional's fixed coherent project with its rigorously
established result. (204)

All of these expressed concerns are consequential of generic expectation.
Criticisms around authorial honesty and objectivity seem legitimate if
In Patagonia is read as a straightforward travelogue; should the reader not
be able to expect an empirical appraisal of the terrain surveyed and the
manner in which it was covered? Is Chatwin not guilty of an authorial
sleight-of-hand in his representation of this journey to Patagonia?

The critical answer to these questions rests on two separate elements:
the understanding taken from the text, and the extratextual information brought to the text. The text itself appears to signal that it is not
to be taken as a traditional work of travel writing in the contemporary
tradition of Wilfred Thesiger or Paul Theroux, both of whom – often
misleadingly – wear their unremitting objectivity as a badge of honour.
This unreliability is manifest even in the opening pages, where Chatwin
presents two contrasting versions of a story accounting for the inclusion
of the sloth skin in his grandmother's cabinet. Of the second, the narrator
observes: 'This version was less romantic but had the merit of being true'
(3).[8] The authorial value system, it is implied, does not prize the virtue of
honesty above all other qualities.

This impression will be reaffirmed later, both in the lapses into novelistic omniscience ('The Bolivian did not want me to go. It was a lovely
day. He did want to go fishing. Going to bed that morning was the
last thing he wanted to do' (44)) and the manifest unreliability of those

intertextual anecdotes relating to characters such as Butch Cassidy, as Andrew Palmer observes:

> The unreliability in the text is extended by Chatwin's partiality for stories which have no single, definitive version ... He devotes several chapters to Butch Cassidy whose death, he tells us, is recorded variously as taking place in Bolivia in 1909, Uruguay in 1911 and Washington State in the late 1930s. There seems no end to the versions of his life and death and, while some are discredited, none has any great degree of authority. (28)

The text, it can thus be seen, sends clear signals to the reader that the general authorial approach is not one of objective reportage; Susannah Clapp observed that 'Nobody reading *In Patagonia* could mistake it for an attempt to give a comprehensive or balanced view of its characters' (1998: 44).

However, it must be accepted that at no point does Chatwin straightforwardly announce the partiality of his narrative technique (as he will, for example, in the preface to *What Am I Doing Here*) and that, just as Chatwin implies the subjectivity of his account, he simultaneously sets up generic expectation through his adoption of formal elements of travel literature (the title, the map and dictation of the narrative by geography, for example).

In terms of extratextual context – significant for a writer such as Chatwin, who managed his writerly image so closely, and who is as well known at this point in history for his biography as he is for his literature – any contemporary reader who comes to *In Patagonia* with more than a fleeting background understanding of Chatwin's approach to his life and work will be sceptical of the literal truth of the accounts presented in his work, even if they fail to register the textual hints. In both his literature and biography, Chatwin has become – rightly or wrongly – known as a fabulist, and it seems hard to imagine that contemporary readers will approach *In Patagonia* as a work of empirical travel writing.

Why then has the issue received so much attention? Without doubt, there is a legitimate question of writerly responsibility to subjects to be answered here; the same as that for any writer who transmutes the lives of those he encounters into a work of creative literature. Chatwin acknowledged the difficulty of balancing this responsibility in discussion with Melvyn Bragg: 'It's a very tenuous and difficult business. And I don't pretend to know the exact answer, because it's a process which you live with and are worried by all the time' (*The South Bank Show*).

Though he changed almost all of the names of those he wrote about in *In Patagonia*, Chatwin did, at times, fall short of the implicit authorial code of conduct; when, for example, he retained Ernest Hobbs' name in an account of Indian killing[9] which led his granddaughter to write a furious letter to Jonathan Cape:

> My grandfather neither killed nor arranged the massacre of any Indians, even such a thought would have been completely out of character.
>
> Please let me know what documentary evidence Mr Chatwin holds for this particular account – or can you confirm that his sole source of information was 'Charlie's' story? As Charles Milward was a well known raconteur confirmation on this point would be welcome. (Box 8)

Generally, however, critical reaction seems motivated not by the reasonable examination of this type of oversight, but rather by resentment that the work has become, in Chris Moss' formulation, 'canonical, unhealthily influential' (278) and 'the only travel book that every traveller to Patagonia feels obliged to read – or at least carry around' (257). As a consequence, critics and observers have felt the need to debunk the myth and dismantle the mystique that Chatwin surrounded himself and his work with; an undertaking which ignores the integrity and ambition of his undertaking, and which has led to a current critical climate where observations of Chatwin's visit to Patagonia such as that recorded by Michael Jacobs are acceded a wholly undeserving credence:

> 'But what was he like as a person?' I continued. 'Insignificant,' she replied without hesitation, 'a small, insignificant man, dull and charmless. He was interested in people only if they could help him, or supply picturesque material.' (512)

The acceptance and publication of *In Patagonia* marked the end of Chatwin's apprenticeship as a writer; in October 1977, he turned professional. As such, the moment provides an opportunity for reflection upon the method of Chatwin's craft for, in his writerly approach to *In Patagonia*, Chatwin established a methodology which would sustain throughout the composition of each of his subsequent texts.

Of central importance to Chatwin's writing process were his notebooks. 'I must just make a note' (qtd. in Shakespeare 2000: 445) is remembered by Patrick Leigh Fermor as one of Chatwin's most oft-repeated phrases, and the five boxes of notebooks which reside in the authorial archive at Oxford are testimony to the truth of this statement. Crammed with jotted anecdotes, fragments of conversation, observations, poems, drawings, quotations – but rarely any personal confession – Chatwin's notebooks contain the raw material of his finished writing. The notebooks are not in any way affected; they are written not to be read by others, but as an aide-memoire for the author; the cramped, frequently illegible handwriting alone is testimony to that.

As such they offer a fascinating insight into the authorial process. In those notebooks dating from Chatwin's visit to Patagonia, the stories which will become fully realised in *In Patagonia* are tersely sketched, often in fragments of thought or conversation. In a red-bound notebook, for example, one finds the initial jottings of the story of José Macías, whose death is described in chapter 88 of *In Patagonia*:

> Wore a clipped moustache. Eyes of a man who has seen horror ... Rose early. Cleaned street – pebbles of foot path. House washed a pale blue modern style tin plates ... Barbers [sic] shop tidy – pale wood cabinet – ... bevelled plate glass mirror – glass vitrines, pomades and brillantines. (Box 31)

Later in the same notebook, we find a far more refined version of this narrative:

> Jorge Mansilla shot himself in his barber's chair on the morning of February 17th. At midday his cook, Margerita Maxim – a careless and spirited woman in gypsy earrings with two sons and never a husband found the front door bolted and the white blinds down, when she came to make his lunch. She enlisted the help of his neighbour, Pepe Vargas. They worked their way into the back garden and broke open his kitchen door. Mansilla had managed to put two bullets through his right temple with a Winchester 1917. He must have sat in the chair and looked at himself in the plate glass mirror – neat new razors, the spirit lamp for sterilizing clippers, bottles of brillantine ...
>
> The impact of the shots had ruined the balance of the composition [and] swivelled the white enamelled barber's chair. Slumped down head resting in the green leatherette seat, blood, which had poured down the white enamelled column was sticky ...
>
> Nobody heard the shots. The police estimated the time of death at 10am. (Box 31)

The final version of this description (*IP* 232–3) contains more establishment of scene, and a better sense of narrative pace (Chatwin announces the death, then delays the discovery of the body for another four paragraphs), but the basic facets of the later story exist intact in Chatwin's noted account. In many ways, the notebook versions offer greater insight into Chatwin's talents than the refined narrative presented in *In Patagonia*; the characteristics which distinguish the finished article are basic writerly embellishments of pace and description and are learnt techniques, whereas the notebook accounts demonstrate that pre-eminent quality of Chatwin's writing – his ability to notice and distill detail. In a Moleskine notebook, for example, Chatwin describes the cartilage of the mylodon skin he discovers as 'embedded in the skin like almonds in honey-coloured nougat' whilst, during a boat journey from Punta Arenas to Chiloé which will become the conclusion to *In Patagonia*, Chatwin notices 'A patchwork of hills punctuated with poplars' (Box 31).[10] These are merely jotted fragments, but they demonstrate the centrality of Chatwin's skill of capturing an image in prose; a talent which affirmed the truth of Paul Theroux's observation that: 'to be [in Patagonia], it helped to be a miniaturist, or else interested in enormous empty spaces' (1980: 429).

Chatwin's period of research in Patagonia lasted from December 1974 through until April 1975. At this point, after a brief Peruvian adventure with his wife and mother-in-law, he relocated to Fishers Island, situated at the eastern end of Long Island Sound off the coast of Connecticut, to begin the process of transmuting the raw material of his notebooks into a draft manuscript. Chatwin would rarely – until the onset of his illness – write at home, preferring to rent or borrow writing retreats, as Elizabeth testified: 'He worked in other people's houses; he'd go to houses all over the Mediterranean: Spain, France, Italy, Greece. Friends' houses, rented houses. Over and over and over again' ('Chatwinesque'). His working day followed a regular pattern:

> He would be awake in bed and thinking already, so he was useless at breakfast. ... He'd go straight to work. He had huge power of concentration; it was really amazing. ... [T]hen he'd come around 11 and have some coffee and then have lunch, and then after lunch he usually wanted some activity. He didn't want to be writing and reading; I think his eyes got tired and he'd have to go off. And he'd either go off for a walk or go for a ride or go and visit somebody. And then come back and possibly write some more before supper. But not usually anything after supper. He'd then read. (E. Chatwin 2010)

He preferred to write longhand on yellow American legal pads, discarding as he went. Often, he would read the prose he had finished that day aloud to whomever he was staying with, as Elizabeth testifies: 'All his books had to sound great read out loud' (2007). Chatwin was not choosy about his audience; Elizabeth remembers him reciting a day's work to her terrier: 'He walked very fast, so she just ran and ran. ... He was going along, shouting sometimes' (2007). Once a first version was completed, the manuscript would be typed and the revision process would begin in earnest. For *In Patagonia*, this process required a large degree of external input, as editor Susannah Clapp recalls: 'The task posed by the manuscript was considerable. It was huge and it didn't have a clear sense of direction; it sprawled, and on occasion it got stuck' (1998: 29).

Clapp would play a crucial role in refining *In Patagonia*, suggesting the addition of brief linking passages ('I left the soprano and went to call on the Germans' (83)), the removal of Chatwin's chapter headings ('A Piece of Brontosaurus and Other Early Interests', etc.) which 'had the quaintness of a Victorian manual; they made the book look like an encyclopedia' (Clapp 1998: 30) as well as generally clarifying the narrative line through the cutting of incidental material: 'My calculation at the time was that we reduced the length by between a quarter and a third of the original' (1998: 31). The cuts were mainly 'administered not to get rid of duff stuff but to tighten the book's shape, give it more pace and focus its subject-matter' (1998: 32), and were engaged upon with as much gusto by the author as the editor: 'He made up his mind quickly and, without being alarmingly acquiescent, would cut a whole section without a minute's brooding' (1998: 29).

All of Chatwin's texts were refined from rough beginnings, though none would require as much external input as *In Patagonia*; as he grew in confidence, Chatwin became a more adept self-editor. The process was intrinsic to Chatwin's art, however; from the raw material of his draft, he would embark upon a process of distillation, refining both the prose – which was, of itself, pared down – and the thematic thrust of a text. He would 'shuffle the contents and subtract and subtract until he had wrought the clarity and resonance of Le Thoronet',[11] (2000: 443) writes Nicholas Shakespeare, to whom Chatwin offered the telling advice: 'Write the first draft, then write the synopsis' (Shakespeare 2010). Chatwin's commitment to the spareness which resulted from this process has occasionally been identified by readers as an artistic flaw, as Elizabeth Chatwin testifies:

> Paddy [Leigh Fermor's] book [*A Time of Gifts*] and *In Patagonia* came out about the same time. And Paddy said to me, 'You know it would be really nice if Bruce would just let up a little bit, just sort of let things go a little bit more, it would be absolutely wonderful.'
>
> And Bruce, in my other ear virtually, said 'Paddy really ought to tighten

it up a little bit, pare it down a bit.' ... They liked each other's books, but each one thought it ought to be like their book: one ought to be more spare, the other ought to be more flamboyant. (2010)

However, as Andrew Palmer has observed, what some have identified as a flaw in his art in fact 'was his art' (32). The vibrancy and individuality of Chatwin's literary voice emerges from its reticence, from those 'awesome GAPS' (*US* 275) which the reader is required to bridge. Occasionally – as in *The Viceroy of Ouidah* – Chatwin's commitment to this approach was overly severe; in later life he admitted to Elizabeth of his African novel: 'I cut it too much' (2010). His intentions were always determinedly artistic, however; he was chasing a purity of theme and prose.

The completed manuscript of *In Patagonia* was submitted to Jonathan Cape in late 1976. By this time, Bruce Chatwin had already embarked on a new story; in December of that year he travelled to Dahomey in order to track down the tale of a notorious slaver named Francisco Felix de Souza. He told Elizabeth: 'There's a fantastic story there; I wish somebody would write it. I mean, it would be like *Salambo* or something' (2010). He wrote to Gerald Brennan of the project:

> The original de Souza was a Portuguese peasant, who went to Bahia, became captain of the Portuguese fort on the slave coast and successively the leading slave-dealer, the Viceroy of the King, and one of the richest men in Africa. At one point he had 83 slave ships and 2 frigates built in the Philadelphia dockyard, but he could never leave his slave barracoon and his hundred odd black women in Ouidah. The family went mulatto and are now *feticheurs* ... Tom Maschler of Cape's says I should go and try and chronicle the gradual blackening of the family. (*US* 257)

NOTES

1 Elizabeth Chatwin, however, does recall the existence of a note; in her preface to *Under the Sun*, she observed: 'He wrote a letter to the *Sunday Times* on a little piece of yellow foolscap now lost or stolen' (*US* 3).

2 As in Australia – which was declared as *terra nullius* (unowned land) despite the presence of the Aborigines – Patagonia's native inhabitants tended to be overlooked.

3 Spain had already attempted to colonise the region in 1779, but withdrew in 1783. They attributed their failure to: 'the unfruitfulness of the region which suggested to the authorities that where Spaniards failed, others would also fail' (Williams 1975: 18).

4 A connection which both Darwin and W.H. Hudson also noted.

5 Though, of course, no small influence on Cassidy's relocation to Patagonia must have come from the increasing difficulty of avoiding police capture in the US.

6 In *In Patagonia*, a version of this line is spoken by 'Anton Hahn', the German (86).

7 Nicholas Shakespeare – who in the course of his biographical work examined many of the same resources as were made available for this study – shares a similar perspective, however. See 2000: 290–1.

8 Later in the text, the reader will discover that this version of the story is far from the definitive account.

9 See *IP* 225–7.

10 This observation is incorporated into *In Patagonia*; Chatwin writes of a 'Lombardy poplar, the punctuation mark of man' (107).

11 Former Cistercian abbey in south-east France. Chatwin greatly admired the simplicity of the abbey's architecture.

4

Skin for skin

— Every day you walk forty miles through the thorns and why are you
barefoot? Don't you have any shoes?
— I don't trust shoes.
— Then why don't you have a horse?
— I'd never trust a horse. I don't trust people either, but I long to go forth
from here to another world.
Cobra Verde

Through a concentration on the individual story, rather than the overarching theory, Bruce Chatwin managed to convey in *In Patagonia* a
compelling emotional understanding of the affliction he had struggled to
define and explain in *The Nomadic Alternative*. The text presents a tableau
of the restless, exploring the tangible disillusion experienced when an
individual, travelling in search of a utopia, instead finds themselves
trapped in a location that fails to meet their expectations.

Chatwin's second published book, *The Viceroy of Ouidah*, addressed
the same subject; it is also, essentially, a work about the perils of restlessly travelling in search of illusory goals – and ultimately getting stuck.
As Nicholas Murray observes, '*In Patagonia* introduced Chatwin's great
theme of human restlessness, and his second book focuses on the life of
another restless spirit' (1993: 56). Chatwin's approach to this theme in
The Viceroy of Ouidah was, however, substantively different from that of
In Patagonia, with a combination of factors provoking a new response to
old problems, and ultimately producing a work which, whilst offering
a purer and more concentrated depiction of the affliction of restlessness, was simultaneously bleaker and less empathetic. The humanity of
In Patagonia was swept away, replaced by a brutally objective authorial
vision from which readers and critics recoiled. Diverse factors provoked
this revised approach; some personal and contemporaneous, others

external and historical. Before undertaking an analysis of the text itself, it is desirable to outline the most significant of these contextual influences.

Of particular significance to the author's approach in *The Viceroy of Ouidah* was location; the story of the novel's protagonist, the slaver and patriarch Francisco Manoel da Silva, is split between Brazil – Da Silva's homeland – and Dahomey – the West African state from which he trades – both of which, by virtue of their culture and history, exerted an influence upon the author quite different from that of the Patagonian pampas.

The Kingdom of Dahomey established over the course of history 'a place in the literary imagination where it functioned as an image of extreme barbarism' (Murray 1993: 52). Nineteenth-century visitors to the land recounted tales of a vicious army of three thousand women soldiers, naked to below the breasts; of the monarchy's penchant for decapitation; and of palace walls lined with the human skulls that were the byproduct.[1] Such were the expectations set by these accounts that Frederick Forbes, who travelled to the kingdom in 1849, felt he had truly reached Dahomey only upon encountering the following compelling display at Allahdah: 'Looking over the wall of the palace, was the skull of one who, too curious, had sought a taste of the pleasures of the mysteries within, now a ghastly warning to sensualists. In the square of the palace stood some fine forest trees, while a row of small trees in the centre bore each a human skull and jawbone; three trees, standing apart from the rest, bore the bleached remains of three brothers' (56–7). Forbes records his similar fascination with the evidence of human sacrifice which he discovers at the king's palace: 'At the foot of the ladder ... lay six newly-cut-off human heads, the blood still oozing; at the threshold of the entrance gate was a pool of human blood. Within, the scene was entirely different from yesterday: in the centre of the Palace-court stood a huge crimson cloth tent ... ornamented with devices of men cutting off others' heads, calabashes full of human heads, and other emblems of brutality and barbarity' (*King Guezo of Dahomey, 1850–52* 60). Richard Burton, who travelled to Dahomey after Forbes, and from whose *A Mission to Gelele, King of Dahome* Chatwin drew much of the historical detail for his novel, attempted to temper what he saw as the 'many popular fancies wide afloat' (1865: 400) concerning the blood lust of the Dahomean palace. '[T]he Europe-wide report that the king floated a canoe and paddled himself in a tank full of human blood' was quite incorrect, asserted Burton, arising instead from the – apparently far less questionable – 'custom of collecting the gore of the victims in pits about two feet deep and four in diameter' (1865: 403).

Such violent associations were not only historical, however. They came to be echoed and reinforced in the present for Chatwin when, in January 1977, during a visit to the newly titled People's Republic of Benin,[2] he was arrested for suspected involvement in a military coup whilst on his way to a football match in Togo. Chatwin later wrote up the story of his detention in a piece for *Granta* magazine in which he reflected on the historical associations his experience provoked:

> Maddened by the heat and excitement, the crowds who had come to gawp were clamouring, '*Mort aux mercenaires! ... Mort aux mercenaires!*' and my mind went racing back over the horrors of Old Dahomey, before the French came. I thought, the slave-wars, the human sacrifices, the piles of broken skulls. I thought of Domingo's other uncle, 'The Brazilian', who received us on his rocking-chair dressed in white ducks and a topee. 'Yes,' he sighed, 'the Dahomeans are a charming and intelligent people. Their only weakness is a certain nostalgia for taking heads.' (*WAIDH* 24)

In the *Granta* version of the coup – significantly subtitled 'A Story'[3] – this overshadowing threat of violence is not realised. The narrator is released after a day's captivity and a procedural tribunal, with a big toe bruised by the boot of a lady colonel and an invitation to 'continue to enjoy my holiday in the People's Republic' (*WAIDH* 30). The narrator subsequently retires to a hotel room, where he is disturbed the following morning by a nervous soldier who demands a bribe. The story concludes with a chance meeting between the narrator and his fellow captor Jacques, who together reflect on the absurdity of the situation over a bottle of Bollinger; the tone of the whole tale is that of amused objectivity.

However, in other accounts, Chatwin hinted that his experience of the coup may have been darker and more profound. His neighbour James Lees-Milne recounted a confession which appears to relate to his detainment in Benin:

> In one little country – I forget which – he was arrested for some misdemeanour, passport not visa-ed, and beaten up. He was hit in the face, stripped of all his clothes – what a pretty sight to be sure – and humiliated in public. 'How awful!' I said. 'Well,' he replied. 'I must confess to having rather enjoyed it.' 'Then you are a masochist, I surmise.' 'Just a bit,' he answered. (qtd. in Shakespeare 2000: 332)

Chatwin told his wife that he was raped by soldiers who broke into his hotel room after his escape from Benin into Sierra Leone; he appears not to have shared this confession – which occupies common ground with Chatwin's tale of the nervous soldier in 'A Coup' – with others close to him. Some – including Nigel Acheson, who met the author on his subsequent flight to Brazil – have cast doubt on the story; given Chatwin's tendency towards self-mythology, the account could owe more to the imaginative influence of T.E. Lawrence's rape at Deraa – itself thought to be a fiction invented by the alleged victim – as well as the author's own expressed sexual proclivities. Whatever the truth of events, the story affirms the general sense that Dahomey and contemporary Benin figured in the author's imagination as the locus of violent and unexpected happenings.

It also invites reflection upon the influence of another manifest aspect of the cultures he encountered during his research – that of the possibility and appeal of erotic transgression. Whilst the veracity of Chatwin's account of his rape in Benin remains questionable, it is indisputable that the sensuality of Brazil and Africa – 'the relaxed latitudes that Sir Richard Burton termed the sotadic zone' (Ryle) – appealed to the sexually explorative aspect of Chatwin's nature, who, despite his marriage to Elizabeth, embarked over the course of his life upon a number of affairs with men.

The author hints in 'A Coup' of the easy opportunities for erotic encounters in Benin:

> I'd asked the waiter what there was to see in town.
> 'Patrice.'
> 'Patrice?'
> 'That's me,' he grinned. 'And, monsieur, there are hundreds of other beautiful young girls and boys who walk, all the time, up and down the streets of Parakou.' (*WAIDH* 23)

In Chatwin's notebooks, too, one finds confirmation of the appeal of such girls and boys. A poem written during a visit to Mauretania goes:

> They are black here
> Mica black
> Obsidian black
> And their mouths are stone hard
> When you pay for their mouths
> Stone hard and pink at the edges
> But the African back
> Expanse of volcanic dunes
> Black and rippling
> And the rump
> And the walk
> Both sexes are irresistible. (*P&N* 40)

Of Brazil, 'Bruce was to talk – sometimes as if it were fantasy, sometimes fact –', wrote Susannah Clapp, 'of a day at the Rio Carnival spent making love first to a girl, then to a boy' (1998: 161). Nigel Acheson confirmed the general truth of Clapp's recollection: 'Bruce cruised around and often went off on his own to make conquests' (qtd. in Shakespeare 2000: 336).

The influence of the exotic sensuality of West Africa was first evidenced in Chatwin's work by the short story 'Milk'. Published in 1977, the tale presents a vision of Africa, which, in its sense of the forbidden exotic and its frank presentation of sexual desire, clearly demonstrates the erotic appeal of the continent. A young American visits Africa and, whilst travelling through a non-specific French-African ex-colony, has an affair with a prostitute. The title, 'Milk', refers to the warnings the young American, Jeb, has received from his family in Vermont to avoid drinking African milk. Jeb, however, chooses to ignore this advice and in his transgression finds pleasure: 'The doctor had given him sterilising tablets and packets of dehydrated food. He had not used them. Jeb drank the milk in spite of and because of the doctor' (AOR 36). His thrill in performing the sexual act is born of a similar delight in the transgressive act of sleeping with a black prostitute:

> 'You have loved an Africaine?' asked Annie.
> 'Never,' Jeb said in an even voice. He had never been to bed with a woman, but he did not want to show this.
> 'You must go with Mamzelle Dela. She wants it.'
> Jeb turned red and felt his self-confidence running away.
> 'Listen,' she said protectively. 'I speak with you as a mother. You are afraid to go with her because you have heard bad things. I tell you, African women are cleaner than white women. They are très pudique. And they are much more beautiful.' (43)

Africa's appeal in the story is centred on the possibilities for impropriety for a western protagonist away from the judging eyes of family and friends. Jeb notes his distance from home: 'It was winter in Vermont. He tried to picture it, but the picture kept slipping from focus, leaving only the heat and light' (37).

Jeb is an unconvincing protagonist; Chatwin's representation of the character never extends beyond a Hemingwayesque caricature: 'Still he worried about Old Herb. In the fall they'd stood on the bridge below the store. They'd been lumbering all day and the leaves fell, red over yellow, into the river' (37). This hollow characterisation sits in contrast to the authenticity conveyed by the story itself, which was based on lived experience; Jeb is a stand-in for Chatwin, whose visit to West Africa in 1972 provided the raw material for the story. Whilst it is impossible to ascertain the ultimate degree of convergence between Chatwin's experience in Niger and the fictionalised version presented in 'Milk', the tale reaffirms the clear connection established between the locations of *The Viceroy of Ouidah* and transgressive sexual behaviour.

The experiences to which these accounts testify exacted a profound influence over Chatwin's imaginative conception of Africa and Brazil. However, they might well have remained at the periphery of the realised story of Da Silva had circumstances not intervened.

The work was originally planned as a straightforward biography of the real Francisco de Souza, a man referred to by Pierre Verger as 'the most notorious slave-trader of all time' (28). Chatwin's research for this project was, however, unexpectedly curtailed by the Beninese coup: 'His research came to a screeching halt' (2007), comments Elizabeth. 'I did not go back to Benin', he wrote in the preface to the novel's first edition – excised from subsequent versions of the text. 'I did come away with the bones of the story and a number of vivid impressions. ... But such was the patchiness of my material that I decided to change the names of the principal characters – and went on to write a work of the imagination' (2–3).[4]

This enforced shift in form freed Chatwin from the restrictions of fidelity to sources; his own imaginative conception of Africa became the main wellspring of the novel's action and the characters' psychology. Consequently, the protagonists of *The Viceroy of Ouidah* become figures in an authorial psycho-drama, wrestling with personal questions inspired by Chatwin's experiences of Africa and Brazil, as well as his persistent interest in the nature of human restlessness.

In creating the fabric of this imaginative world, Chatwin turned to new models for formal inspiration. Early in his 1976 trip to Benin, Chatwin had written to his wife of his hopes for the text, commenting that to succeed 'it will have to be written in the high style of *Salammbo*' (*US* 259). Flaubert was an eternal touchstone for Chatwin, as Elizabeth observes: 'He adored Flaubert, he thought Flaubert was absolutely fantastic. He must have practically memorised *Madame Bovary*. He used to carry it around with him' (2007). *Salambo* had been the follow-up to *Madame Bovary* – Flaubert's own glittering literary debut – and the dynamic shift between the two works prefigures that evident in the contrast between *In Patagonia* and *The Viceroy of Ouidah*. Whereas *Madame Bovary* is linguistically minimalist and fundamentally human, the world of *Salambo* is ornate and exotic, peopled by characters who seem from an age of myth, and whose behaviour appears inscrutable. Flaubert's prose indulges luxuriantly in the decadence of the world he describes:

> Oxen were roasting at great clear fires in the middle of the garden, which thus looked like a battlefield when the dead are being burned. Loaves dusted with aniseed vied with huge cheeses heavier than disks, and great bowls of wine with mighty water tankards, set close to gold filigree baskets full of flowers. (14)

Chatwin's prose in *The Viceroy of Ouidah* is directly inspired by this model:

> Pigs' heads were anointed with gumbos and ginger. Black beans were frosted with cassava flour. Silver fish glittered in a sauce of malaguetta pepper. There was a ragout of guinea-fowl and seri-flowers, which were reputed to have aphrodisiac properties. There were mounds of fried cockscombs, salads of carrot and papaya, and pastes of shrimp, cashew nuts and coco-flesh. (20)

Flaubertian allusions abound in the text; the initial description of Ouidah's first medical man, Dr Marcos Brandão Ferraez, and his wife Dona Luciana manages to simultaneously reference both *Madame Bovary*'s M. Homais and Felicité's parrot in *Un coeur simple*: 'The couple were childless and lived in two neat rooms above their pharmacy, where they put a plaster bust of Hippocrates and rows of blue pottery drug jars inscribed with Latin names; and they had a macaw called Zé Piranha' (135).

The influence extended beyond the superficial, however. Chatwin mimicked Flaubert's objective indifference to his characters' fate; the description of the actions and thoughts of the protagonists of *The Viceroy of Ouidah* is conspicuously devoid of any authorial judgement or sympathy. Chatwin maintained a distance in all of his texts, of course; he consciously refrains from passing authorial comment or judgement, or from reflecting emotionally on his characters' situation. *The Viceroy of Ouidah* is, however, a more barbarous tale than anything else in his oeuvre, and hence the distanced authorial position is set in dramatic relief. The critic John Thompson reflected upon the objectivity of Chatwin's approach in a review for the *New York Times*, comparing *The Viceroy of Ouidah* with Chinua Achebe's *Arrow of God* (which Thompson, mistaking it for Conrad's late novel, refers to as *Arrow of Gold*): 'That novel of West Africa has violence enough, and cruel superstition too, yet it is suffused with the common humanity of which I find not one dried drop in *The Viceroy of Ouidah*' (28).

Francisco Manoel da Silva is born into the harsh and unforgiving
environment of the arid Sertão, in north-east Brazil: '[l]ike all people
born in thorny places', Chatwin writes, he dreams of 'green fields and
a life of ease' (51). Da Silva's early life is marked by tragedy; his father
dies when the boy is one, and he is brought up by his mother and an
Indian called Manuelzinho, whom his mother takes as a companion. His
first memories are of 'watching the pair, creaking night and day in a sisal
hammock: he never knew a time when he was not a stranger' (52). The
harshness of his upbringing cultivates a spirit of fierce independence in
Da Silva; he has the pedigree of a wanderer. His mother is killed by a
fierce drought; of her death, Chatwin writes, in an observation that will
come to apply to all of the novel's characters, that 'Her oases were not of
this world' (55). Subsequent to his mother's death, Da Silva drifts around
the Sertão, 'taking odd jobs as butcher's apprentice, muleteer, drover and
gold panner. Sometimes he knew a flash of happiness, but only if it was
time to be departing' (59).

Da Silva is subject to a profound restlessness; he briefly marries, but
cannot submit to domesticity, which provokes violent emotions; in a
portent of his future behaviour, Da Silva, upon discovering a frog shel-
tering under a cactus, takes a stone and kills it. As the character sinks
further into settlement and domesticity, these violent tendencies grow
exponentially; the protagonist first kills his wife's cat,[5] then almost
murders his own child: 'He held the guitar above the cradle, waited for
the crash of splintering wood, then checked himself and broke it across
his knee' (63). He is at least sufficiently self-aware to extricate himself
from confinement, and in the aftermath returns to his peripatetic life:
'He went back to his solitary wanderings. Believing any set of four walls
to be a tomb or a trap, he preferred to float over the most barren of open
spaces' (63).

The violent tendencies which inspire his wandering are briefly
tempered by the possibility of contentment which he glimpses in the lifestyle of his rich young friend Joaquim Coutinho. The sight of Coutinho's grand house, Tapuitapera, conjures the belief for Da Silva that 'he
had stumbled on Paradise' (68), and he becomes obsessed with the trappings of wealth:

> [T]hey would leaf through volumes with vistas of European cities, or
> visit rooms where precious objects were strewn in disarray: Venetian glass-
> ware, silver from Potosí, crystal and cinnabar and black lacquer cabinet
> sloughing pearlshell.

> Francisco Manoel could not account for what he saw. He had never thought of owning more than his knives and a few silver horse-trimmings. Now, there was no limit to his thirst for possessions. (69)

Africa seems to provide the easy possibility of attaining this worldly treasure: 'The most valuable slaves came from Ouidah', Da Silva is temptingly informed, 'and Ouidah, by terms of the Prince Regent's treaty with England, was the one port north of the Equator where it was legal to trade: the only problem was the King of Dahomey, who was mad' (75). Africa also appeals to Da Silva on an imaginative level, in its very difference to Brazil:

> Jerónimo told him stories of mudbrick palaces lined with skulls; of tribes who exchanged gold dust for tobacco; a Holy Snake that was also a rainbow, and kings with testicles the size of avocados.
> The name 'Dahomey' took root in his imagination. (71)

Da Silva departs Bahia for Africa aboard the *Pistola*, astonished by the sensual world of the ocean: 'He saw boobies. He saw fleets of medusas, ribbons of sea-wrack, the prismatic colours on the backs of bonitos and albacores and the pale fire of phosphorescence streaming into the night' (81). The ocean functions throughout the novel as a metaphor for escape, and Da Silva is initially afraid of setting eyes on it (67); subsequent to his establishment at Ouidah, however, it comes to represent the impossible passage to an unattainable paradise:

> Whenever a ship sailed, he would watch the yardarms vanish into the night, then light a pipe on the verandah and sink into a reverie of the future: he would have a Big House, a view of the sea, grandchildren and the sound of water tinkling through a garden. But then the mirage would fade. The sound of drumbeats pressed against his temples and he had a presentiment that he would never get out of Africa. (91)

Da Silva's situation appears to consciously echo that of Conrad's Almayer in *Almayer's Folly*, who dreams similarly of escaping his enforced tropical settlement by effecting a voyage across the water: 'He absorbed himself in his dream of wealth and power away from this coast where he had dwelt for so many years, forgetting the bitterness of toil and strife in the vision of a great and splendid reward. They would live in Europe, he and his daughter. They would be rich and respected', Conrad writes (7). 'Such were Almayer's thoughts as, standing on the verandah of his new but already decaying house – that last failure of his life – he looked on the broad river' (7). Where Conrad's character responds to his fate with disarming passivity, however, Chatwin's Da Silva projects his frustrations outwardly.

In *The Nomadic Alternative*, Bruce Chatwin put forward the theory that enforced settlement of an individual could lead to aberrant behaviour, including violence and sexual perversion: 'Violent solutions to complicated problems attract him; for diabolic energy is less insupportable than torpor', he observed (3), whilst in an early essay for *Vogue* he cited claims that 'Monotonous surroundings and tedious regular activities wove patterns which produced fatigue, nervous disorders, apathy, self-disgust and violent reactions' (*AOR* 100). The character of Da Silva in *The Viceroy of Ouidah* is the personification of these theories, and the early violence of his time in the Sertão comes to seem an innocent prelude to his behaviour in Africa:

> Each year, with the dry season, he would slough off the habits of civilisation and go to war. ...
>
> He crossed burning savannahs and swam rivers infested with crocodiles. Before an attack on a village, he would lash leaves to his hat and lie motionless till cockcrow. Then, as the dawn silhouetted the roofs like teeth on a sawblade, a whistle would blow, the air fill with raucous cries and, by the end of the morning, the Amazons would be parading before the King, swinging severed heads like dumb-bells.
>
> Dom Francisco greeted each fresh atrocity with a glassy smile. He felt no trace of pity for the mother who pleaded for her child, or for the old man staring in disbelief at the purple veil spread out over the smouldering ruins. (116–17)

Violence is not the only consequence of Da Silva's frustration at his enforced settlement, however; the character also indulges in sexual promiscuity in order to alleviate his torpor. In *The Nomadic Alternative*, Chatwin wrote of the settled individual that: 'Pinned to one place he verbalizes or enacts his sexual fantasies. (The Marquis de Sade is pre-eminently the product of confinement)' (3). *The Viceroy of Ouidah* – for which the original title, tellingly, was 'Skin for Skin' – realises this notion in the almost insatiable sexual desire of Da Silva: '[H]e would lie in his nightshirt, waiting for the creak of boards on the verandah: on the bad nights, the game of breaking virgins was his only hope of consolation' (122).

For the majority of the novel, Da Silva's relationships with women fail to transcend this superficiality, eclipsed in significance, as they are, by those he establishes with his male companions.[6] Da Silva embarks upon a number of significant male liaisons in the course of the novel; first with

Joaquim Coutinho in Bahia, then with the Major-Domo of the fort at Ouidah, Taparica, and finally with the Dahomean King, with whom Da Silva swears a blood pact: 'The two men knelt facing each other, naked as babies, pressing their thighs together: the pact would be invalid if their genitals touched the ground' (106). Echoing Chatwin's own experiences in West Africa, in *The Viceroy of Ouidah* Dahomey is transmuted, to paraphrase Edward Said, into a 'living tableau of queerness' (103).

In his senescence, and finally abandoned by the king, Da Silva does embark upon an equable relationship with a woman; he falls in love with Dona Luciana, the widow of Ouidah's first doctor. However, the attraction seems at least partly inspired by Da Silva's growing restlessness – Dona Luciana, is, like Da Silva, from the Sertão, and her shared heritage and longing for Brazil constitutes a significant influence on Da Silva's interest in her. He first encounters her reciting songs of their homeland: 'She had sung them as a girl, when she ached to get out of the backlands – to which she was aching to return' (135). Together, Francisco and Dona Luciana make plans to go back; Da Silva wishes to die in his home country.

Da Silva's Brazilian repatriation is an impossibility, however: the king refuses to let him leave and, in any case, his prospects in South America have been brought to ruin; despite years of service, he is a bankrupt in his home country. His confinement in Africa leads him to seek consolation in the promise of spiritual rehabilitation after death – his final opportunity to attain the golden land he has dreamt of. He seeks to 'uphold the decencies of the Church' (119) by insisting on Christian baptism for his children, whilst Dona Luciana conceives his beatification: 'In her imagination she saw the great golden church, the choirs, the angels and the sunlight slanting sideways on the altar. The smell of incense already tingled in her nostrils. Then a figure in shining white would get up from his throne, and raise his hand in benediction, and say, "Rise, Francisco! Reborn in the body of our Saviour!"' (143). Dona Luciana is not the only character who is conflicted in imagining Francisco Da Silva's prospects in the afterlife; in the present day of the novel, which bookends Da Silva's narrative, his daughter Eugenia organises the conversion of Da Silva's bedroom into a shrine. The syncretist result draws a traumatised response from the holy men who visit: 'They saw the head of Holophernes,[7] the head of the Baptist, the slave chains, a toilet mirror and the nails and bloodstained feathers. Father Zérringer, who was an amateur zoologist, looked over the reliquaries and identified a vulture's claw, a python vertebra, a fragment of baboon skull and the eardrum of a lion' (44).

Da Silva does not experience beatification upon his exit from the material world, however. Chatwin depicts his death in prosaic and definitive terms: 'He opened his mouth to speak, but his lower lip hung slack, and the music whirled, round and round his skull, as he reeled from the room, out into the light and dust and hawks and dark and nothing' (150). His oases are neither of this world, nor the next.

Da Silva emerges as a profound and affecting embodiment of the pernicious effects of restlessness, convinced throughout his life that paradise is elsewhere. However, the slaver is far from the only character in the novel to suffer in this way. Subject to similar disorientation are Da Silva's modern-day descendants, who perversely romanticise the era of their progenitor as a 'lost Golden Age when their family was rich, famous and white' (9), an age that – were they as black Africans to return to it – would no doubt enslave them. Eugenia da Silva, whose grasp of theology has already been demonstrated as tenuous, comes to conflate Bahia with the heavenly realm; she envisages the soul of her adopted son flying back to Brazil:

> Then she laughed and held her hands wide and waved a black scarf at the birdless sea.
>
> He asked what she was doing and she said, 'He's gone to Bahia.' (41)

Even the slaves themselves (despite Eugenia's assertion that her father 'sent them to PARADISE!' (44)) are motivated to return to Africa in search of some lost utopia: 'They landed near Lagos, hoping to go upcountry to their old homes in Oyo. But the fetid swamps were far from the paradise of their grandmothers' tales. Villagers stoned them and let loose their dogs. They panicked at the thought of being sold again. They were homesick for Brazil but, with one-way passports, had nowhere else to go' (134).

The chosen structure of *The Viceroy of Ouidah* established a template which would recur in Chatwin's oeuvre; both *On the Black Hill* and *Utz* would – to different artistic ends – employ the same narrative device of beginning in the 'present' before flashing back to earlier events. Confusingly, at the time of writing *The Viceroy of Ouidah*, Chatwin attributed his choice of this schematic to the influence of Balzac's novel *Eugénie Grandet*, which, though sharing areas of vague commonality with *The Viceroy of Ouidah* (both novels concern a central protagonist whose wealth is speculated upon; both contain characters who sail to exotic lands to make their fortune immorally), does not appear a structural match for that work, beginning instead with a long flashback section which brings the reader to the novel's 'present'. Irrespective of influence, however, Chatwin's choice of structure for *The Viceroy of Ouidah* rewards examination.

The novel is split between two separate narrative locations: present-day Benin of the early 1970s and late eighteenth-century/early nineteenth-century[8] Brazil and Dahomey. Chatwin's account of the Requiem Mass and dinner held in memory of Da Silva by his descendants book-ends a chronologically linear narrative of the slaver's life; in the first of these sections there is also a shorter flashback section which recounts the biography of Mama Wéwé.

The central interest of this structural framework emerges from the comparison of ideological systems it invites; Chatwin likes to point up the contrasts and similarities between the worlds he depicts. This device is introduced in miniature in the opening paragraphs of the novel, where Chatwin juxtaposes the two central religious ideologies of the novel: 'the Cathedral of the Immaculate Conception, a stuccoed monument to the more severe side of French Catholicism that glared across an expanse of red dirt at the walls, the mud huts and trees of the Python Fetish' (7). This proposed binary opposition between Catholicism and fetishism will later be demonstrated to be highly porous – as will the larger juxtapositions that the introductory section prefigures.

Of these, particularly significant is the connection drawn between the Marxist ideology of present-day Benin and the rampant capitalism of the slave era in Dahomey. Marxism is seen as an imposition masking a more universal – though fundamentally misguided – impulse for wealth: the young Marxists come out of the 'Bar Ennemi du Soir' to ogle Madam Hélène da Silva's cream Mercedes-Benz as it passes, whilst the descendants of Francisco Manoel, obliged to listen to the Marxist propaganda of the presidential broadcast on the radio, sit avidly discussing the fate of their ancestor's fortune. The contrast drawn ironises both Marxism and capitalism, echoing Chatwin's philosophical belief – expressed throughout his work – that such systems are founded upon flawed principles.

Chatwin employs numbered chapters in organising the narrative of *The Viceroy of Ouidah*; there are only six in the whole novel, and are consequently the longest of any of Chatwin's books – yet the narrative feels fragmented as a result of the brevity of the paragraphs and sentences. This extreme brevity, and the swiftness of action which is its consequence, was inspired by Racine's *Bajazet* – name-checked in

1 Nomad tent: 'The tent is an ideal machine for living in. Earthquakes cannot destroy it. Problems of sanitation do not complicate its structure. It is simple to replace, rests lightly on the earth and does not wound the soil with its foundations.' (76) *The Nomadic Alternative.*

3 Nomad flocks, Sudan 1965.

2 Nomad woman, Sudan 1965: 'I went to the Sudan. On camel and foot I trekked through the Red Sea hills.' (11) *Anatomy of Restlessness*.

5 Asado: 'He carried the five carcasses to the fire and crucified each one to its iron cross, set on an incline to the flame.' (76) *In Patagonia.*

4 The Germans at Río Pico, Patagonia: 'Apart from its metal roof nothing distinguished it from the houses of a South German village, the half-timbering infilled with white plaster, the grey shutters, the wicket fence.' (84) *In Patagonia.*

6 Playing 'taba': 'The *taba* is the astragalus bone of a cow. The player throws it ten paces on to a prepared circle of mud or sand. If it falls on its concave side, this is *suerte* (good luck) and he wins; on its rounded side, this is *culo* (arse) and he loses ... I was *culo* many times and lost a lot of money.' (76) *In Patagonia*.

7 Patagonian bar.

8 Abomey, Dahomey.

9 Dahomey.

10 West Africa.

11 China, 1985. 'I have put off going to China for so long, for fear that the China of my imagination, a kind of ideal China composed of such congenial spirits as Li Po and Tu Fu did not exist. But they are still there!' (425–6) *Under the Sun: The Letters of Bruce Chatwin.*

12 South Africa, 1984.

13 Boat building: 'Chatwin had a capacity for finding and revelling in extraordinary, rare and beautiful objects. He liked things which were functional and utilitarian and unusual; rare not simply in the sense of rare fine art, things that would be put in museums or art galleries, which would automatically fetch large sums of money, but rare in the sense of overlooked, ordinary.'
Susannah Clapp, 'Chatwinesque'.

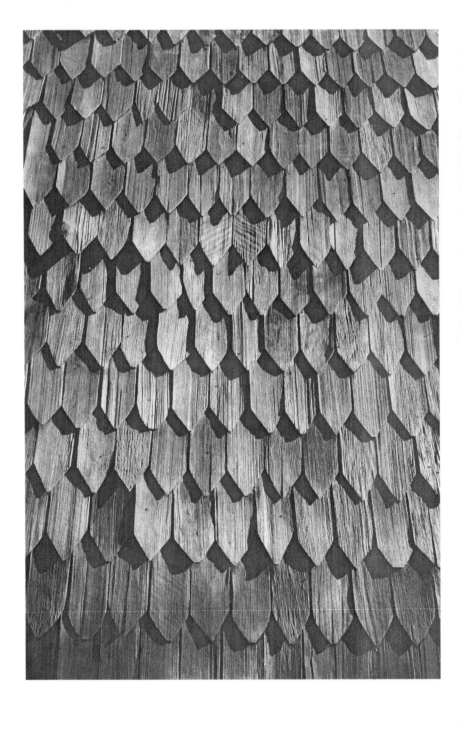

15 Graffiti.

14 Wood surface.

16 The chapel at Chora. Chatwin's ashes were buried near this tenth-century Byzantine chapel on the Peloponnese peninsula. Patrick Leigh Fermor: 'We dug a hole with a trowel, poured a libation of wine … and said a prayer: "May the earth rest lightly upon him. May his memory rest eternal." So there he is. The end of his travels.' *In the Footsteps of Bruce Chatwin.*

17 Chapel view.

the text as one of the few volumes kept by the modern-day *Librairie Moderne*. Where Flaubert inspired prose style and authorial position, Racine inspired narrative structure and pacing.[9] Chatwin wrote in his notebook: 'Racine: note the astonishing swift reversals of fortune. The outcome of Andromache is fated from the start ... There is no way out for the players. Yet in act II scene iii Orestes is buoyant with hope for the future: only to be dashed 2 stepped stanzas in the next scene' (*US* 469). The influence is evident throughout the novel; take, by way of example, this passage recounting Da Silva's eventual demise, with its remarkable compression of plot:

> Without warning the King's tax-collectors swarmed into Simbodji and removed all the silver and gold. A month later, a steam-frigate of the West Africa Squadron boarded the last Baltimore clipper: it was obvious that Jacinto had tipped the British off.
>
> The women of Simbodji said, 'The Big Tree is falling,' for quite suddenly the master was old. (138)

There are substantive differences, however, between the formal conventions of plays and novels, and Chatwin's incorporation of Racine's swift pacing occasionally lends *The Viceroy of Ouidah* an incoherent air; characters come and go, and action unfolds in such a way as to leave the reader trailing in the novel's wake; as Susannah Clapp observes, 'it isn't always easy to know what is going on' (1998: 160). Both *Utz* and *On the Black Hill* would balance the conflicting demands of novelistic convention and Chatwin's treasured narrative brevity more successfully; it would, however, remain a hallmark of his literary style throughout his career.

Yet, the brevity of *The Viceroy of Ouidah* was not solely borne of stylistic choice. In the summer of 1978, Chatwin wrote to his friend Sunil Sethi of the frustrations of the writing process: 'Five hours of work and I'm exhausted. I will the words to come, but they won't; don't like what I've already done: feel like burning the manuscript' (*US* 290). Paul Theroux was generally sceptical of his friend's claims of such difficulties: 'Bruce was at his least interesting bemoaning his writer's block, and I often felt that he was not really bemoaning it at all, but rather boasting about the subtlety of his special gift. His implication was that it was so finely tuned it occasionally emitted a high-pitched squeal and seemed to go dead; but no, it was still pulsing like a laser – it had simply drifted a fraction from his target' (385). However, there can be little doubt as to the profundity of the challenges Chatwin experienced in piecing the story of Francisco da Silva together. The novel 'was squeezed out sentence by polished sentence' (1998: 165), wrote Susannah Clapp. The brevity of *The Viceroy of Ouidah* is at least partly attributable to these challenges.

Shortly after the publication of *The Viceroy of Ouidah*, Chatwin wrote to Clapp: 'Phew! Yes, we seem to have *just* almost got away with it' (*US* 328). The comment reflected a general sense that the work was not all that the author would have wished. 'I didn't quite pull it off', he told Martin Wilkinson (qtd. in Shakespeare 2000: 374).

The critics' view was similarly qualified. Mary Hope wrote in *The Spectator* that 'It is flawed as fiction but has such an obsessional quality, such vigour and exactitude in the description of life beyond conventional boundaries that it is intensely powerful stuff. Chatwin is fascinated by the flamboyant savagery, the barbarity of the African kings matched only by the barbarity of the Christian slave-traders who deal with them.' Graham Hough, damning the novel with faint praise, wrote in the *London Review of Books* that he thought the work a 'grimly remarkable piece of writing' (20).

Some critics were troubled by the stylistic qualities of the novel; Charles Sugnet commented that its 'lurid prose belongs on the shelf somewhere between Conrad and H. Ryder Haggard' (73), whilst Karl Miller observed: 'This is the jewelled prose of the upper-class English traveller, carried to the threshold of burlesque – and maybe across it, to produce a variety of Camp and a latter day Wildean largesse' (405). Others were concerned by the objectivity with which Chatwin presented his story of the slave trade: 'We should be able to endure reminders of its horrors', John Thompson wrote, '[b]ut should we relish them or leer at what is repellent to us?' (28). Chatwin himself later acknowledged the ambivalent reception of the style of the work, commenting that the novel engendered 'bemusement' in reviewers 'some of whom found its cruelties and baroque prose unstomachable' (*WAIDH* 138).

In November of 1982, the equivocal contemporary critical response to *The Viceroy of Ouidah* was reinforced by the announcement that *On the Black Hill* – Chatwin's third book, and second novel – had won the Whitbread award for best *first* novel. Such a course of events consolidates a prevalent sense of the work as the orphan child of Bruce Chatwin's oeuvre. The novel remains the least read of his books.[10]

Yet, despite the qualified critical and readerly opinion of the novel, there is an admirable purity of theme and subject in *The Viceroy of Ouidah*. It offers perhaps the most unremitting version of Chatwin's theme of restlessness; circumstances and influences combined to engender a text which offers a brutal elucidation of some of the darker elements of the authorial world view. A year after its publication, Chatwin asked Elizabeth Sifton, who would edit *On the Black Hill* and *The Songlines*, what she thought of *The Viceroy of Ouidah*. 'I danced around', she told Nicholas Shakespeare. 'I said I thought it was beautiful, but cold and repellent.' 'But it's *meant* to be', Chatwin said (qtd. in Shakespeare 2000: 374).

The unremitting nature of *The Viceroy of Ouidah* would be amplified in the future film version of the novel, retitled *Cobra Verde* (1987) by its director, Werner Herzog. Herzog was in many ways the obvious choice to direct the adaptation of Chatwin's novel of exotic frustration; he had already established himself as a director preoccupied by the impact of the singular colonial vision upon remote cultures in his films *Aguirre, The Wrath of God* (1972) and *Fitzcarraldo* (1982).

Herzog contacted Chatwin whilst both were in Australia in the early 1980s with the idea of their collaborating on Herzog's film concerning Aboriginal culture, *Where the Green Ants Dream* (1984). Though the collaboration never came off, their meeting in Melbourne was a notable success: 'From the airport, before we even stepped into the car he was telling stories from Central Australia and, for forty-eight hours almost non-stop, we kept telling stories to each other, 80 per cent of the time him telling stories and, whenever he had to take a breath, I would tell stories that I had' (commentary to *Cobra Verde*).

Both shared a passion for travelling on foot. Herzog famously walked from Munich to Paris upon hearing that his friend, the film critic Lotte Eisner, was unwell; Chatwin wrote in an article for *Interview* magazine, later reprinted in *What Am I Doing Here*, that Herzog was 'the only person with whom I could have a one-to-one conversation on what I would call the sacramental aspect of walking. He and I share a belief that walking is not simply therapeutic for oneself but is a poetic activity that can cure the world of its ills' (138–9). Before Chatwin died in 1989, he gave Herzog his precious leather rucksack, telling the filmmaker: 'You carry this on now' (commentary to *Cobra Verde*). 'It is such a dear thing to me', Herzog told Nicholas Shakespeare. 'Let's say if my house was on fire, I would throw my children out the window, that would be the first one, but of all belongings that I have, it would be the rucksack that I would save' (*Footsteps*).

Like the novel on which it is based, *Cobra Verde* does not make an attempt towards realism; it offers a vision of a singularly afflicted character, played with manic intensity by Herzog's nemesis and muse, Klaus Kinski (described by Chatwin as 'a sexagenarian adolescent all in white with a mane of yellow hair' (*WAIDH* 143)) in what would be their last collaboration. Herzog emphasises, through long silent scenes, the loneliness of the slaver's enormous, deserted fort and, through the casting of Kinski, the fundamental instability of the character. Da Silva seems content, like Kurtz, only when wielding his power over the native population; he takes particular delight in the training of his army of topless Amazons. The film strips all extraneous plot and characterisation, leaving a vision of a character that is, if anything, even purer and more unremitting in its representation of the themes of restlessness and exile than Chatwin's novel.

Herzog was unable to finish the film as he wished due to the pressures of working with Kinski, yet the enforced conclusion can be seen as a metaphorical image, conceptualising the whole narrative impulse of Chatwin's vision for the work. The scene shows Da Silva desperately straining, like Crusoe, to pull a too-heavy boat out to sea, desperate to escape, yet finally conceding, allowing himself to be tossed in the surf, resigned to his fate: '[C]onscious that he was playing the final scene, Kinski allowed himself to be dragged back into the waves and rolled back, time after time, onto the sand' (*WAIDH* 143). It is perhaps of interest to note that Herzog viewed this ending as so unremitting that he felt compelled to add a final scene of young African singers in an effort to mitigate the brutality and loneliness of the preceding image.

NOTES

1   See W. Winwood Reade, *Savage Africa*; Archibald Dalzel, *The History of Dahomy* [sic]; and J.A. Skertchly, *Dahomey as It Is: Being a Narrative of Eight Months' Residence in That Country.*

2   The establishment of the People's Republic of Benin occurred in 1972; the integrity of the Marxist state lasted until 1990.

3   A word 'intended to alert the reader to the fact that, however closely the narrative may fit the facts, the fictional process has been at work' (*WAIDH* xi).

4   Chatwin had also been put off the prospect of a full-blown biography by the paucity of records pertaining to the slave trade; the coup is, of course, a better story.

5   See 63. Tortured cats recur in *The Viceroy of Ouidah*; in the office of the modern Lieutenant-Colonel there is a 'stuffed civet cat, nailed, in mockery of the Crucifixion, with its hind legs and tail together and its forelegs stretched apart' (154). Nicholas Shakespeare connects this with Chatwin's own dislike of Elizabeth's cats. See Shakespeare 2000: 234.

6 Close relationships between male protagonists recur in Chatwin's work. In *On the Black Hill*, the twins Lewis and Benjamin Jones share a relationship which extends beyond the merely fraternal, whilst *The Songlines* also places two male protagonists at the centre of the narrative.

7 Significantly, Holophernes, whose beheading at the hands of Judith was depicted by Caravaggio, amongst others, reappears later in the novel. Da Silva's Brazilian agent sends a canvas of the image as a present for the king; Dom Francisco keeps the painting back, however, commenting: 'His Majesty might not be amused' (126). Holophernes also appears in Dante's *Purgatorio* as an example of punished pride.

8 The novel is conspicuously cagey regarding dates. Towards the end of the novel, Chatwin incorporates references which allow the reader to infer the timescale of earlier events.

9 Letter to Sunil Sethi, 18 June 1978: 'I have chosen to go to the Spanish Pyrenees (Pray God, they are as I remember them) to hole up in some cheap hotel, with Racine, Flaubert and a manuscript' (*US* 289).

10 As of December 2010, Chatwin's UK paperback sales are as follows: *In Patagonia*: 323,661; *The Viceroy of Ouidah*: 101,014; *On the Black Hill*: 350,185; *The Songlines*: 433,546; *Utz*: 128,357.

5

Those blue remembered hills

A man travels the world over in search of what he needs and returns home
to find it. (122)
George Moore, *The Brook Kerith*

New Year's Day 1980
The ground hard and dusted with hoar frost. The Radnor Hills in a white
streak on the horizon with dappled black patches, which are the fir planta-
tions of the forestry commission. A streak of pale turquoise sky darkening
in the west. The Clee Hill.
Chatwin Archive, Box 35

In the proposed schema that this volume has thus far argued for – of a
disparate body of work united by the theme of restlessness – there would
appear to exist an obvious exception. Bruce Chatwin's third book, *On
the Black Hill*, seems manifestly unconcerned with the issues which define
the rest of his oeuvre. The novel's story is of a rural family who live out
apparently contented sedentary lives on a small farm in the hills of the
Welsh borders. Their narrative seems free of the grand restless drama of
Chatwin's other books, marked by a notable sense of continuum rather
than upheaval; of fulfilment rather than disillusion.

On the Black Hill undoubtedly does offer something of a contrast to
the reader in its depiction of a contented, settled life. It is, however,
fallacious to assume that this new aspect of Chatwin's literary vision
signals a wholesale abandonment of more familiar artistic territory. At
its creative centre, *On the Black Hill* shares a philosophical commonality
with both those works that immediately preceded it, and those which
would follow it. For – though *On the Black Hill* relates the story of stable,
rural existence in a familiar and comfortable environment – it is simultaneously a novel of the imaginative power of abroad, of the compromises
of materialism, of the sense of liminality invoked by life at the edge, and

of the restless frustrations of settled existence.

Such a richness of meaning is engendered by the structural conceit upon which the novel is founded. For *On the Black Hill* is a novel of opposition, of doubles; it is a story in which every significant element of the narrative has an opposite. As such, it offers an insightful dialectic between the contrasting positions which demarcated Chatwin's central intellectual preoccupations. The concept of duality becomes the stylistic and thematic hallmark of the work, referenced in a proposed early title, 'The Vision and the Rock', and allegorically incorporated into all aspects of the novel's construction. When subjected to interrogation along these structural lines, this seemingly aberrant novel reveals itself instead as perhaps the most subtle, complex and profound examination of Chatwin's grand theme of restlessness in his entire oeuvre.

The structuring device of dualism is most obviously apparent in the characterisation of the protagonists of *On the Black Hill*, the identical twin brothers Lewis and Benjamin Jones. The central narrative of the novel follows the lives of the twins as they tend to their family farm, The Vision, which sits secluded in the hills above the fictional market town of Rhulen. The farm has been inherited by Lewis and Benjamin from their parents, Amos and Mary Jones, whose tumultuous married life forms the other narrative interest of the novel.

Chatwin based Lewis and Benjamin in large part on a real-life pair of farming brothers, Jonathan and George Howells, who tended a farm on the eastern side of the Black Mountains called New House. Chatwin was first introduced to the Howells whilst staying in the borders in the late 1970s, and he returned to visit them on a number of occasions whilst researching *On the Black Hill*. The influence of his encounters with them was to be keenly felt on the novel; in early drafts, Chatwin even named one of his brothers 'Jonathan'.

Like Lewis and Benjamin, Jonathan and George lived a life rooted in family and rural tradition. New House had been their home since the 1920s, and was – with the exception of a television purchased to watch the news[1] – barely altered from the early decades of the century, as Chatwin recorded in his notebook sketches of the brothers:

They showed me the Granary and Stable that they built in 1937 ...
In the house – nothing changed. ...
There was a side of bacon hitched up in the rafters: I imagine they must cure their own.

(Box 35)

Their relationship with the modern world was as distant as that of the twins; Chatwin wrote that they '[n]ever went to Hereford' (Box 35) and suffered from a fear of antique dealers and the short skirts of the Hay-on-Wye fair: 'They came back with crestfallen faces, never having seen girls in short skirts before. This put them off forever' (*US* 347), Chatwin wrote to Graham C. Greene of Jonathan Cape. Their hopes for the future, like those of the twins, revolved around their nephew, Vivian, who came 'up from Dorstone on his motorbike' (Box 35) to help on the farm, and to whom it was to be handed down.

However, despite the resonant comparison, Lewis and Benjamin are far from simply direct biographical transcriptions of the Howells brothers. Rather, they are extended beyond figures in a *roman-à-clef* by the 'imaginative reordering of experience' (Murray 1993: 62) which Chatwin undertook in deploying his documentary material. As he would with many other elements of the novel, Chatwin imbued the lives of his brothers with an allegorical resonance, with Lewis and Benjamin coming to separately represent the central arguments of the novel. In particular, they embody conflicting philosophical positions in Chatwin's ongoing investigation into the nature of human restlessness.

In adopting this allegorical approach, Chatwin was significantly inspired by the German novel *On the Marble Cliffs*, by Ernst Jünger. Published in 1939, *On the Marble Cliffs* (note the titular similarity) is a work that Chatwin first encountered in translation during his time at the *Sunday Times*. John Russell told Nicholas Shakespeare that Chatwin had an 'unlimited and obsessional regard' (qtd. in Shakespeare 2000: 276) for Jünger's work, and in later life the author wrote an admiring review of Jünger's diaries for *The New York Review of Books*. In this review, Chatwin wrote of *On the Marble Cliffs* as 'an allegorical tale, written in a frozen, humourless, yet brilliantly coloured style that owes something to the nineteenth-century Decadents and something to the Scandinavian sagas' (*WAIDH* 303).

Jünger first came to public prominence as a result of his military service; copiously decorated for his heroics in the First World War, he subsequently published a celebrated autobiography, *Storm of Steel*, which related his wartime experiences. His position towards the National Socialist party in Germany in advance of the Second World War was not one of active support and he was later associated with the Stauffenberg bomb plot of 1944. However, unlike many of those involved with that attempt on Hitler's life, Jünger was not executed, and he later told the translator Stuart Hood that he believed that 'someone high up held a protecting hand' over him.

On the Marble Cliffs concerns two brothers living in rural seclusion high on marble cliffs above a populated area bordering the sea known as the Marina. The brothers, who are 'brethren both in the flesh and in a fraternity of elect spirits' (Steiner 9) hold themselves generally aloof from the prosaic reality below them, working as botanists, and enjoying little company. Ultimately, however, their repose is disturbed by the senseless acts of slaughter performed by the Chief Ranger, who resides above the cliffs in the black forests and who, with his hordes of hired thugs, the Mauretanians, begins to destroy the cultured way of life enjoyed by those who live on the marble cliffs. Though the brothers join the uprising against the Chief Ranger, it is ultimately defeated, and they are forced to retire to Alta Plana, across the sea, on a boat mysteriously prepared for their departure.

There are a number of notable similarities between *On the Marble Cliffs* and *On the Black Hill*, aside from their close titles. Both drew inspiration from personal fraternal relationships: the brothers depicted in Jünger's novel are explicitly based on Ernst and his sibling Friedrich Georg, whilst, as shall be seen, the fraternal exploits of the young Lewis and Benjamin were inspired by the childhood experiences of Bruce and his younger brother Hugh. The occupation of Jünger's brothers as botanists (also drawn from Jünger's life) was one which Chatwin himself aspired to: 'This is my ambition – BOTANIST written in my passport' (*US* 60), he wrote to Cary Welch in 1964. Crucially, however, both novels share the sense that it is dangerous and counterproductive to involve oneself in the civilised world. The brothers of *On the Marble Cliffs* feel they are right 'to keep clear of affairs in which no honour was to be won, and to return peacefully to the Marina; there by the sunny banks we would devote ourselves to flowers, those fleeting coloured signals which in their secret painted script express the unchangeable order of things, and are like timepieces that never fail to tell the hour' (54), just as Chatwin's brothers feel no compulsion to involve themselves in the ordeal of two world wars, and willingly attempt to return themselves to unchanging nature.

As well as the evident influence on the plot of *On the Black Hill*, however, Jünger's novel also provided Chatwin with a fictional template for a literary mode where the character's actions transcend their environment, and become representative of a wider philosophical stance. In an introduction to the volume, George Steiner referred to a widespread assessment that *On the Marble Cliffs* is 'the only major act of resistance, of inner sabotage, carried out by German literature under Hitler' (11) as a result of the clear allegorical resonances of fascism and resistance evident in the text. Much less is at stake in *On the Black Hill*, of course – this is a novel about the author's personal anxieties, rather than his political concerns – but, nonetheless, Lewis and Benjamin's characterisation is significantly refined in the novel to sustain an allegorical reading. This reading is encouraged by the author's significant – though apparently unconscious – decision that the brothers were to be identical twins: '[H]e said "Suddenly, they turned into twins"', comments Elizabeth Chatwin. 'They took on their own life – they became twins. And it wasn't going to be a short story any more after that. It got longer and longer' (2007). That Lewis and Benjamin share an identical genetic heritage will, as shall be seen, serve to further extend their allegorical significance in the novel.

The opening pages of *On the Black Hill*, which depict Lewis and Benjamin in their old age, introduce the dualistic framework which Chatwin sets up in the conceit of the twins, with the author detailing the physical differences between them:

> Lewis was tall and stringy, with shoulders set square and a steady long-limbed stride. Even at eighty he could walk over the hills all day, or wield an axe all day, and not get tired. …
>
> Benjamin was shorter, pinker, neater and sharper-tongued. His chin fell into his neck, but he still possessed the full stretch of his nose, which he would use in conversation as a weapon. He had less hair. (2)

These physical differences are the overt manifestation of the subtler divisions of personality and preoccupation which will become evident as the novel progresses. Lewis, for example, has little or no interest in acquisition of material possessions, and leaves all financial matters to Benjamin – who has a mania for buying land. Lewis is practical, straightforward, heterosexual; whereas Benjamin is bookish, morbid and a cross-dresser.

Within the context of this volume, however, the most profound and resonant contrast delineates their attitude to the settled lifestyle they lead. The brothers separately embody the opposing impulses of the familiar debate: to stay or to go. Free of possessions, and not subject to the burden of materialist desire, Lewis is, along with the minor character Theo the Tent,[2] the allegorical representative in the novel of the 'nomadic alternative'. Lewis's restless instinct is first provoked by a picture of a Red Indian sent to the family from Canada by the expatriate Uncle Eddie: '[I]t was this picture, with its Red Indian, its birchbark, its pines and a crimson sky – to say nothing of its association with the legendary Uncle Eddie – that first awoke in Lewis a yearning for far-off places' (5). Lewis's desire to travel is encouraged by a youthful trip to St David's on the Pembrokeshire coast – the furthest that either of the brothers travel in the course of their lives.[3] Whilst on holiday, Lewis and Benjamin strike up a friendship with a local fisherman: 'As a young man, he had sailed on the Cape Horners. He had seen the Giant Patagonians and the girls of Tahiti. Listening to his stories, Lewis's jaw would drop with wonder, and he would go off alone to daydream' (68). When he returns to his home, Lewis tells his parents: 'When I grow up, I'm going to be a sailor' (69).

Lewis's desire to travel the world never comes to fruition, though the strength of his passion, repressed by his enforced settlement, is ameliorated by a lifelong ability to travel in his mind. Provoked by an image, a scent or a story, Lewis is able to transport himself to another place and time:

> An aroma of coffee beans caused him to halt before a bow-fronted window. On the shelves sat little wicker baskets heaped with conical mounds of tea: the names on the labels – Darjeeling, Keemun, Lapsang Souchong, Oolong – carried him away to a mysterious east. The coffees were on the lower shelves, and in each warm brown bean he saw the warm brown lips of a negress.
>
> He was daydreaming of rattan huts and lazy seas, when a butcher's cart rolled by; the carter yelled, 'Watch it, mate!' and chutes of muddy water flew up and dirtied his breeches. (101)

Lewis's Proustian ability to travel in his mind is inherited from his mother, Mary, who travelled in her youth, and who comes to struggle psychologically against her enforced settlement. Upon receiving a flowerhead of Mimosa from the aristocratic matriarch Mrs Bickerton, stuffed into the envelope which brings the Jones family permission to buy their farm for a reasonable price from the estate to which it belongs, Mary recalls a Mediterranean spring, 'the sea, the olives blown white in the wind, and the scents of thyme and cistus after rain ... Yet this letter, the letter she had prayed for, was it not also a sentence to stay, trapped for ever and ever, for the rest of her existence, in this gloomy house below the hill?' (150).

Mary never does escape her life on the Black Hill, and on her deathbed visions of her peripatetic past preoccupy her: 'Images of India kept passing before her eyes. She saw a shimmering flood-plain, and a white dome afloat in the haze. Men in turbans were bearing a cloth-bound

bundle to the shore. There were fires smouldering, and kitehawks spiral-
ling above. A boat glided by downstream' (190).

Lewis, on the other hand, does finally manage, at the tail-end of his
life, to transcend the restrictions of his sedentary existence; motivated
by his uncle's passion for aviation, Lewis and Benjamin's nephew, Kevin,
organises a flight over the Welsh hills on the occasion of the twins' eight-
ieth birthday: 'And suddenly he felt', Chatwin writes of Lewis, 'even if
the engine failed, even if the plane took a nosedive and their souls flew
up to Heaven – that all the frustrations of his cramped and frugal life now
counted for nothing, because, for ten magnificent minutes, he had done
what he wanted to do' (254).

Whilst Lewis's restless frustration is soothed by this short plane
journey, his brother Benjamin has no need of consolation, eminently
satisfied, as he is, within the boundaries of the farm: 'He never thought
of abroad. He wanted to live with Lewis for ever and ever; to eat the
same food; wear the same clothes; share a bed; and swing an axe in the
same trajectory. There were four gates leading into The Vision; and, for
him, they were the Four Gates of Paradise' (88). Benjamin is the voice of
contented settlement in the novel – the first within Chatwin's oeuvre,
revelling in domesticity: 'He creamed the butter, beat the eggs, sifted
the flour, and watched the brown crust rise. Then, after filling the two
layers with raspberry jam, he dusted the top with icing sugar and, when
Lewis came back ravenous from school, he carried it, proudly, to the
table' (62). Benjamin represents, along with the reclusive family of neigh-
bouring farm The Rock and the happiness found in the early married life
of the twins' parents, Amos and Mary, a model of rural living in which
Chatwin clearly saw the possibility of living contentedly in one place.

Part of Benjamin's ability to find satisfaction at home can be located
in his overt love for his brother, and any consideration of the opposi-
tional representations of the twins cannot ignore the homosexual aspect
of Benjamin's character. In his notebooks for *On the Black Hill*, Chatwin
wrote: 'Twins one queer – the other not' (Box 35), and originally the
novel was to have made much more of this issue of homosexuality.
Chatwin apparently hinted to Edmund White of a more explicit version
of the story, and his notebooks contain clues as to the form the novel
could have taken: 'Yes: They did it 2 brothers involuntary at night, and
afterwards it was a shame. 2 placed a bolster between them. Incapable
of talking about sex. Sometimes they hunched against one another.
Never spoke about it. Only to confessor' (Box 35). Chatwin retains the

image of a physical barrier between them in the opening description of the shared double bed: 'Under the goose-feather mattress, there was a second mattress, of horsehair, and this had sunk into two troughs, leaving a ridge between the sleepers' (1), and there are strong hints as to the feelings Benjamin hides from his brother: 'Benjamin loved his mother and his brother, and he did not like girls. Whenever Lewis left the room, his eyes would linger in the doorway, and his irises cloud to a denser shade of grey: when Lewis came back, his pupils glistened' (88). On the brothers' intermittent visits to Rhulen, Benjamin — like the Howells brothers — is reviled by the female flesh on display, the bare legs of the girls reminding him of 'his one and only visit to an abattoir and the kicks of the sheep in their death throes' (164).

However, whilst Benjamin undoubtedly conveys a homosexual desire towards his brother, which intensifies his wish to stay put, it is significantly counterbalanced by the repressed heterosexuality of Lewis, which is likewise a key factor motivating his desire for escape. It is no coincidence that, in the tropical fantasy inspired by the coffee beans cited above, he perceives the 'warm brown lips of a negress' (101).

Consequently, though the issue of sexuality is key in motivating Lewis and Benjamin's differing responses to settlement and travel, Chatwin does not make it the focus of the work. The complexity of the brothers' relationship would have been reduced to one dimension had Chatwin chosen to make homosexual love the central narrative impulse of the novel, and would have led to a reductive critical and reader response. Indeed, even before the novel was written, it was being referred to by Chatwin's friends as 'the novel about the incestuous brothers' (qtd. in Shakespeare 2000: 383).

In dividing the sexuality of his brothers, Chatwin further extends their overt dualism, and simultaneously reaffirms a sense, suggested by their characterisation as twins, that they represent two sides of one personality.[4] This interpretation is strengthened by the evident spiritual connection that the brothers share; their secret childhood language is 'the language of the angels' (40) whilst their physical bond — referred to by John Updike as a 'mysterious, infrangible connection' (128) — can be seen as paranormal, with the twins being able to communicate physical distress over long distances.[5] The connection is so profound that 'if either twin caught sight of himself — in a mirror, in a window, or even on the surface of water — he mistook his own reflection for his other half' (87). As Benjamin learns to shave, he sees his brother's face in the mirror and, as he holds his razor 'at the ready and glanced up at the glass, he had the sensation of slitting Lewis's throat' (87).

If it is true that, together, the brothers represent the conflicting natures of one individual, then there is, of course, a prime candidate for the model of this individual. All of the personality traits evident in the twins were seemingly present in the personality of the author himself, who veered throughout his life between restless travel and a desire for stability and refuge, as well as struggling with the lure of materialism and the confusion of his own sexuality. Chatwin's friend Jonathan Hope observes: 'The novel is between Bruce and Bruce' (qtd. in Shakespeare 2000: 382), whilst Susannah Clapp calls the novel a 'submerged piece of autobiography. They are two parts of himself' (2007).

On the Black Hill, with its dualistic structure, might then seem a deliberate interrogation of the author's divided personality; certainly, the biographical resonances of the work are overt, as shall become even clearer later in this chapter. However, despite the relevance of *On the Black Hill* to the author's life, the reader is left unsure as to the degree to which the thematic material of the novel was inspired by any conscious desire on the part of the author to explore the intricacies of his own personality. This ambiguity is present in each of his books, and leads to a peculiar uncertainty on the part of the reader, for, though Chatwin's work is so obviously and constantly investigating himself and his own personal neuroses, he rarely acknowledges the source of his preoccupations. As Susannah Clapp observes: 'There's a sort of paradox in someone who tries to scrape away all biographical details from his work whilst constantly investigating himself' (2007). This tension is present in all of Chatwin's work, but is none more evident than in *On the Black Hill*, which, despite being undoubtedly the most personal of Chatwin's works, retains the disdain of overt authorial self-reflection that permeates the entirety of his oeuvre.

If the characters of Lewis and Benjamin act as allegorical vectors for the emotional conflict inherent in the individual, then the wider division of landscape and culture in the novel can be seen as a comparable vehicle for the author's sense of uncertainty regarding the material world which surrounds that individual.

The action of *On the Black Hill* is divided between two opposing physical and moral worlds. On one side of the divide stands the civic world: represented by England, and all its associated institutions and associations: the Anglican church, the aristocracy and middle class, and the urban centres of Rhulen, Hereford, Coventry and London. On the other stands the rural world: Wales, the nonconformist chapel, the agricultural class and the asceticism and seasonal virtues of country life.

The contrasting qualities of these worlds find their overarching meta-phorical expression in the novel in the print of *The Broad and Narrow Way*, which hangs on the Jones' farmhouse wall. This nineteenth-century painting, based on Matthew's account of the Sermon on the Mount, represents two paths. The first, to the left, represents the civic world and its attendant corruptions, and depicts a wide road flanked with casinos and theatres and pursued by people fighting and drinking who travel a road towards a pitched battle below flaming battlements 'which looked a bit like Windsor Castle' (89). To the right, the Narrow Way is less popu-lated, and bordered by chapels and Sunday schools; it is crowned by a troop of trumpeting angels. The Narrow Way is identified by the twins as 'unmistakably' Welsh: 'In fact, the Chapel, the Sunday School and the Deaconesses' Institution – all with high-pitched gables and slate roofs – reminded Benjamin of an illustrated brochure for Llandrindod Wells' (89). Their examination of the print leads them to believe that 'the Road to Hell was the road to Hereford, whereas the Road to Heaven led up to the Radnor Hills' (89). This belief is manifest in the contrasting walks the twins take with their grandfather, one up the mountain into Wales, the other down into the grounds of Lurkenhope Park, and England. The English walk represents the sins of settlement: decadence and tempta-tion, symbolically represented by Lurkenhope Castle, residence of the Bickerton family, which, like the castle crowning the Broad Way, later burns to the ground. It is on the latter walk that Lewis first succumbs to temptation of the flesh upon sight of Nancy Bickerton, and professes to his mother: 'Mama, when I grow up I'm going to marry Miss Bickerton' (46) – a confession that brings his brother to tears.

The Welsh walk, by contrast, takes the twins up past The Rock, home of Meg and Jim, who embody the frugal existence implied in the Narrow Way. Meg, in particular, is portrayed in the novel in idealised terms; she appears to exist in virtuous symbiosis with the natural world which surrounds her: 'On frosty mornings she sat on an upturned bucket, warming her hands around a mug of tea while the tits and chaffinches perched on her shoulder. When a green woodpecker took some crumbs from her hand, she imagined the bird was a messenger from God and sang His Praises in doggerel all through the day' (237). In the farmhouse of The Rock, Chatwin places an overt reminder of the metaphor of the print in

the framed text: 'The Voice of One Crying in the Wilderness. Prepare
Ye the Way of the Lord, make His Paths straight...' (47). The Welsh walk
follows the path to salvation, and the implication is that in following
the frugal traditions of the Welsh hills one avoids the sins of settlement
represented by the 'civilised' urban centres of England. It is no coincidence that, during the Second World War, Coventry under bombing is
described as 'a red glow on the horizon' (192).[6] The description is a direct
allusion to the flaming battlements which crown the Broad Way.

The division between physical worlds implicit in *On the Black Hill*,
and which finds a visual metaphor in the print of *The Broad and Narrow
Way*, directly refers to the allegorical division expressed in *The Nomadic
Alternative*, contrasting civilised existence with a system predicated on
seasonality, anti-materialism and profound engagement with the natural
world. However, the alternative proposed in *On the Black Hill* differs
significantly in one crucial aspect. Chatwin sees in the asceticism and
frugality of rural life a material solution to his question of how best to
live which is, for once, not predicated on travel. The life lived by many
of the rural characters of *On the Black Hill*, though far from easy, offers
an alternative to the peripatetic existence which Chatwin had previously
seen as the only cure for his proposed endemic restlessness.

Chatwin's faith in this manner of life finds its most explicit expression
in the sermon delivered by Mr Isaac Lewis at the chapel service held to
celebrate the Harvest festival:

> They had gathered in this humble chapel to thank the Lord for a suffi-
> ciency. The Lord had fed them, clothed them, and given the necessities of
> life. He was not a hard taskmaster. The message of Ecclesiastes was not a
> hard message. There was a time and a place for everything – a time to have
> fun, to laugh, to dance, to enjoy the beauty of the earth, these beautiful
> flowers in their season ...
>
> Yet they should also remember that wealth was a burden, that worldly
> goods would stop them travelling to the City of the Lamb ...
>
> 'For the City we seek is an Abiding City, a place in another country
> where we must find rest, or be restless for ever.' (259)

The virtues of rural life as depicted in *On the Black Hill* embody the
key tenets of Chatwin's philosophy – a seasonal approach to life, the
casting off of unnecessary possessions, the possibility of escape from the
urban environment – but with the advantage of a rootedness which the
travelling life necessarily precludes. In the cyclical, frugal mechanics of
a rural existence outside the 'mainstream of twentieth-century mate-

rialism' (*The South Bank Show*), Chatwin discovered a new model of living.[7]

That Bruce Chatwin perceived such a model in the material world of the Welsh hills was the result of a deep seated affection for the area which originated early in his life. The border country around Hay-on-Wye and the Black Mountains of Wales had been known to the author since a youthful trip with his father to Rhayader. It was an area to which he would return frequently throughout his life and for which he felt great fondness; Chatwin told Melvyn Bragg that he 'thought of this landscape ... as my home in many ways' (*The South Bank Show*), whilst his wife Elizabeth calls the Black Hill 'his favourite place' (2007).

Written testimony to the appeal of the area to the author came early in his career; indeed, Chatwin's very first attempt at travel writing dates from a school visit to Capel-y-Ffin on the Welsh borders. It takes the form of a short letter written to his parents describing Blytonesque bike rides and camping adventures: 'We charged down Hay Hill and went straight onto Glasbury where we stopped to buy some ice-cream ... We arrived in Rhyadder [sic] and were very thirsty and so invested in ice-cream ... and more "pop" at a café where a very heavily made-up and extremely ugly girl served us' (qtd. in Shakespeare 2000: 377). These youthful experiences are echoed in *On the Black Hill*'s idyllic account of Lewis and Benjamin's own walking expeditions with their grandfather: '[O]ld Mrs Godber would come out with mugs of lemonade for the twins. She made them bawl into her ear-trumpet and, if she liked what they said, she'd give them a threepenny bit and tell them not to spend it on sweeties – where upon they would race to the Post Office, and race back again, their chins smudged over with chocolate' (45).

In later life, Chatwin wrote explicitly on the influence exercised by these youthful encounters with the border landscape, describing in his essay 'I Always Wanted To Go To Patagonia' another childhood visit to the area:

> By 1949 the hard times were over, and one evening my father proudly drove home from work in a new car. Next day he took my brother and me for a spin. On the edge of an escarpment he stopped, pointed to a range of grey hills in the west and then said, 'Let's go on into Wales.' We slept the night in the car, in Radnorshire, to the sound of a mountain stream. At sunrise there was a heavy dew, and the sheep were all around us. I suppose the result of this trip is the novel I've recently published, *On the Black Hill*. (*AOR* 8)

However, it was not solely the specific influence of the Welsh landscape that led to the advocation of possible settlement in *On the Black Hill*; much of what was precious from Chatwin's general childhood experience also filtered into the book. Chatwin was born in 1940, and, as a result of the impositions of war, spent much of his life travelling around Britain between various relatives. One of the Chatwin family's many temporary wartime homes was in the Derbyshire village of Baslow, situated on the eastern flank of the Peak District, where the young Bruce lived with his mother and brother. With his grandfather, Sam Turnell (who appears in the novel as the twins' grandfather 'Sam the Waggon'), Bruce would walk the moors and explore the local area. The young Bruce's favourite walk with his grandfather took the pair up to the Eagle Stone above the village, a large gritstone outcrop which was traditionally a point of pilgrimage for young men who would climb the rock to prove their suitability for marriage. In *On the Black Hill*, this edifice is transplanted to Wales: 'On fine summer evenings, Sam walked them as far as the Eagle Stone – a menhir of grey granite, splotched with orange lichen, which, in the raking light, resembled a perching eagle' (49). In a notebook he kept whilst writing *The Songlines*, Chatwin recounts his reaction to those he found walking the same path: 'I was very possessive about the path to the Eagle Stone and if ever we passed a walker "Get off my path"' (Box 35). The twins, of course, react identically to intruders on their own 'Welsh' walk: 'The twins looked on the path to the Eagle Stone as their own private property. "It's Our Path!" they'd shout, if they happened to meet a party of hikers. The sight of a bootprint in the mud was enough to put them in a towering rage, and they'd try to rub it out with a stick' (50).

Chatwin often recounted Proust's assertion in *The Way by Swann's* that the walks of our childhood provide 'the substance of our "mental soil" – to which for ever after we are bound' (Box 35). These youthful pathways are, for Chatwin and Proust's narrator alike, inexpressibly personal, forming bonds which remain fundamental throughout one's life: 'It is because I believed in things and in people while I walked along them, that the things and the people they revealed to me are the only ones I still take seriously today and that still bring me joy' (Proust 184). Chatwin wrote in *The Nomadic Alternative* that '[t]he scene of a child's first explorations binds him in a way no subsequent experience can. An exploring child sees his territory as a complex network of paths linking his observations and experiences. These combine to form the raw material of his intelligence' (232). *On the Black Hill* is testimony to the profound influence exacted by

Chatwin's youthful experiences on the intellectual territory of his later creative output.

Also incorporated into the positive representation of the Welsh borders in *On the Black Hill* was the bucolic atmosphere of Chatwin's most permanent childhood home at Brown's Green Farm, near Tanworth-in-Arden in Warwickshire, where Bruce and Hugh lived from 1947 onwards. Brown's Green was a working smallholding, not dissimilar, in its rural isolation, to the farm that Lewis and Benjamin grow up on, as Hugh observes: 'our detachment from the rest of life was absolutely total; there was a B-road, there were five cars a day and one had to make one's own entertainment' (CCMM). Life on a working farm had a tremendous impact on the young Chatwin, who thrived in the countryside, delighting in the possibilities for exploration and adventure. One can perhaps see *On the Black Hill*'s romantic casting of Benjamin's life as a fictional version of what the author's own life might have constituted had he managed to curtail his restless affliction and follow through his rural beginnings in Tanworth-in-Arden.[8] As his father observes: 'Bruce liked this life [at Tanworth] very much, but I think he probably realised that as he got older, this life would slip away from him. ... Indeed, it turned out to be London, and after that, anywhere in the world' (*Footsteps*). Chatwin employs much of this youthful experience in *On the Black Hill* and, indeed, the allusions to his bucolic youth are made overt in the novel by the mention of Umberslade, the very estate that the Chatwin family farm in Tanworth formed part of: '[Mrs Bickerton] had also planned to be present, with her family and house-party, but the guest-of-honour, Brigadier Vernon-Murray, had to drive back to Umberslade that evening; and he, for one, wasn't wasting his whole day on the hoi polloi' (121).

Chatwin's youth in Tanworth meant so much in part because it represented a move away from not only the peripatetic existence of the war years, but also, more specifically, the industrialism of Birmingham, where the author had spent an unhappy two years after his father Charles had returned from the war in 1945. His younger brother Hugh observes:

A special flavour of our childhood is that while we enjoyed romping in Lewis and Benjamin's rural playground – damming the infant River Alne with pebbles, pausing to wave at the passengers in passing puffer-trains so that they would be bound to wave back – we were also rejoicing in a much better time than we had known, had heard about, had witnessed at Birmingham's bomb sites. We knew that everything was getting better. (qtd. in Shakespeare 2000: 47)

From 1945 until 1947 the Chatwin family had lived in a terraced house, used during the war as a brothel, on Stirling Road in Birmingham. Chatwin had suffered here, as Robert Louis Stevenson did in his early life in Edinburgh, from a bronchial illness that coloured his attitude to urban landscapes. Chatwin harboured a fundamental dislike of his home town of Birmingham for the whole of his life; after leaving the Midlands for London, Chatwin returned to the city only twice. As he sat on a waiting train one afternoon at Birmingham's Moor Street station, he looked out at the grey concrete of the city and wrote in his notebook: '25 years ago? The last time I came on this train 1955? I would think so', noting the 'puddles on top of a flat roof ... The absolute hideousness' (Box 35). In an interview with the *Sydney Morning Herald*, the author reiterated the profound psychological effect of his early upbringing in the city: 'My bedroom looked out on a Satanic mills landscape, with factories belching smoke and a black sky. The curtains had a fearful pattern of orange flames and like many children I had terrible dreams of the Bomb, of wandering through that blackened landscape with my hair on fire.' This is a dream shared by the Jones twins who, on the night after hearing news of the bombing of Hiroshima and Nagasaki: 'had an identical nightmare: that their bed-curtains had caught fire, their hair was on fire, and their heads burned down to smouldering stumps' (198). This is, in Karl Miller's formulation, 'a world from which it is right to retire' (406).

Chatwin's childhood experiences can thus be seen to have been key formative influences on the adult author's affection for the Welsh borders. This affection, however, was bolstered by Chatwin's stay in the area in 1980. His trip was coincidental with a period of profound uncertainty in his personal life, for, after a number of years of strain and uncertainty, Bruce and Elizabeth had decided to informally separate. As he wrote to Sunil Sethi, 'The trouble with living separate lives, as we have done for so long, is that you end up with totally different conceptions of life' (*US* 323). For Bruce, the Welsh Borders offered a refuge in the aftermath of the break up: 'On train to Newport. Ah! The joy of not going places by car. The relief to find that you are in possession of yourself' (Box 35), he wrote after having parted from Elizabeth in London.

During this period, Chatwin divided his time mainly between two friends, Diana Melly and Penelope Betjeman. In her strikingly honest memoir, *Take a Girl Like Me*, Melly, wife of jazz singer and legendary raconteur George Melly, describes the experience of having an author in residence:

I had met him before, but I found his blond good looks and the stream of often unintelligible chatter quite intimidating. I was both impressed by and shy of him. On that early visit Bruce spotted that I could cook, and that the top room, with only a small window and rather cut off from the rest of the house, would be ideal for writing. Early the following year he wrote to me from America tentatively inviting himself to stay; he enticingly suggested that we could take it in turns to make supper as then we could both write.

Bruce stayed with me off and on for five years and never even made a cup of tea, although he did occasionally boil up some rather disgusting-smelling Mexican leaves into a brew which he said gave him energy – not something I thought he lacked, rather he fizzed with it. But if Bruce, with his endless demands for coffee, company, meals and an ear for his latest pages, did nothing to enable me to write, he did get me out of the house. We went to Pembrokeshire and climbed around on the Preselis, the mysterious hills where the stones for Stonehenge were quarried. We climbed a few mountains, Bruce talking all the time as he strode ahead. (163–4)

In the absence of Elizabeth and upon his return to his youthful idyll, Chatwin was restlessly searching for maternal figures: 'He was very childish and needed looking after' (qtd. in Shakespeare 2000: 388), Melly told Nicholas Shakespeare. In Melly's autobiography, Chatwin appears to fill, in some small way, the hole left by her son Patrick, who died in 1980 as a result of a heroin overdose. The sense is of two damaged individuals seeking solace in one another's company; his wife Elizabeth commented of Melly: 'She was crazy about Bruce' (2007).

Whilst Melly offered Chatwin maternal comfort in a time of anxiety, the author's other host, Penelope Betjeman, offered the author something more immediately relevant to the production of On the Black Hill. Betjeman provided Chatwin with introductions to many of the local farmers and rural workers in the border area where she lived, including the Howells brothers. The means of life he uncovered as a result of these relationships would crucially influence Chatwin's positive assessment of rural existence.

One of the key factors which influenced his appreciation of the border region was the liminality of the area; its sense of being in between two worlds. The inhabitants of the Welsh marches struggle with dual national and cultural identity; they are neither truly English, nor truly Welsh and thus must choose between languages, between religions, between cultures. Indeed, until 1974 the border county of Monmouthshire was often considered to be part of England, so confused by the vacillations of history were its borders. The traditional coat of arms for the county shows the gold fleur-de-lis of Gwent being supported on the left by the lion of England and on the right by the dragon of Wales. The motto below reads *Utrique Fidelis* – 'Faithful to Both'. The struggle for cultural identity was a literal and pressing concern; diarist Francis Kilvert, who documented rural life during his chaplaincy at Clyro near Hay-On-Wye, recorded the contortions of a mother in labour: 'remembering the extraordinary story which old Betty Williams of Crowther used to tell me about the birth of a child in this house (the Pant) and the care taken that the child should be born in England in the English corner of the cottage. "Stand here, Betsey, in this corner," said the midwife. And the girl was delivered of the child *standing*' (96). Chatwin enjoyed the anecdote so much that he incorporated the idea of a nationally divided house into his description of The Vision. The uncertain national status of the border dwellers was certainly a key attraction of the area for Chatwin, who was always interested in those who felt – like himself – that they did not quite belong.

However, perhaps the central appeal of border life for Chatwin can be located in its impression of timelessness, of having been unaffected by the impositions of the modern age. The way of life of those he encountered on the borders had hardly changed in the previous century; Hugo Williams recounts Chatwin's surprise on one visit to a local farm, where he discovered 'one of the first tractors to be used in this country, a Fordson, probably imported from America in 1914 as part of the war effort'. The tractor was, Williams relates, 'buried up to its axles in earth and nettles'. Chatwin asked the boy whether he realised how rare the machine was – observing that the tractor belonged in a museum. 'Oh, don't worry about that', the boy told Chatwin. 'I'll soon have that going again' (18). In her discussion of Welsh history, *The Matter of Wales*, Jan Morris confirms the essential truth of this impression, describing individuals:

> [L]eading lives that have not changed in fundamentals since the nineteenth century. The advent of electricity, the car and the telephone has hardly frayed their unbroken attachment to their own particular patch of soil, or their loyalty to the unwritten rural traditions, good or bad, that govern their affairs. Their ring of mountains, their few acres of valley floor, their *bro* and all the creatures in it constitute a world for them. (43)

The ascetic virtues which Chatwin perceived as embodied in this way of life, whilst evident generally in his visits to the various farms and small-holdings of the area, were most pertinently exemplified for the author in the frugal existence of a couple whom Chatwin met during a visit with

Betjeman to a crumbling grey stone farmhouse on an ill-tended hillside smallholding, named Coed Major, near Capel-y-Ffin. The inhabitants of Coed Major, Joe and Jean the Barn, would become the specific models for Meg and Jim the Rock, as well as generally influencing Chatwin's burgeoning appreciation of the border way of life.

Joe was something of a local character – Chatwin records a story, transcribed in the novel with little alteration,[9] of his evading an Income Tax officer, 'only to meet him in the road and say: Joe the Barn be out for the day' (Box 35). He is vividly described in Chatwin's notebook on the occasion of their first meeting as having 'Sandy green eyes. ... Tobacco breath. Wide smile. Shaved – hair once fair now straggly almost like lichen' and a 'turned up nose like an imp' (Box 35). Jean was much younger than Joe, and the exact nature of their relationship was the source of some local speculation. Chatwin wrote of her 'Eyes that caught the sun and shone back at the sun', observing that she 'could have been beautiful with all her upper incisors and no eye *teeth*' (Box 35).

However, Chatwin's relationship with Joe and Jean may very well have remained at a superficial level were it not for the fact that, shortly after their first meeting, Joe was taken to hospital having suffered a stroke:

> 17th Jan
> Joe the Barn was taken last Thursday night at 2 in the morning with a stroke. Jean the Barn said how it happened: she got up in the night to put more coal on the fire and found him fallen off the settle where he slept and caught his head.
> 'I hope 'e comes back –
> We've been together all our lives, like & doin' the work, like together – .'
> (Box 35)

As a result of Joe's illness, Chatwin became crucially involved in the life of Jean and Joe, in a fashion quite unfamiliar to a writer used to parachuting into people's lives to uncover material and as swiftly moving on. It is clear that the author felt great affection and admiration for the couple and their frugal life; a life which they sustained in spite of its evident anachronism and hardship: 'Damn the Marxist interpretation of history', Chatwin wrote in his notebook following a visit to Jean. 'Damn Darwinism and the survival of the fittest' (Box 35).

Chatwin evidently felt in some way duty bound to help Jean as she struggled with the day-to-day upkeep of the smallholding in Joe's absence: 'She offered me £1 for cleaning the chimney but I would take only 50p. She was very distressed because she hoped I'd come back to do

more odd jobs – and was worried she wasn't paying enough' (Box 35).
Chatwin's assistance to Jean is fictionalised and embellished in the novel:

> He borrowed a set of rods to clean her chimney. Halfway up, the brush
> snagged on something solid. He pushed, harder, and clods of soot came
> tumbling into the grate.
> Meg chortled with laughter at the sight of his black face and beard: 'And
> I'd think you was the devil hi'self to look on.' (242)

Chatwin developed a great affection for Jean during his visits, and took
copious notes, capturing her patterns of speech and idiosyncrasies of
lifestyle, many of which find their way wholesale into the text of *On
the Black Hill*: '"I tell you what I done" – I done all the foddering and
the feeding – she is complaining of pains in her arms and legs. ... She
said she could have some eggs if she could only find where 'em girls is
laying' (Box 35). Some have seen the spectre of *Cold Comfort Farm*, Stella
Gibbons' ironic pastiche of the fatalistic rural novels of Thomas Hardy,
D.H. Lawrence, Mary Webb et al., in the representation of the Watkins
family, particularly Meg, who bears some comparison to *Cold Comfort
Farm*'s 'nature spirit' Elfine; Nicholas Murray refers to a critical response
to Meg's 'comic Starkadderish idiom' (1993: 79), whilst Andrew Palmer
locates in the character of Meg a source of generic instability: 'Is Meg's
language', Palmer asks, 'an accurate representation of Radnorshire dialect
(i.e. agrarian record)? Or is it an extension of Meg as the earthy, simple,
wise woman of the land (pastoral convention)? Or is it too marked to be
serious, a parody, poking fun, undermining convention?' (74).

The reality is that Meg's dialogue, along with many of the physical
details of The Rock, is taken verbatim from Chatwin's encounters with
Jean and Joe the Barn. The description of the farmhouse of The Rock is
virtually identical to Chatwin's notated descriptions of Coed Major, even
down to the row of toy soldiers on the window sill. The dilapidated state
of the buildings, and the desperate lack of materialism of Jim and Meg
in the novel were not fanciful authorial impositions, but rather drawn
directly from the realities of Joe and Jean's life, as evidenced by Chatwin's
contemporaneous notebooks:

> Calendar from the 1950s.
> The fire was drawing better today because it seems that the sun iced over
> the chimney pot and caused the smoke to fill the room – the whole of the
> back of the house has fallen out and there is nothing but a few zincs to
> keep it in place.
> No evidence whatever of another room. (Box 35)

The deeply anachronistic life that Chatwin uncovered during his time with Joe, Jean and the Howells brothers, pursued as much of the population of Great Britain began a decade of material indulgence, provided what seemed to be another means of establishing a viable lifestyle: 'I wanted to take these people as the centre of a circle and see the rest of our century as somehow abnormal' (*The South Bank Show*), he told Melvyn Bragg. They represented the possibility of a sedentary version of the life he had first identified as the ideal in *The Nomadic Alternative* – of existence unencumbered by material possessions, and in tune with the seasonal and annual fluctuations of life. Chatwin's vision of such a life now seems little more than a fleeting glimpse – for the author was off again in search of the travelling ideal in his next book, *The Songlines* – but the rural contentment evident in *On the Black Hill* provided its own balance to a literary perspective most commonly focussed on the horizon.

NOTES

1 They knew 'all about Yugoslavia – how it was divided' (Box 35) and were concerned about events in Afghanistan.

2 Of Theo, Chatwin writes: 'He remembered, in Africa, seeing the Kalahari Bushmen trekking through the desert, the mothers laughing, with their children on their backs. And he had come to believe that all men were meant to be wanderers, like them, like St Francis; and that by joining the Way of the Universe, you could find the Great Spirit everywhere' (241).

3 A brief note records an excised plot point, which would have had the Jones brothers embark upon an aborted trip to London: 'The lady archaeologist?/ butterfly hunter from Hampstead. Determined out of sheer willingness to do good that they should visit the sights of London, but when they got to the railway station they turned back' (Box 35).

4 Chatwin's notebook refers to the '[t]acit, ashamed oneness of brothers' (Box 35), whilst also recording a proposed alternate title which he considered for the novel – 'Mr and Mr Jones' (Box 35).

5 Chatwin had personal experience of this telepathic sibling connection. In 1967, Hugh had been seriously injured in a car accident in Birmingham; he was unconscious for two days, during which time he dreamt of Bruce. Shortly after the accident, as Hugh was convalescing, his older brother wrote to him on the subject: 'All this business about dreams. I never knew we were telepathic. Believe it or not I had a dream about you to coincide with yours about me. It's this wild Celtic blood. Very sinister' (*US* 110).

6 As with so much in *On the Black Hill*, this detail was drawn from Chatwin family history; Margharita Chatwin had watched the red sky above Coventry

from her and Bruce's temporary home in Barnt Green, Worcestershire.

7 Chatwin's perspective was crucially influenced by the work of the Shropshire writer, Mary Webb (1881–1927). Of particular significance to the thematic content of *On the Black Hill* was her novel *Gone to Earth* (1917), which can also be seen to have partly inspired the characterisation of Meg the Rock.

8 Hugh Chatwin certainly believes that the novel is reflective of biographical fact. Of the physical description of Lewis, he commented: 'That's definitely Bruce', and of Benjamin, 'That's definitely me' (*Footsteps*).

9 '[W]hen the Tax Inspector came asking for a "Mr James Watkins", Jim poked his head over the stockade and shook his head: "Aven't see'd him in a good while. 'Im be gone to France! Fightin' the Germins, as I did 'ear it"' (207).

6

Transformations

Changes of shape, new forms, are the theme which my
    spirit impels me
now to recite. Inspire me, O gods (it is you who have even
transformed my art), and spin me a thread from the
    world's beginning
down to my lifetime, in one continuous poem. (5)
Ovid, *Metamorphoses*

Bruce Chatwin's first three published works offer profound and varied insight into the authorial conception of restlessness. *In Patagonia* details a place and community that has become a very metaphor for the affliction, examining the psychology of those who journeyed to the peninsula in search of a better life: a life that they saw receding before them – or behind them – upon their arrival. *The Viceroy of Ouidah* narrows the author's focus, offering an uncompromising vision of an individual afflicted by a raging internal dissatisfaction that emerges from sublimation in acts of violence and sex. *On the Black Hill*, meanwhile, tentatively articulates an ascetic solution to the conundrum, positing the rural life as a possible alternative to civilisation, whilst simultaneously continuing to explore the debates between travel and settlement present in the author's previous works.

However, despite the evident preoccupation these works manifest with the subject of restlessness, all deal with the subject obliquely. There is rarely any attempt to engage with the subject head on. Chatwin's fourth published work, *The Songlines*, abandons this reticence, full-bloodedly re-engaging with the project that Chatwin had failed to bring to completion in *The Nomadic Alternative*. *The Songlines* attempts once more to delineate the origins of – and possible solutions to – restlessness.

The specific genesis of the novel – as Chatwin insisted[1] it be called – can be traced to an obscure work of Australian anthropology that Chatwin encountered in the course of his reading for that earlier volume, entitled *Aranda Traditions*, and written by an Australian linguist named Theodor Strehlow. Chatwin had incorporated its account of Aboriginal culture into a short section of *The Nomadic Alternative*, concentrating particularly on the then unfamiliar concept of 'dreaming tracks':

> All over Australia zig-zagged the mythical tracks of the ancient ancestors, who had wandered about the sub-continent 'in the dreamtime' creating topographical features as they went. One could only see the tracks if one knew they were there. To an outsider they were invisible, and today these untrodden paths pass through sheep-stations, cities, rocket ranges planted by white men. An Aboriginal could 'read' a track as he memorized a song. He knew each crag, totemic tree, river crossing, waterhole or bend in the way in due succession. He could find his way along the track even if he had never travelled that way before. The paths of the ancestors meandered from coast to coast through territories of people whose language and customs he could not necessarily understand. (*NA* 164–5)

Though *The Nomadic Alternative* touches but briefly upon the subject of Aboriginal traditions (the passage is a short diversion in a long section detailing the various virtues of the hunting lifestyle), Chatwin's encounter with Strehlow's work provoked a profound interest in both the concept of these dreaming tracks and Strehlow himself. In early 1983, Chatwin travelled to Adelaide and met with the author's widow, Kath (Strehlow had died in 1978). Kath sold Chatwin an unbound copy of *Songs of Central Australia*, Strehlow's summational work of Aboriginal anthropology. It was this book which would provide the primary intellectual inspiration for *The Songlines*.

Theodor Strehlow was uniquely placed to study Aboriginal culture, having been raised as part of the Aranda tribe on the Hermannsburg mission, south-west of Alice Springs, of which his father, Pastor Carl Strehlow, was superintendent. As well as tending to the mission, Carl had spent a lifetime documenting the language and customs of the Aranda and Luritja tribes whom he lived amongst; he had even embarked upon the compilation of a dictionary of the Aranda language. Following in his father's footsteps, Theodor, who by school leaving age spoke fluent German, Aranda, Latin and Greek, went up to the University of Adelaide to study Classics and English; upon graduating, he began his own anthropological investigations into Aranda culture.

Songs of Central Australia is Theodor Strehlow's magnum opus. A colossal book, running to nearly 800 pages, it collates a lifetime of research, documenting in astonishing detail the Aboriginal tradition of what Chatwin would popularise as the songlines. The work outlines the origins, form and structure of Aranda song, offering new insight, through the use of transcription and musical scores, into the totemic songs of the tribe. However, Strehlow extended his examination beyond the specifics of Aranda linguistics. Encouraged by his research, and his instilled classical knowledge, Strehlow was inspired to extrapolate tentative hypotheses concerning the commonality of narrative preoccupation which he had uncovered in his study of the songlines. Strehlow believed that the extant tradition of Aboriginal dreaming tracks was related to the myths of the rest of the world:

> He wanted to show how every aspect of Aboriginal song had its counterpart in Hebrew, Ancient Greek, Old Norse or Old English: the literatures we acknowledge as our own. Having grasped the connection of song and land, he wished to strike at the roots of song itself: to find in song a key to unravelling the mystery of the human condition. (*TS* 69)

Strehlow viewed the Aboriginal tradition of the songlines as the last remaining echo of a common poetic heritage: 'In the ancient verse proper of our country,' Strehlow wrote, 'we find raw material not very dissimilar to that from which our own European verse once sprang into being in the distant lands whence our white forebears came to this continent' (728).

The songlines as documented by Strehlow appeared to provide confirmation of many of the theories that Chatwin had attempted to set out in *The Nomadic Alternative*. That work had argued that humankind's innate nomadic instinct was codified in the stories which preoccupy the species – in particular those which adopt the structuring device of the voyage. However, at the point of writing, Chatwin was extrapolating backwards, inferring a shared nomadic heritage from a contemporary preoccupation with the literary trope of the voyage or quest. The significance of the songlines was in the connection they confirmed between narrative and travel in the present day. In Aboriginal culture the link between journeys and the narrative of those journeys had yet to be severed. Thus, if there was provable commonality between the songlines and western myth, and if the songlines were predicated on the travelling heritage of the Aboriginal people, then ergo once we were all travellers – a conclusion which both explains and evidences our restlessness. Strehlow's work appeared to provide a way back in to the subject which had continued to obsess Chatwin for the previous twenty years. He wrote in *The New York Review of Books* that the songlines offered him a 'springboard from which to explore the innate restlessness of man' ('The Songlines Quartet' 50).

The primary narrative impulse of *The Songlines* is ostensibly the journey undertaken by the narrator into the Australian outback in order to research the songlines. However, as the novel progresses, it becomes clear that the true intention of the work is the expression of a more universal authorial vision. When the narrator of the novel is asked his purpose in Australia, he replies vaguely to his interlocutor that he 'came here to test an idea' (16). Though the narrator does not finish outlining this idea in the moment – he is interrupted by his questioner's wandering attention – the curtailed description proffers familiarly generalised theories of nomadic life: 'The more I read, the more convinced I became that nomads had been the crankhandle of history, if for no other reason than that the great monotheisms had, all of them, surfaced from the pastoral milieu' (19). Chatwin seeks in the novel to forge a broad connection between the songlines and these theories of nomadic life, and employs Strehlow's hypothesis of cultural commonality as an initial justification for doing so. He extrapolates from the tentative assertions regarding the connections between Western and Aboriginal myth put forward in *Songs of Central Australia* to establish the songlines as synecdochical of a universal network of poetic tracks, established in an ancient phase of human development: 'I felt the Songlines were not necessarily an Australian phenomenon', he writes in the novel, 'but universal: that they were the means by which man marked out his territory, and so organised his social life. All other successive systems were variants – or perversions – of this original model' (282).

This appeal to the universal is repeatedly reaffirmed in the novel by the invocation of classical myth as a point of comparison for the songlines. Ovid's *Metamorphoses*, in particular, becomes a frequent point of reference.[2] Chatwin wrote in his notebook: 'I had an idea that Ovid's *Metamorphoses* would be the key book for this journey' (Box 35), and the eclectic volume of tales, a copy of which is bought for the narrator in the course of the novel, provides the author with a neat Western corollary to the songlines themselves:

> Using my leather rucksack as a pillow, I leaned back against a tree-trunk and leafed through Ovid's *Metamorphoses*.
>   The story of Lykaeon's transformation into a wolf took me back to a blustery spring day in Arkadia and seeing, in the limestone cap of Mount

Lykaeon itself, an image of the crouching beast-king. I read of Hyacinth and Adonis; of Deucalion and the Flood; and how the 'living things' were created from the warm Nilotic ooze. And it struck me, from what I now knew of the Songlines, that the whole of Classical mythology might represent the relics of a gigantic 'song-map': that all the to-ing and fro-ing of gods and goddesses, the caves and sacred springs, the sphinxes and chimaeras, and all the men and women who became nightingales or ravens, echoes or narcissi, stones or stars – could all be interpreted in terms of totemic geography. (117)

The stated appeal to universality, codified in these recurrent references to classical mythology, forms a central philosophical thrust of *The Songlines*. It extends through the various sections of the novel to reach its apotheosis in the authorial vision which concludes the novel's theorising:

I have a vision of the Songlines stretching across the continents and ages; that wherever men have trodden they have left a trail of song (of which we may, now and then, catch an echo); and that these trails must reach back, in time and space, to an isolated pocket in the African savannah, where the First Man opening his mouth in defiance of the terrors that surrounded him, shouted the opening stanza of the World Song, 'I AM!' (282)

However, as the quotation above implies, this assertion is founded on a parallel proposition, which locates the genesis of humankind's poetic and nomadic instinct in a distant evolutionary moment. The presentation and explanation of this proposition forms the other philosophical thrust of the novel, and was prompted by Chatwin's discovery of the work of Charles Kimberlin Brain, a South African taphonomist who, at the time Chatwin was writing *The Songlines*, was excavating a number of South African caves for the fossils of *Australopithecus africanus*, an early hominid precursor of *Homo sapiens*. In 1981, Brain had published a book detailing his research titled *The Hunters or the Hunted?*; this volume became, along with Strehlow's *Songs of Central Australia*, a central influence on the final argument expounded in *The Songlines*; it was, wrote Nicholas Shakespeare, 'the last piece of his puzzle' (2000: 429).

Brain's work was explicitly designed to explore the assessment of hominid evolution raised by the Australian anthropologist Raymond Dart, who, in 1924, had made what has been referred to as the most important archaeological discovery of the twentieth century; it was also to be amongst its most controversial. At that point, Dart was working as the head of the anatomy department at the University of the Witwatersrand in Johannesburg. Through a peculiar chain of circumstance,

Dart had received for analysis a large number of fossils from a quarry in north-west South Africa. Amongst them was one which would become famous the world over – that of the Taung child. Taung was the first example of the species Dart named as *Australopithecus africanus* and was subjected to scrupulous analysis. The skull was conjectured to have belonged to a small child of no more than three or four years old who would have stood approximately 3'6" (107 cm) tall. Of particular interest was the damage sustained to the skull, which led Dart to speculate that the child had perhaps been killed by a sudden, severe blow to the head. That the Taung child – at that point the earliest hominid specimen to have been discovered on the continent of Africa – could have been subject to a violent, seemingly weapon-related, death led Dart to later extend a hypothesis which was known as the Osteodontokeratic (bone/tooth/horn) tool culture theorem, and which asserted that internecine violence had formed the mainspring of hominid evolutionary change, that 'our species had emerged from its simian background because we were killers and cannibals; that the Weapon had fathered the Man' (*TS* 237). Dart speculated that the area from which the Taung child skull had come was the refuse area of early men, who had killed the child:

> From an analysis of more than 7,000 bones from Makapansgat, Dart concluded that the collection represented food remains of *Australopithecus*, who had apparently been a highly effective hunter, capable of killing the largest and most dangerous animals of the times. The unusually high proportion of cranial remains among the fossils was taken to indicate that australopithecines had been headhunters, sometimes practicing their art on their own kind. (Brain 3)

Dart's theorem seems chilling in its implications for a modern audience, but, after being first aired in the 1920s and 1930s, his assertions concerning man's origins would find some considerable sympathy amongst the academic community, partly as a result of the contemporary context of his research. As Charles Bergman observed: 'Dart's view of the australopithecines as murderous hunters was accepted, not because he adduced evidence, but because it must have explained something to us about ourselves. We seemed to believe it instinctively, perhaps out of the horrors inspired by the unprecedented bloodshed of World War I' (38).

Brain's work, documented in *The Hunters or the Hunted?*, openly contradicted Dart's assessment of man's instinctively aggressive nature. Brain settled on an alternative explanation for the deaths of the animals, putting forward an hypothesis which argued that the killer in the cave responsible for the preponderance of skeletal remains was not *Australopithecus*, but rather a specialist predator of primates. Brain proposed *Dinofelis*, or the false sabretooth tiger,[3] as the most likely candidate:

> To my mind, *Dinofelis*, would have been well suited for the task: it was clearly a cat that hunted by stealth, it had powerful forequarters to hold the prey in position and long canines to ensure rapid killing. A combination of robust jaws and a well-developed crushing component in the dentition would have allowed *Dinofelis* to eat all parts of a primate skeleton except the skull. The hypothesis that *Dinofelis* was a specialized killer of primates is persuasive. (270–1)

However, at some point in hominid evolution, Brain argues, this threat was mastered; the hominid species developed technology to protect themselves from the attacks of *Dinofelis*. In *The Hunters or the Hunted?* Brain proposed that the use of fire was the most likely technology employed in warding off their predator. However, at the time Brain was writing *The Hunters or the Hunted?* no firm archeological evidence had been uncovered to prove the employment of fire that early in hominid evolution.

On a day in early 1984, however, Bruce Chatwin visited Brain's excavation at the Swartkrans cave, near Sterkfontein in South Africa. He observed as Brain and his site foreman, George Moenda, spent the morning and early afternoon excavating a patch of hardened earth. Shortly after lunch Moenda uncovered a small piece of bone which seemed to show signs of having been burnt. Bruce had speculated earlier that day as to 'how nice it would be to discover the human use of fire in the cave' (*US* 385). In a remarkable coincidence – so typical of Chatwin's life – his wish was realised. Analysis would confirm that the small piece of antelope bone had been burnt; Chatwin had been present at the discovery of the earliest human hearth yet found.

The discovery of evidence suggesting the management of fire by these early hominids reinforced Chatwin's faith in the argument he was developing. Based on Brain's research, Chatwin expounded a theory that, at some point in the species' past, an evolutionary jump had occurred, prompted by the overwhelming threat posed by the specialist predator *Dinofelis*, and that the results of this evolutionary jump had been the simultaneous development of language as a means of strategising against the beast and the emergence of a nomadic system of existence. Our evolutionary past was thus not one of internecine aggression, but rather of cooperative defence against the beast – a defence in which fire played a crucial role. Both the songlines and the universal system of myths

Chatwin describes are connected legacies of this moment – and thus prove this peaceful nomadic heritage.

Possibly the most lucid account of this complex argument came in interview with Michael Ignatieff:

> Ignatieff: Let me see if I understand this. Human beings originate on the desert plains of Africa three million years ago...
> Chatwin: Yes...
> Ignatieff: ... and they gradually acquire a set of instinctual behaviours that enable them to survive on the grasslands and vanquish their predators...
> Chatwin: Yes...
> Ignatieff: ... and as they acquire a set of instinctual nomadic patterns of behaviour they also acquire a meaning system, a set of myths which are imprinted on the brain over millions of years...
> Chatwin: Yes...
> Ignatieff: ... and these are the story patterns that keep recurring even in the modern day.
> Chatwin: Absolutely. (1987: 29–30)

The evidence Chatwin uncovered in the work of Theodor Strehlow and Bob Brain allowed him finally to connect the dots which he had been attempting to match for twenty years. The details are sketchy, the argument rife with question marks, but in satisfactorily evidencing his theory that 'Once we were all nomads. Nomadic existence was peaceful' (Shakespeare 2000: 429), Chatwin felt that he had finally located the source of humankind's restless instinct.

Yet, in many ways, Chatwin had been in this position before. The writing of *The Nomadic Alternative* was similarly borne of a conviction that he had uncovered certain profound insights into both the nomadic origins of our species and the role these origins play in explaining the contemporary condition of restlessness; however, he conspicuously failed in that work to express those convictions in a convincing, or even compelling, way. This new work – founded on an even vaguer philosophical bedding – appeared, in many ways, to be simply a new battle in the same conflict. In early 1985, Chatwin wrote to Diana Melly of his new project in terms reminiscent of those in which he discussed the writing of *The Nomadic Alternative*: 'I now realise the full enormity of this book, which seems to stretch before me like an endless tunnel. The only thing to do is press on regardless without looking back even, and then – only then – see if one can sort out the mess. It may take years' (*US* 409).

It *did* take years; Chatwin published *The Songlines* in 1987, five years after *On the Black Hill* had appeared. However, though the challenges of its gestation in many ways mirrored those of *The Nomadic Alternative*, the book itself, in terms of its artistic success, could not have contrasted more profoundly.

Chatwin had learnt the lessons of *The Nomadic Alternative*: 'I had a go at laying down the law', he told Michael Ignatieff, in obvious reference to the writing of his first book, 'I can't tell you how pretentious you sound' (1987: 24). *The Songlines* consequently adopted rhetorical and literary strategies in conspicuous contrast to those employed in *The Nomadic Alternative*, fashioning the impression of an argument through dialogue, anecdote and character. This approach ensured that the novel generally avoided detailed academic scrutiny, appealing instead to the reader's enthusiasm for the romance of restlessness. As Andrew Palmer has observed: '*The Songlines* is not posing as an objective or definitive enquiry. The conceptual apparatus through which the subject was constituted is represented in the text itself. *The Songlines* begins by embracing the poetic mode of cognition and this recognition informs the whole' (102).

Key amongst the rhetorical strategies adopted in *The Songlines* is the extensive use of dialogue to express ideas. Conversations flow back and forth throughout the novel; they form the central mechanism which Chatwin employs to describe the intricacies of the songlines. Over the course of the book, we hear opinions on the subject from Father Flynn, Marian, Titus and Kidder the 'Gym Bore' amongst others, all of whom contribute separate elements to the reader's overall comprehension of the songlines. However, the central dialogic relationship of the novel is between the 'Bruce' who functions as narrator and Arkady Volchok, a 'Russian who was mapping the sacred sites of the Aboriginals' (1), and who accompanies the narrator during his trip to the outback.

Arkady is the novel's main voice of authority on Aboriginal matters, mediating between the narrator and the world he is attempting to describe. His presence allows Chatwin to outline the concept of the songlines without claiming any personal insight or authority; a strategy which both avoids didacticism and lessens the political impact of any statements made in the novel regarding Aboriginal affairs: 'The point of inventing a character like Arkady is that I was able to take a load off my back as an observer' (1987: 34–5), Chatwin told Michael Ignatieff.

Arkady forms only one side of the dialogue, however, and, in the '"I" named Bruce' (Shakespeare 2000: 417) which takes the other, Chatwin created an admirable, erudite interlocutor who acts as a knowing ingenue in the Aboriginal world, asking all the right questions and supplying all the right references:

> 'So the land,' I said, 'must first exist as a concept in the mind? Then it must be sung? Only then can it be said to exist?'
> 'True.'
> 'In other words, "to exist" is "to be perceived"?'
> 'Yes.'
> 'Sounds suspiciously like Bishop Berkeley's Refutation of Matter.'
> 'Or Pure Mind Buddhism,' said Arkady, 'which also sees the world as an illusion.' (14)

Chatwin claimed that the inspiration for the structure of this dialogue came from two sources. He wrote to Elizabeth from Patmos with his vision for the work:

> It's to be called, simply, OF THE NOMADS – *A discourse*. And it takes the form of about six excursions into the outback with a semi-imaginary character called Sergei during which the narrator and He have long conversations. Sergei is incredibly well-informed, sympathetic but extremely wary of generalisations – and is always ready to put the spoke into an argument. The narrator is a relentless talker/arguer. I've done two chapters and it really seems to work in that it gives me the necessary flexibility. Needless to say the models for such an enterprise are Plato's *Symposium* and the *Apology*. (*US* 371)

Chatwin's specific choice of classical reference points is of interest, as *The Apology* is a rare Platonic work without strict dialogue (constituting an account of Socrates' speech in his defence during his trial) whilst *The Symposium* presents a discussion of romantic love which involves a number of people. Neither would seem to provide a direct model for the work Chatwin seems to be describing in his letter to Elizabeth – of a strict two-person dialogue.

A more persuasive comparison seems the eighteenth-century novel *Jacques the Fatalist* by Denis Diderot. Chatwin told Michael Ignatieff of his admiration for the ability of the '*philosophes* of the eighteenth century' to express 'serious concepts very lightly indeed. That was one of the things I was trying' (1987: 24). Hugh Chatwin traces this admiration and impulse back to an aphorism of a history master at Marlborough, the delightfully titled Reginald A.V. 'Jumbo' Jennings: 'Always be disposed to treat serious subjects lightly', he instructed the young Chatwins. 'If not lightly, you may not be able to deal with them. If not lightly, they may end up dealing with you' (H. Chatwin 2011).

The influence of Diderot's genre-defying novel upon *The Songlines* is marked. *Jacques the Fatalist*, written by Diderot over a long period in the second half of the eighteenth century, presents a sustained dialogue between a master (significantly unnamed) and his valet, the eponymous Jacques, a superstitious individual who believes that 'Everything which happens to us in this world, good or bad, is written up above' (25). The pair travel around the French countryside together, suffering, like Don Quixote and Sancho Panza, frequent distractions from their narrative purpose – which is nominally to outline the course of Jacques' one experience of love. The novel scrupulously avoids didacticism, and instead chooses to make its philosophical point – the seriousness of which the reader is frequently invited to question – through dialogue, character and action. Chatwin did not cleve exclusively to Diderot's model – in *The Songlines* the two participants in the debate are more closely matched, both in narrative importance and intellectual stature, than Jacques and his master, and the dialogic structure is predominant only in the early sections of the novel. However, Diderot's method of presenting philosophical ideas provided a key model for Chatwin, and offered a partial solution to the intractable problems he had faced in the composition of *The Nomadic Alternative*.

A related strategy, hinted at above, employed by Chatwin in presenting the philosophical material of *The Songlines* is found in the idealisation of the narrator of the novel, the '"I" named Bruce' who guides the reader both through the outback and along the various theoretical byways the novel takes. Bruce's function in rhetorical terms may be that of sophisticated interlocutor, but in the context of the whole novel his most significant role is that of the romantic yet humanised hero who personifies the theoretical assertions at the heart of the novel.

Chatwin told Michael Ignatieff that he did not believe 'you can invent yourself … All one hopes to be is the first-person narrator who is like a camera shutter, taking flashes on the story as it develops in front of his eyes' (1987: 24). Chatwin's wife, Elizabeth, has given similarly short shrift to the idea that he in any way romanticised his literary persona; of the tendency towards narrative idealisation, she commented: 'I don't think that impressed him much' (2010). Yet, consciously or not, Chatwin did exercise scrupulous editorial control over the way in which he represented himself in his work – and no more so than in *The Songlines*. As

Nicholas Shakespeare observes: 'If there is anyone who is truly fiction-alised in this cast, it is the novel's all-seeing narrator' (417). The public image of Chatwin as a solitary and refined traveller of style and erudition, fearlessly traversing the blank places of the earth was constructed, to great degree, by his characterisation in *The Songlines*.

The character of Bruce is presented in the early pages of the novel as a wanderer of long pedigree. He offers a litany of those familial antecedents who have felt the call to travel: 'Cousin Charlie in Patagonia; Uncle Victor in a Yukon gold camp; Uncle Robert in an oriental port; Uncle Desmond, of the long fair hair, who vanished without trace in Paris; Uncle Walter who died, chanting the suras of the Glorious Koran, in a hospital for holy men in Cairo' (6). Yet, Bruce has his own biographical compulsion – his experience as a war baby: 'I remember the fantastic homelessness of my first five years. My father was in the Navy, at sea. My mother and I would shuttle back and forth, on the railways of wartime England, on visits to family and friends' (5). Later, Chatwin describes the inevitable consequence of this heritage; a sudden revulsion from the settled world (another recasting of his flight from Sotheby's) and a turn towards nomadism: 'I slept in black tents, blue tents, skin tents, yurts of felt and windbreaks of thorns. One night, caught in a sandstorm in the Western Sahara, I understood Muhammed's dictum, "A journey is a fragment of Hell"' (18–19). As the novel progresses, this image of the narrator as a fearless, sophisticated modern nomad is continuously extended and burnished.

A pertinent example of this project is observed by Toly Sawenko, an Australian of Ukrainian ancestry who served as the model for the character of Arkady. Sawenko related a journey made by himself, Chatwin and a group of Aboriginals during which the party was forced to make camp on open ground. Chatwin was fearful of snakes, and, out of concern for his companion, Sawenko rigged a snake-proof groundsheet for him to sleep on. In the novel, however, it is the narrator himself who prepares the groundsheet, with Arkady electing to sleep on top of the Land Cruiser; a decision which elicits a cry of 'Chicken!' (104) from Bruce.

Not only is this fictionalised account consciously self-aggrandising, it also appears to deliberately allude to an account of a meeting with Wilfred Thesiger in Eric Newby's *A Short Walk in the Hindu Kush*. Thesiger is encountered by Newby's party at the tail end of their journey through Nuristan. By this stage the group is in a fairly depleted state, and suffering from dysentry, bleeding feet and exhaustion. The expedition has, by and large, been a poorly organised, amateur affair, and Newby draws a telling contrast between their and Thesiger's contrasting approach to exploration:

> All that evening he was opening and shutting boxes so that I had tanta-lizing glimpses of the contents of an explorer's luggage – a telescope, a string vest, the *Charterhouse of Parma, Du Côté de Chez Swann*, some fish-hooks and the 1/1000000 map of Afghanistan – not like mine, a sodden pulp, but neatly dissected, mounted between marbled boards. (247–8)

Thesiger invites Newby's party to camp with him, and Newby and his companion Hugh Carless begin their preparations for the night – to be spent on ground 'like iron with sharp rocks sticking up out of it' (247) – by inflating their air mattresses. Watching them, Thesiger comments: 'God, you must be a couple of pansies' (247).

Chatwin's impulse to align himself with Thesiger speaks of the general approach to self-representation taken in *The Songlines*. It is easy, in the light of the biographical work done latterly on Chatwin, to be dismissive of the characterisation developed in the novel. However, there can be little dispute that the constructed character – despite the obvious idealisation undertaken – figures alluringly in *The Songlines*, both as the personification of the author's theoretical assertions regarding restless-ness and also, more straightforwardly, as a figure who calls to the reader's romantic sense of self.

To some extent, all of the contemporary characters of *The Songlines* can be seen as elements in Chatwin's overall strategy of presentation. They do not play any crucial role in the serious business of the novel and their fates become to some extent attendant, unimportant concerns, cast into shadow by the philosophical edifice at the heart of the work. They function mainly as vehicles for dialogue and, simultaneously, as compelling, romantic figures who capture the reader's interest and, like those characters presented in *In Patagonia*, come to embody the tenets of Chatwin's philosophy of restlessness.

There is Rolf, the polymathic store keeper of Cullen, who, like the Bruce of the novel, has renounced the cosmopolitan life of the city for the solitude of Central Australia, retreating into intellectual seclusion in the desert:

> He belonged, on his father's side, to a lineage of Barossa Valley Germans – eight generations of Prussians, solid Lutheran with solid money, the most rooted community in Australia. The mother was a Frenchwoman who

had landed up in Adelaide during the war. Rolf was trilingual, in English, German and French. He got a grant to go to the Sorbonne. He wrote a thesis on 'structural linguistics' and later had a job as 'cultural correspondent' for a Sydney newspaper.[4] (147–8)

There is Father Terence, for whom 'the Desert Fathers had been his spiritual guides: to be lost in the desert was to find one's way to God' (64) and who had left Australia to make his home in a tumbledown hermitage. He is an explicit voice of the 'nomadic alternative' in the novel, advocating a life of constant movement and corresponding asceticism: 'Today, he said, more than ever before, men had to learn to live without things. Things filled men with fear: the more things they had, the more they had to fear' (64).

There is also Hughie the barrister, born in New Zealand, schooled in England, plying his profession in the outback and questioning what he is doing there: 'I ask myself, my dear. Every time I brush my teeth, I ask the same question. But what would I do in London? Prissy little dinners? Pretty little flat? No. No. Wouldn't suit me at all' (47).

However, in terms of Chatwin's grand theme of restlessness, perhaps the most resonant character of the novel is Arkady, who embodies so many typically Chatwinesque traits that he functions essentially as the alternate side to Bruce's personality, as Salman Rushdie observes: 'Bruce is Arkady as well as the character he calls Bruce' (233). As in *On the Black Hill*, Chatwin divides himself between two characters.

From the very opening of the novel, Arkady's Chatwinesque qualities are manifest. He is described in the early paragraphs of the novel as both 'a Russian' and 'an Australian citizen' (1), and this instability of nationality informs a pervasive restlessness. A visit to Europe leaves him, as it will Joachim Utz in Chatwin's final novel, 'feeling flat' (3), whilst his marriage disintegrates '[a]fter a single summer' (3): 'Now that he lived alone he liked to spend most of his time "out bush". When he did come to town, he worked from a disused newspaper shop-floor where rolls of old newsprint still clogged the presses' (3–4). At his apartment, he has 'few possessions apart from a harpsichord and a shelf of books' (1); a very model of Chatwinesque asceticism.

However, Arkady never transcends this figuration; he remains throughout the novel as merely a sounding board for Chatwin's theories and a stylised embodiment of endemic restlessness. As with all of the characters of *The Songlines*, his story is subordinate to the wider philosophical narrative which Chatwin expounds in the course of the novel;

it is merely another element in the author's sophisticated method of presentation.

However, perhaps the most significant – and certainly the most commented upon – presentational strategy employed by *The Songlines* in articulating its theory is the *From the Notebooks* section. The extracts contained within this interlude – drawn from both Chatwin's notebooks and the manuscript of *The Nomadic Alternative* – are artfully arranged to act as the main vehicle for Chatwin's wider argument in *The Songlines*. Through these sections, he attempts the presentation of the romantic theory of human evolution outlined above, and draws a connecting line to his notion of contemporary restlessness.

The *From the Notebooks* section is ninety pages long – almost a third of the work – and split into seven separate sections. These sections are interspersed with brief passages of narrative; however, by this stage of *The Songlines*, the plot is clearly secondary to the intended purpose of the novel. Some extracts are quotations from other sources (including familiar figures such as Robert Burton, Baudelaire and Rimbaud); some are anecdotes or reflections from the author himself. The effect of the whole is deliberately impressionistic; the reader is left to draw their own inferences from the material. The technique sits in deliberate contrast to the didactic approach taken in *The Nomadic Alternative*.

However, though the form of *From the Notebooks* was a deliberate artistic choice – encouraged by his editor, Elisabeth Sifton,[5] and in part inspired by Chatwin's fondness for compendia such as Edith Sitwell's *Planet and Glow-worm* – Chatwin had originally intended the section to be far shorter. In the novel, Chatwin describes the *From the Notebooks* section as being assembled *in situ*, working in an air-conditioned caravan in Cullen. The description of the writing of this erudite and polymathic kaleidoscope of nomadism fosters an idealised vision of the authorial process: 'There was a plyboard top which pulled out over the second bunk to make a desk. There was even a swivelling office chair. I put my pencils in a tumbler and my Swiss Army knife beside them. I unpacked some exercise pads and, with the obsessive neatness that goes with the beginning of a project, I made three neat stacks of my "Paris" notebooks' (160). This trope of the author writing *in situ* has emerged as a defining characteristic of the modern travelogue, much emulated (and to some extent mocked as self-evidently artificial) in the genre,[6] a fact for which Chatwin, who is constantly flourishing a notebook in *The Songlines*, must take at least partial responsibility:

My reference books are laid out in a line on the floor; the pads containing my library notes are open. Files full of photocopied articles lie piled up below the window; my pencils are sharpened and upended in a glass. A matchbox lies ready beside the paraffin storm lantern: the monastery generator is turned off after compline, and if I am to write tonight I will have to do so by the light of its yellow flame. (4)

The above passage is taken from *From the Holy Mountain: A Journey in the Shadow of Byzantium*, by William Dalrymple, an author who so consciously emulates Chatwin that he began the writing of an earlier work, *City of Djinns*, at the very desk at which Chatwin in part composed *The Songlines*. However, as so often with the apparently objective genre of travel writing, this vision of the creative process is a construct of the imagination, for Chatwin's claim that *From the Notebooks* was composed whilst in Australia is a conceit. In fact, the notebooks section was assembled in the Chilterns under somewhat pressing circumstances, as was disclosed in an article Chatwin wrote for *The New York Review of Books* entitled 'The Songlines Quartet', itself subject to some artistic licence: 'In the summer of 1986 I completed my book *The Songlines* under difficult conditions. I had in fact picked up a very rare fungus of the bone marrow in China. Certain I was going to die, I decided to finish the text and put myself into the hands of doctors. My work would then be done. The last third of the manuscript was a commonplace book of quotations and vignettes intended to back up the main line of argument. I put this into shape on sweltering summer days, wrapped in shawls, shivering with cold in front of the kitchen stove. It was a race for time' (50). Elizabeth recalls Bruce's tremendous dedication to the completion of this element of the novel: 'He just went on and on. And I remember one time when he was wrapped up in blankets and things and I said, "I don't know how you can go on working like this, you're so ill," and he said "I'm a trooper"' (2010).

Chatwin's rare bone fungus was in fact a manifestation of the disease that he concealed successfully for many years behind varying exotic afflictions and of which he died – Aids. The debilitating effects of the disease led, inevitably, to artistic compromises in the course of writing the novel. Chatwin had never intended to make the notebooks section so entirely separate and so comprehensive. A hand-written plan, stored amongst his papers at the Bodleian library, shows the notebooks originally constituting far less of the total work than was the case upon publication.

Given its idiosyncrasy and the circumstances surrounding its composition, there have been inevitable debates as to the success of the *From the*

Notebooks section. For some, the extracts offer an opportunity for the reader to make his or her own mind up, to construct from inference a personal interpretation of Chatwin's grand ideas on nomadism and rest- lessness. Howard Morphy makes this case: '[W]hat he sets up is a resource for speculating about the human condition which centres on the theme of nomadism' (19). For others, the notebooks present a substantial narra- tive problem; John Ryle commented of 'the strange irruption of extracts from Chatwin's notebooks in the middle of the narrative', adding that, as a result, '[t]he book is misshapen; there is no suspension of disbelief'. Susannah Clapp observes similarly of this section: 'I think he might have reconsidered it if he was fully himself' (2007). When temporarily recov- ered, Chatwin himself would come to express a sense that, overall, the work was not as fully realised as it would have been had he not been unwell, telling Colin Thubron that, believing he would 'never live to see it polished' he 'let it go through in a rough state that he would have altered' (*Footsteps*). However, he wrote to Charles and Brenda Tomlinson: 'I have an idea that what's written is written with all the glaring defects: and if I'd tried to deliver everything I had in mind, the result might be even more incoherent than it is' (*US* 485).

However, the *From the Notebooks* section of *The Songlines* was not the most controversial aspect of the novel. In appearing to have approached the individuals he met and the information he uncovered during his time in Central Australia as merely resources for his work, Chatwin, as he had done in Patagonia, engendered considerable bad feeling.

There were a number of transgressions which Chatwin was accused of having committed. The first related to his approach to the real-life characters he met on his travels. As in *In Patagonia*, Chatwin had used these individuals as the basis for the characters who populate his fiction- alised story. They were not direct transcriptions – but there was also little doubt in Alice Springs as to who was who. Perhaps the most bitter of those whom Chatwin fictionalised in *The Songlines* is Philip Toyne, who in the novel becomes the dislikable Kidder, the 'Gym Bore': 'He was, it had to be said, good-looking in a sourish way. His name was Kidder. The shrill, upward note on which he ended his sentences gave each of his statements, however dogmatic, a tentative and questionable bias. He would have made an excellent policeman' (42). Toyne discussed Chatwin's perceived transgressions with Nicholas Shakespeare: 'It caused enormous upset, confusion, disappointment, pain. People felt heavily betrayed by many parts of it' (*Footsteps*), Toyne says of the novel. Such is often the fate of the writer in those communities they visit and transcribe, however; as Thomas Keneally observed in a comment on the novel, employing other people's stories in service of your own is 'almost the job description of writing' (*Footsteps*).

The second accusation levelled at Chatwin, related to, though perhaps more serious than, the first, is that he in some way used the Aborigines and Aboriginal culture as a springboard from which to launch a discussion of his own personal theories of restlessness; that he failed to show proper respect for the personal, spiritual and political aspects of the world in which he was involving himself, focussing instead upon attaining a super-ficial understanding of the concepts involved which he could then exploit.

Chatwin was certainly well aware of the potential for upset. There were repeated warnings from those with whom he discussed the project, including Salman Rushdie, who joined him on a trip through the outback in 1984, and who, after reading the finished book, told Chatwin 'You realize many of the sort of people you've written about will be pretty cross about some of this?' (234). Chatwin was also acutely conscious of the contention which continued to swirl around the life and work of the figure who had inspired *The Songlines* – Theodor Strehlow.

Strehlow had become a polemical figure in Australia during his life-time as a result of the collection of sacred Aboriginal material he had amassed during the period of his working and living with the Aranda. This material included recordings, transcriptions and photographs[7] of tribal rituals and song, as well as – most controversially – approximately 1,200 sacred artefacts of the Aranda tribe, which had been bequeathed to him by elders who considered their sons and grandsons to be untrust-worthy of the responsibility of continuing to protect them. Strehlow commented of this bequest: 'Many of them were, in fact, almost patheti-cally eager to pass on their totemic secrets to someone whom they trusted, and in whom they placed their confidence that he would do his best to preserve these secrets from oblivion' (Strehlow xlv). Feeling he had been trusted with a role of custodianship, Strehlow refused to return these artefacts to their 'owners', and the issue dogged him until – and beyond – his death in 1978.

It was not that Chatwin callously disregarded such implicit warnings to exercise caution in involving himself in Aboriginal affairs. Rather, he was, as always, focussed upon his larger aims. The songlines were of interest, both of themselves and within the context of Chatwin's expansive theories of restlessness, and hence he wanted to explore them. They were, put simply, good material. He never intended to deeply involve himself in his subject: 'I just didn't want to' (1987: 34), he told Michael Ignatieff, who subsequently put the obvious question:

> Ignatieff: An accusatory voice would say, you've managed just enough entanglement with the Third World to get some fiction out of it, but you've never actually got involved.
> Chatwin: Now you've caught me on tricky ground. (Pause.) If I had become involved, I wouldn't write the books I do. (1987: 34)

There were, inevitably, consequential gaps in Chatwin's understanding of the intricacies of Aboriginal culture which resulted from his approach, and these gaps are manifest in the novel. It is also true that Chatwin took very little interest in the immediate politics of the Aboriginal call for land rights – an issue which was all consuming at the time of Chatwin's visit. Some have said that his approach was negligent: that he should have spent longer with the Aborigines; that he should have placed their political concerns centrally in the novel. Others take a longer-term view; asserting that by avoiding the political and writing a book which – however inaccurately – offers a more profound view of Aboriginal culture, Chatwin managed to raise the profile and understanding of it in a manner in which a strictly anthropological or political text would have failed. The anthropologist Howard Morphy makes this case: '[A]s a book for the "public" to read on the contemporary context of Aborigines in the Northern Territory that provides insights into their cultural values and world view, *Songlines* [sic] has no rival. If an anthropologist feels that a better book should be written then it's up to him or her to write one' (20). Thomas Keneally feels similarly:

> If you understand the concept of songlines, then you understand native title perfectly. So I think he actually did, in so far as a European can – it's a dangerous thing to say – but I think he did Aboriginal Australia a service. I think he did all of us a service. I mean, if there were 10 books I had to set for every Aussie to read, not for the sake of nationalism, but for the sake of coming to terms with where we are on earth, *The Songlines* would be one of them. (*Footsteps*)

In completing his Australian novel, Bruce Chatwin had achieved nothing less than the composition of his own songline; a narrative record of his own personal and intellectual journey, from birth to the point of 'going back in'. Such a reading is supported by the narrative arc of the novel,

which begins with a biographical outline of the narrator's youth and restless pedigree, and which ends with a reflection on death which implies
the end of one journey, and the beginning of another:

> Arkady folded his arms, and watched.
>   'Aren't they wonderful?' Marian whispered, putting her hand in mine
> and giving it a squeeze.
>   Yes. They were all right. They knew where they were going, smiling at
> death in the shade of a ghost-gum. (295)

This conclusion mirrored Chatwin's own personal situation – *The Songlines* marked a number of endings and beginnings. There were, of course,
the intimations of mortality that overshadowed this period. Chatwin's
illness was, as noted above, a prevalent concern as he completed the
novel: 'I wrote that last chapter about three old men dying under a gum
tree, when I was just about to conk myself' (1987: 35), he told Michael
Ignatieff. However, even before his illness had manifested itself, there
were harbingers that resonated emotionally.

In April 1986, as Chatwin worked on the manuscript of *The Songlines*
in Bhimtal, India, he received news of the death of Penelope Betjeman.
She had suffered a heart attack whilst leading a trek in the Kullu valley,
near to where he was staying. Chatwin travelled to attend her funeral ten
days later, and as he took his leave following her cremation, he encountered a Sadhu[8] who asked to tell his fortune. Having looked at Chatwin's
palm, the holy man refused to speak: 'Obviously the Sadhu could see it,
in his palm, or in his face maybe' (2010), comments Elizabeth.

The sense of conclusion also, however, attended the completion of
a project which had occupied Chatwin's intellect for twenty-five years.
The Songlines was a summational text, a manifesto outlining the conclu-
sions Chatwin had arrived at concerning the causes, effects and possible
cures for restlessness. Having finally relieved himself of 'the burden he's
been carrying all his writing life' (235), as Salman Rushdie described it,
he was free to move on to new subjects.

Finally, there was a personal new beginning marked by the completion of *The Songlines*. During their visit to Ayers Rock, Chatwin had
told Salman Rushdie: 'I've been very unhappy lately and for a long time
I couldn't work out why, and then I suddenly realised it was because
I missed my wife' (qtd. in *US* 364). The writing of *The Songlines* was
concurrent with a rapprochement which occurred between Chatwin and
Elizabeth, and which came to strongly influence the emotional subtext

of the novel. The conclusion of *The Songlines* depicts the marriage of Arkady and the idealised Marian (for whom the narrator himself has earlier appeared to harbour romantic feelings). It is difficult not to read Chatwin's description of the couple as a sublimated commentary on his own recent reconciliation with Elizabeth, to whom, of course, the novel is dedicated:

> We watched them go off to bed. They were two people made in heaven for each other. They had been hopelessly in love since the day they met, yet had gradually crept into their shells, glancing away, deliberately, in despair, as if it were too good, never to be, until suddenly the reticence and the anguish had melted and what should have been, long ago, now was.[9] (285–6)

It is a conclusion that would be echoed in Chatwin's next novel, *Utz*, and which confirms an emergent faith – inspired by his own experiences – in the power of the human to act as a curative for the effects of restlessness.

NOTES

1 Letter to Murray Bail, 3 November 1986: 'I finished the book – title *The Songlines* – which, to all the publishers distaste, I insist on calling a novel' (*US* 467).

2 See 12–13. *Metamorphoses* is not the only classical source referred to. The work of Homer is alluded to in both the novel's image of a 'spaghetti of Iliads and Odysseys, writhing this way and that' (13) and in the later account of the Lizard Man: 'The distance from here to Port Augusta, as the crow flew, was roughly 1,100 miles, about twice the distance – so we calculated – from Troy to Ithaca. We tried to imagine an Odyssey with a verse for every twist and turn of the hero's ten year voyage' (107).

3 This hypothesis has recently been contradicted by Professor Lee Berger, whose research indicates that crowned hawk eagles were most likely to be responsible for the death of the Taung child. See Berger.

4 This description has its origin in a note from one of the author's Moleskine notebooks: 'red haired Lutheran 8th generation Australian yet indomitably East Prussian. From the Barossa Valley. Father didn't speak English till he went to school' (Box 35).

5 See Shakespeare 2000: 448.

6 See Grant 257 for further evidence of this trope.

7 Strehlow generated further controversy by selling some of these photographs to the German magazine *Stern* in 1977.

8 A Hindu mystic.

9 Chatwin was, to a degree, ambivalent about the inclusion of this passage; it would be excised from the French edition, presumably as a result of its frank emotional tone.

7

The Harlequin

'The collector' was another of Bruce's big categories: the opposite of the nomad; the person who – he declared every now and then – it was important to stop being. (228)
Susannah Clapp, *With Chatwin*

Art is never enough. Art always lets you down.
Michael Ignatieff, 'On Bruce Chatwin'

Bruce Chatwin frequently expressed his personal belief in the perils of materialism, a belief rooted in his conviction that we are evolutionarily programmed to follow a nomadic model: 'Travel well, travel light', Chatwin wrote in *The Nomadic Alternative*. 'A wandering man owns what he can carry and cannot own anything else' (152). Following this model approach to material wealth was a key element of Chatwin's oft-expressed strategy for avoiding the restlessness induced by settlement; to ignore the nomadic model was to find oneself entrapped and frustrated by one's collection of acquired belongings: 'We sacrifice our freedom of action to become its privileged guardian, and we end its imprisoned slave' (*AOR* 171), he wrote in a speech delivered to a Red Cross charitable art auction in 1973 entitled 'The Morality of Things'.

Such is the situation of Joachim Utz, the central protagonist of Chatwin's final full-length work, trapped as he is by his collection of Meissen porcelain which, established as a means of protecting himself from the world, comes to hold 'him prisoner' (*U* 75). Utz presents a slight story which illustrates a significant facet of Chatwin's philosophical notions – namely that settlement, and its attendant materialism, is contrary to our nomadic heritage, and thus renders restively anxious those who submit to it.

Chatwin repeatedly identified the genesis of this conviction in the epiphanic trip he made to the Sudan in 1965, discussed in Chapter One. In interview, he outlined the appeal of the life he had discovered during that journey, part of which was spent with the Beja, a nomadic tribe of the Red Sea Hills in Eastern Sudan: 'I was ... overwhelmed by the simplicity of the lives of those people, and fascinated by the idea that you were much happier if you had nothing, if you carried nothing with you, in the classical sense of the term' ('Chatwinesque'). This narrative of the craven materialist awakened from his sinful ways by the simple wisdom of the nomads has, as was noted in Chapter One, an obvious romantic appeal. Yet, in reality, the intellectual certainty that this epiphany inspired – of the virtues of the nomadic life, and its attendant asceticism – was always pitched against Chatwin's strongly felt aesthetic (and, indeed, sedentary) desires.[1] Though his conviction was absolute, Chatwin struggled throughout his life to master his appreciation of and passion for beautiful objects. When he wrote of the problematic nature of collection: 'All civilisations are by their very nature "thing-oriented" and the main problem of their stability has been to devise new equations between the urge to amass things and the urge to be rid of them' (AOR 171), he wrote from a personal, rather than social, perspective; he describes his own anxieties.

The source of these anxieties can be located in Chatwin's early life. His youth was defined by two tendencies, one towards movement – emerging from his transient upbringing during the years of the war and described in previous chapters – and the other towards acquisition. Early letters sent to his parents testify to a developing interest in the value and provenance of *objets* and antiques. Aged ten, he wrote to Charles and Margharita with the satisfied air of the collector: 'I have just discovered that my bird-books are worth £10 for the set', he wrote from Old Hall School, 'and will soon be very valuable' (US 30). The young Chatwin would later become notorious amongst antique dealers within cycling distance of Marlborough School.

Child Bruce's enthusiasm for collection was to find its most resonant expression, of course, in his documented fascination with the cabinet of curiosities belonging to his Grandmother, Isobel. In one of W.G. Sebald's final essays, the German writer identified this cabinet as central to Chatwin's development, both personal and literary, describing:

> [T]hose early moments of pure fascination when the boy crept into his grandmother Isobel's dining room and, looking past his own blurred

reflection, marvelled at the jumble of curios arranged on the shelves of the glass-fronted mahogany cupboard, all of them from very different lands. It could not even be said where some of them came from or what they had been for; apocryphal stories clung to others. (183)

Most coveted of these objects, of course, was the piece of mylodon hide which Chatwin sought to recover in *In Patagonia*, and with which he had developed a 'fetishistic obsession': 'Whenever I came to the house I had to make sure the piece of brontosaurus was still there and screamed until I was shown it' (Box 41). Less well known is the fact that the skin was to form part of a childhood collection constructed in the author's own image, as recounted in a passage ultimately cut from the published *In Patagonia*: 'Already I had a Museum, a cabinet with Roman glass, a miniature penknife, a Tsarist rouble, a real piece of eight and the skull of a field mouse, waiting only to receive its prize exhibit' (qtd. in Clapp 1998: 33). Chatwin retained a fascination with the concept of the cabinet of curiosities; later in life he would make several small 'God Boxes' containing items from his travels. Only one now remains extant at his home in Oxfordshire; it is a pale green wooden box with a glass frontage, stencilled with the initials 'B C'. Inside is stored: 'the eardrum of a lion, a dried gecko, a guinea fowl feather, an unidentified internal organ and two toes from a bird's claw wrapped in indigo cloth: there used to be a monkey's skull but it has disappeared' (*P&N* 16).

The cabinet of curiosities[2] can thus be seen as metaphorical of Chatwin's wider impulse to collect and acquire; as Andrew Palmer observes: 'The moment when the young Bruce sees the sloth skin in his grandmother's cabinet can be seen as another "poetic moment" like the ones described in the opening pages of *The Songlines*. Those in the later book led Chatwin to restlessness, but the one in his first book led him to collect, to hoard' (135).

His enthusiasm for works of art was, of course, further cultivated by his time at Sotheby's. His work at the firm allowed unparalleled access to a repository of rare and beautiful objects, and would introduce him to a social circle – including the antiquities dealer Robert Erskine, collector George Ortiz and the art dealer John Kasmin – who prized such objects above all else, and who would remain his friends for the rest of his life. The work also flattered his talents, in particular his noted ability to recognise items of quality, as Katherine Maclean observes: 'Bruce was like a cross between an enfant terrible and a prodigy ... [I]t became apparent that he had this uncanny eye; he was able to recognise things without any intellectual working out, which was unnerving but very useful' (CCMM). Chatwin's own pride in this prenatural ability emerges in his autobiographical writing; in a short piece titled 'The Bey', Chatwin recounts with obvious pleasure the recognition of his talents: "'Ha!" said the old gentleman. "I see you have The Eye. I too have The Eye. We shall be friends"' (*WAIDH* 358). Chatwin would, of course, dramatically turn his back on his art-world life in 1966. Yet, despite Chatwin's obvious intention in so severing his connections with the world of art and acquisition, he never managed to escape its influence and appeal. He would remain a collector for the whole of his life.

He did, however, manage to alight upon a compromise position that appeared to mollify, temporarily at least, the restless anxiety which attends collection. Chatwin wrote of this approach in an essay on the architect John Pawson, referencing his 1965 trip to the Sudan: '[I]n my late twenties, I was sick of things; and after travelling some months in the desert, I fell for a kind of "Islamic" iconoclasm and believed, in all seriousness, that one should never bow before the graven image. As a result, the things that have survived this iconoclastic phase are, for the most part, "abstract"' (*AOR* 19). Chatwin here struck at a moderate position; rather than adopting true asceticism, as advocated in other accounts of his Sudanese journey, he instead sought to rationalise his acquisitive behaviour by exercising the aesthetic he saw as intrinsic in the craft of the nomad.

Such an aesthetic, in Chatwin's interpretation, centred upon the stripping away of decoration and filigree; returning objects and environment to an essence. The use of unworked materials was central; wood and stone left relatively unadorned, save for, perhaps, a splash of colour. Or else beautiful portable objects of great tactile and visual quality. Yet his aesthetic was never casual or inconsidered; despite the purity of his taste, Chatwin's decorative schemes – like his writing – were always finely worked. Susannah Clapp describes Chatwin's flat at Grosvenor Crescent Mews:

> A small octagonal room had a round table for the host's minute portions of delicious food. There were two painted Swedish chairs with blue-and-white eighteenth-century saddlecloth on the seats; there was another table made of a slab of marble balanced on two trestles; and there was the Japanese Screen ... which went on to feature in the picture Howard Hodgkin painted of Chatwin ... Fragments of marble were scattered around, and a trunk contained various prized items, such as ancient pieces of lacquer, bundled up in scraps of silk tied with leather. (15–16)

Perhaps the most revealing exposition of the possibilities and perils of this nomadic aesthetic comes in a short story by Chatwin published first in the *Saturday Night Reader* in 1979 called 'The Estate of Maximilian Tod'. This story, which carries its emulation of the Argentinian writer Jorge Luis Borges almost to the point of pastiche[3] – indeed, Iain Stewart wrote an essay on the similarity titled 'The Sincerest Form of Flattery' – offers an intriguing view, obscured, as always in Chatwin's confessional writing, by the veil of fictionality, of his profound ambivalence to this approach.

The story opens with a statement of geographical and chronological specificity which prefigures that of *Utz*, presenting a statement of specific fact from a narrator who turns out to be fundamentally unreliable: 'On 6 February 1975, Dr Estelle Neumann fell down a crevasse of the Belgrano Glacier in Chilean Patagonia' (*AOR* 54). The story continues with an explanation of Neumann's life and death by a colleague; the dead woman had been a glaciologist at Harvard University, researching a controversial topic: 'She had proved', the colleague narrator observes, 'beyond question that the injection of fossil fuels into the atmosphere had no effect whatever on the temperature of glaciers' (55). This assertion had led to generous funding from petrochemical companies and the guaranteed continuation of the research undertaken by Neumann and the – at this point – unnamed narrator. This narrator does, however, bear a passing resemblance to the author himself; certainly, like Chatwin, he prides himself on his good taste – in contrast to that of his deceased colleague who, the narrator observes, 'was addicted to "primitive" jewellery of the worst kind – Navajo turquoise, African bangles, amber beads. That morning a golden eagle of the Veraguas Culture was flapping between her breasts; I did not have the heart to tell her it was a fake' (56). Chatwin himself was in the habit of joyously declaring inauthenticity, as Nicholas Shakespeare discovered when interviewing colleagues from the author's days at Sotheby's: 'Bruce had been away on a trip at the wrong time of the year. On the first day of the sale this hurricane comes in and very grandly points at a Renoir drawing of a nude: "Oh, that's ghastly, I even think it's a fake." He looked around and said, "That's a fake. That's a fake. That's a fake," and walked on' (qtd. in 2000: 101). Notions of authenticity were identified by Chatwin – both in his essay 'The Morality of Things' ('Is it a fake?' (*AOR* 172)), and in *Utz*, where the eponymous protagonist momentarily questions the authenticity of his piece *The Spaghetti Eater* – as a central cause of the restless anxiety that afflicts the sedentary collector, constituting part of the psychopathological mania that afflicts those who put their faith in works of art. In 'The Estate of Maximilian Tod', however, there is no question as to the authenticity of the vast and tasteful collection belonging to the narrator; it is the character himself who proves to be a fake.

It emerges in the course of the story that, in fact, the narrator and the Maximilian Tod[4] of the title are one and the same, and that he murdered Neumann in order to prevent her from revealing a secret which she had recently uncovered: Tod has been filtering off the funds supplied for their academic research towards the construction of a decadent Patagonian retreat. Stuffed full of the most desirable books and antiquities, this South American refuge is situated in a hidden valley which, like that housing the Washington mansion of Fitzgerald's *The Diamond As Big As The Ritz*, has never been mapped.

In this valley the narrator describes a dwelling of stunning simplicity and good taste:

> Mr Tod's house ... was an airy pavilion built on a knoll about one hundred yards from the water. It was thirty-five feet square, aligned to the cardinal points, and had five sash windows on each face except for the north. The walls were of battered vertical planks painted the colour of pewter. The glazing bars were a warm ivory.
>
> No structure could be simpler. It owed its severity and perfect proportions to the utopian projects of Ledoux and the houses of Shaker communities in New York State. (60-1)

The description of this dwelling is reminiscent of that envisaged as a retreat by the narrator of *In Patagonia* just two years earlier: 'I pictured a low timber house with a shingle roof', Chatwin wrote in the early pages of that work, 'caulked against storms, with blazing log fires inside and the walls lined with the best books, somewhere to live when the rest of the world blew up' (4). Even the motivation behind the establishment and location of such a retreat is identical: 'I began work on my "refined Thebaid" in the southern summer of 1947–8, believing at the time that nuclear war was inevitable in the Northern Hemisphere' (69), Tod informs the reader. In his later short story, Chatwin is simply extrapolating the reclusive vision of *In Patagonia* to its imaginative limits.

Mr Tod has amassed in this extraordinary dwelling place a collection of exquisite good taste which, despite the narrator's observation that '[i]nventories make tiresome reading' (63), is described at some length: a 'Shang bronze fang-i with the "melon-skin" patina; a Nuremberg sorcerer's mirror; an Aztec plate with a purple bloom; the crystal riliquary of a Gandharan stupa; a gold mounted bezoar; a jade flute; a wampum belt; a pink granite Horus falcon of Dynasty I and some Eskimo morse ivory animals which, for all the stylised attenuation of their features, seemed positively to breathe' (63). It is a list which is again reminiscent of the author, and, in particular, the inventory presented by Chatwin in his essay on John Pawson, in which he lists the beautiful objects which survived his 'iconoclastic' phase:

> I also have a sheet of Islamic Kufic calligraphy, from the eighth-century Koran – which has a certain talismanic value for a writer, in that Allah first cut a reed pen and with it he wrote the world. There is an Indian painting of a banana tree; a Sienese fifteenth-century cross in tempera and gold; and a gilt-bronze roundel from a Japanese Buddhist temple. Other than that, I have a small collection of Japanese *negoro* lacquers, which once belonged to a German called Ernst Grosse. (20)

Yet, despite the obvious sensual pleasure taken in these descriptive inventories, there is a tension in both which is brought into clear relief by one of Tod's most treasured possessions: 'a calligraphy by the Zen Master, Sen Sotan, with the tenet: "Man originally possesses nothing."' Both Tod and Chatwin understand the moral and personal implications of collection; that 'man is the sum of his things, even if a few fortunate men are the sum of an absence of things' (65). Tod has attempted, like Chatwin, to circumvent this absolute by possessing objects devoid of ostentation, decoration or show. He cites the Japanese concept of *Wabi* as a guiding aesthetic principle: 'Literally the word means "poverty", but applied to a work of art it means that true beauty, "the beauty that breaks away from this world", must rely on the use of its humblest materials' (67). It is a description which is, again, reminiscent of the author's personal approach. As Elizabeth testifies of Bruce's collection: 'He didn't tend to have rococo things at all. They were very plain: marvellous proportions or texture' ('Chatwinesque').

Ultimately, however, Tod admits that for all his efforts in constructing a minimalist paradise, he has been forced away, seemingly by the anxieties of restlessness attendant upon settlement and aestheticism, from his collection and the place of settlement he so zealously guarded; the outcome all the less surprising given the presence of Baudelaire's poem 'Anywhere Out of The World' in his library. Despite the ascetic existence he emulated, relief can only be found in moving on: 'I had intended to settle for ever in my valley; I have left it for others to pillage. I have left my young companion. I have left my things. I, who with bedouin rigour abolished the human form from my possessions ... I, who did everything to protect my retina from the visual affronts of the twentieth century, now I too am prey to hallucinations. Women with red faces leer at me. Wet lips slaver over me. Monstrous blocs of colour smother me. Je dus voyager, *distraire les enchantements assemblés dans mon cerveau'* (69).

The citation of Rimbaud's *Une Saison en Enfer* – a key text for the author – confirms the impression, clearly conveyed throughout the piece, that 'The Estate of Maximilian Tod' is ultimately a commentary by the author on himself. The conclusion of the story appears to confirm that, despite his ambitions, Chatwin fundamentally recognised the impossibility of securing a compromise between the binary positions of aestheticism and asceticism – that, however tasteful or refined one's collection, acquisition ultimately leads to restlessness. It would be another ten years before the author alighted upon a true solution for the impositions of collection.

In the summer of 1967, Bruce Chatwin embarked upon a journey through Central Europe. His trip took him from Brussels to Aachen in the West of Germany, then through Cologne, Bonn and Nuremberg – and on to Zàvist, near Prague, where he was to take part in an archeological dig as part of his studies at Edinburgh. Chatwin used the opportunity of this time on the continent, both before and after his dig at Zàvist, to explore the museums of Central Europe; of his visit to the Schatzkammer at Aachen, he wrote to Elizabeth: '[T]here are some objects that nearly made me die, especially the engraving on the back of the cross of Lothar and Richard of Cornwall's sceptre' (*US* 98). This journey, and his brief experiences of Prague, would be resurrected twenty years later, as Chatwin recuperated from a fierce onslaught of his illness, as the inspiration for *Utz*.

During his time in Czechoslovakia, the young archeologist met for four hours with Dr Rudolph Just, a Czech businessman – and obsessive collector of porcelain. Chatwin had secured an introduction to Just from a colleague at Sotheby's, Kate Foster, who had, a year earlier, travelled to Prague during two months of paid leave from the firm, which she intended to use to improve her German – the language of porcelain. At his apartment Just quizzed Foster as to the values of his collection, and for news of the porcelain world. The narrative of her experience that day would be combined with Chatwin's brief encounter one year later to provide the framework for the story of *Utz*.

Kaspar Joachim Utz, however, is a far more obsessive individual than Rudolph Just. Chatwin transmutes Just – who in reality collected an eclectic mix of porcelain, silver and glass – into a single-minded Meissen neurotic, with an amassed porcelain collection which comes to both obsess and frustrate him. As in Chatwin's other work, the character became a vector for the author's own personal anxieties, his situation being extrapolated in fiction to its extreme limits.

As with Chatwin, Joachim Utz's drive to collect emerges from a youthful poetic moment. In a scenario powerfully reminiscent of Bruce Chatwin's own fascinated encounter with Charley Milward's sloth skin, Utz is described 'standing on tiptoe before a vitrine of antique porcelain', in his grandmother's house, transfixed by one particular object:

> [A] figure of Harlequin that had been modelled by the greatest of Meissen modellers, J.J. Kaendler.
>
> The Harlequin sat on a tree trunk. His taut frame was sheathed in a costume of multi-coloured chevrons. In one hand he waved an oxidised silver tankard; in the other a floppy yellow hat. Over his face there was a leering orange mask.
>
> 'I want him,' said Kaspar. (16)

In the novel, Utz finally receives the piece four years after this first encounter, in consolation for the death of his father. The gift of the Harlequin is the initiating influence which begins Utz's obsession with porcelain: 'He had found his vocation: he would devote his life to collecting – "rescuing" as he came to call it – the porcelains of the Meissen factory' (17). However, in George Sluizer's 1992 film adaptation of the work, the two events are exactly concurrent, with the young Utz stating his desire for the Harlequin in the immediate aftermath of his father's death, reinforcing the text's clear implication that Utz's later fascination with porcelain is born of its compensatory effect in the face of childhood trauma.

This connection between the experience of a tragedy in early youth, and the victim's later propensity to collect has been well documented. Werner Muensterberger, in his volume *Collecting: An Unruly Passion*, writes of the relationship:

> Provoked by early, possibly unfavorable conditions or the lack of affection on the part of not-good-enough mothering, the child's attempt towards self-preservation quickly turns to some substitute to cling to. Thus, he or she has a need for compensatory objects of one or the other kind. This can also be interpreted as a self-healing attempt. In later life, this attitude leads to a biased weighting for more money or more possessions, as if they could

provide magic protection and shield the individual from new frustrations and anxieties.

To put it in another way, such a person requires symbolic substitutes to cope with a world he or she regards as basically unfriendly, even hazardous. (21)

Muensterberger's conclusion is that the impulse to collect develops in the aftermath of childhood trauma as a means of shoring up against further difficulties; of building a protective environment where one cannot be threatened. Chatwin also sees the power of the collection as consoling in the face of early loss: '[T]he work of art', Chatwin writes, 'is a source of pleasure and power, the object of fetishistic adoration, which serves in a traumatised individual as a substitute for skin-to-skin contact with the mother' (*AOR* 174). Utz's life closely follows the model suggested by Muensterberger; his father's death establishes a preoccupation with porcelain which develops in adult life as a comprehensive strategy for limiting his involvement and exposure in the wider world.

This defence is constructed partly against the profound social and political upheaval with which Utz is faced during the course of his life. Utz lives through a period of significant turbulence: his lifetime encompasses the stock market crash of 1929, both world wars, the imposition of communist rule in Czechoslovakia in 1948 and the Prague Spring of 1968. Like the Jones twins, who watch the distant glow of Coventry from their window, Utz screens himself from these events, retreating from the outside world into the created and controlled environment of his apartment:

> [F]or him, this world of little figures was the real world. And that, compared to them, the Gestapo, the Secret Police and other hooligans were creatures of tinsel. And the events of this sombre century – the bombardments, blitzkriegs, putsches, purges – were, so far as he was concerned, so many 'noises off'. (94)

To some degree, the narrator sees Utz's stance as both politically virtuous, and also indicative of the Czech attitude to imposition. The narrator's historian friend, who provides the necessary introduction to *Utz*, observes that 'The Czechs' propensity to "bend" before superior force was not necessarily a weakness. Rather, their metaphysical view of life encouraged them to look on acts of force as ephemera' (13). The narrator views Utz's passivity towards communist rule as an act of rebellion far more powerful than overt political protest; he comes to concur with the opinion that 'the true heroes of this impossible situation were people who wouldn't raise a murmur against the Party or State – yet who seemed to carry the sum of Western Civilisation in their heads' (13). This approach, the narrator concludes in an aside which seems eerily prescient of the Velvet Revolution, is that most likely to bring about the desired result: '[I]n the end', Chatwin writes, 'the machinery of repression is more likely to vanish, not with the war or revolution, but with a puff, or the voice of falling leaves' (99).

Utz's collection is not merely a politically laudable mechanism to defend against the outside world, however; it is also intended to protect him from the emotional consequences of human relationships. His insecurity in this arena has been initiated, of course, by the traumatic loss of his father – a loss which immediately leads the young Utz to distance himself from his remaining relations. His mother and grandmother become ancillary figures in Utz's life; their main significance to the protagonist is found in the opportunity their deaths provide to bolster his collection, allowing him 'to bid against a Rothschild' (18).

Utz's emotional reticence suffers further reinforcement by his first experiences of the opposite sex, whom he approaches in the spirit of Augustus the Strong: 'the girls', however, 'were perplexed by the scientific seriousness of the young man's approach, and collapsed with giggles at the minuscule scale of his equipment' (18). In the face of this humiliating rejection, Utz turns to the 'warmer welcome of the antiquaires' (18), and – like many of Chatwin's protagonists – retains a passive suspicion of the opposite sex throughout his life.

In his Red Cross auction speech, Chatwin observed this tendency of the collector to replace the human with the material: 'The true collector, they imply, is a voyeur in life, protected by a stuffing of possessions from those he would like to love, possessed of the tenderest emotions for things and glacial emotions for people. He is the classic cold fish' (AOR 171). This analysis is certainly true of Utz; so profound is the relief he finds in the company of his collection that he begins to view his porcelain as actual living beings; the collection comes to form, in the narrator's words, a 'miniature family' (47). The real world is replaced by a fantasy environment populated solely by minute inanimate beings who cannot change, and hence cannot inflict trauma.

The reader is first made aware of Utz's conception of his collection as alive in a passage quoted from a fictional journal article written by the character: 'An object in a museum case', he writes, 'must suffer the de-natured existence of an animal in the zoo. In any museum the object dies – of suffocation and the public gaze – whereas private ownership confers on the owner the right and the need to touch' (17). This suggestion is expanded upon in a later conversation between the narrator and Utz, in which the collector spells out his belief in the life inherent in his figures:

> 'So you see,' said Utz, 'not only was Adam the first human person. He was also the first ceramic sculpture.'
>
> 'Are you suggesting your porcelains are alive?'
>
> 'I am and I am not,' he said. 'They are alive and they are dead. But if they were alive, they would also have to die. Is it not?' (33–4)

The concept of figures fashioned from inert material who come to life is, of course, strongly reminiscent of the folk-story of the Prague Golem: 'that man-made being that long ago a rabbi versed in the lore of the Cabbala formed from elemental matter and invested with mindless, automatic life by placing a magic formula behind its teeth' (Meyrink 42). The Golem, shaped from the clay of the River Vltava, was designed to be an aid to Rabbi Loew, created as 'a servant to help him ring the synagogue bells and do other menial tasks' (56). Yet, in the Jewish myth, the Golem ultimately went out of control one sabbath, running amok in the streets, causing damage and 'crushing everything that happened to be in its way' (56) before finally being subdued by his creator.

The Golem features prominently in *Utz*; Marta is described as a female version of Rabbi Loew's creation, whilst Utz is himself fascinated by the myth, concluding that the story of the Golem is a warning against idolatory. The Golem in *Utz* can be seen as a metaphor for both the consolatory and destructive nature of collection; formed in the image of his creator as an aid, the automaton becomes a burden which ultimately demands its destruction.

The insulation provided by Utz's miniature family is irrevocably disrupted in 1952 by the unwelcome visit of the staff of the state museum. Their intrusion leaves Utz feeling 'abused and assaulted. He felt like the man who, on returning from a journey, finds his house has been burgled' (47). In the aftermath of this disturbance – the spell of his protective shield broken – Utz begins to speculate on the possibility of a life free of his current ties: '[C]ould he bring himself to leave the collection? Make a clean break? Begin a new life abroad? He still had money in Switzerland, thank God!' (47). He decides to leave, organising a trip to Vichy for his health from which he plans not to return. This impulse to travel is, of course, predictable for a character in a novel by Bruce Chatwin; it is the first recourse of the restless. However, Utz finds little solace in his journeying. The intended pleasures of his trip are savourless, and he comes to realise that, despite the attendant compromises, his settled life in Prague is that which will make him 'least unhappy' (66). The revelation strikes him, simultaneously, that what he misses most is not his collection of Meissen, but rather Marta. As Kerry Featherstone observes: 'the importance of the collection diminishes in the light of the first genuinely affectionate relationship that the adult Utz experiences' (2000: 253). 'What am I doing here?' (72) Utz asks himself – an echo of Rimbaud's question from *Une Saison en Enfer* that will lend its title to Chatwin's final book – as he rouses himself for return to Prague and to Marta.

Yet, in the narrator's account of events, Utz cyclically continues to make this pilgrimage every year, driven by his recurrent 'resentment against the regime', his 'acute claustrophobia, from having spent the winter in close proximity to the adoring Marta', and 'the boredom, verging on fury, that came from living these months with lifeless porcelain' (74). Abiding restlessness has set in; the psychopathology of the collector has condemned Utz to a lifetime of listlessly alternating between adoration and hatred for his collection. As the narrator takes his leave of Utz on the streets of Prague, the protagonist appears unwillingly committed to a Chatwinesque existence of unsuccessfully searching for a solution to the 'tricky equation between things and freedom' (*AOR* 183).

However, at this juncture of the narrative the reader is made aware that what has thus far passed is not necessarily to be relied upon; that the arc of Utz's life may not conform as closely to the model of the neurotic collector as the novel has indicated. This moment of realisation is consequential of the tricky narrative structure which Chatwin employed in *Utz*.

The novel begins, of course, with the remarkably specific, third-person account of Utz's funeral:

> An hour before dawn on March 7th 1974, Kaspar Joachim Utz died of a second and long-expected stroke, in his apartment at No.5 Široká Street, overlooking the Old Jewish Cemetery in Prague.
> Three days later, at 7:45 a.m., his friend Dr Václav Orlík was standing outside the Church of St Sigismund, awaiting the arrival of the hearse and clutching seven of the ten pink carnations he had hoped to afford at the florist's. (7)

The effect of this opening is not dissimilar to that of a novel by Balzac; it is intended to conform to the stylistic conventions of realism in order to reassure the reader as to the reliability of the narrative. Immediately, however, this reliability is undermined when the novel switches away in the second chapter from this third-person omniscience to a first-person account of the encounter between the narrator and Utz.

Having been provided with an introduction by his historian friend, the narrator, Utz and palaeontologist Dr Orlík – himself a collector – go for lunch at the Restaurant Pstruh, where they deal awkwardly with the issues of translation presented by the menu – a detail drawn from Kate Foster's experience with Just. The narrator and Utz then return to Utz's apartment to examine his porcelain. It is at this point that the narrative slips back into the third person, where, in a long section, the narrator outlines the biographical details of the central protagonist discussed above. This section is bookended by the narrator's contemporary encounter with Utz at his apartment; the implication is that the journalist narrator has constructed his account of Utz's life from the information supplied to him during this meeting.

There are hints throughout this section of the novel that the account presented is not entirely to be trusted. There is the narrator himself – an unnamed figure who, whilst sharing some similarities with the author, seems, even at this early stage, slightly untrustworthy. He describes his 'idleness' and 'ignorance of the languages' of Middle Europe, commenting that his trip to Prague – intended to support a journalistic study of the psychopathology of the collector – turned out instead as 'a very enjoyable holiday, at others' expense' (11). The sense of unreliability is reinforced by the narrator's early admission that he is unable to accurately recall Utz's physical appearance; 'His face was immediately forgettable', he writes. 'Did he have a moustache? I forget' (23). Yet, to some degree, the reader's sense of anxiety at these revelations is assuaged by the authoritative nature of the third-person account that follows. It is only when the narrative returns to the first person – and the tenuous basis for the story presented is revealed – that these early hints come into clear focus.

The switch back to the first person moves the narrative through to March 1974, and the revelation that Utz has died. The slight foundation for the preceding account is exposed, with the narrator reminding the reader that he had only 'known Utz for a total of nine and a quarter hours, some six and a half years earlier' (97). The narrative then jumps once again to the 'present day' of the late 1980s, with an account of the narrator's return to Prague – a return which will entirely destabilise the story presented thus far.

From this visit, and the narrator's consequent conversations with Dr Orlík, Dr Frankfurter, Utz's porcelain-dealing friend, and the curator of the Rudolfine museum, a number of startling insights emerge. Utz, it is revealed, was far from the 'ineffectual lover' (112) that the narrator envisioned; rather, for many years, he had pursued a successful romantic career seducing operetta starlets:

> A succession of Merry Widows and Countess Mitzis passed through his bed. And if the usual sources of erotic arousal left him cold, he would be driven to frenzy by the sight of a lower larynx, as the singer threw back her head to hit a high note. (112)

His conquests continued until the mid-1960s, when the ageing collector's advances were rebuffed by a young soprano. Chastened, Utz renounced his romantic pursuits, and turned instead to the patient love of Marta, who had 'adored Utz with a hopeless and blinkered passion' (112) from the occasion of their first meeting.

In order to avoid the loss of his apartment, Utz and Marta had wed in a marriage of convenience in 1952 and, through the subsequent years of seduction, Marta had acted as a resigned facilitator of Utz's conquests. Subsequent to his humiliation at the hands of the young opera singer, however, the couple come to live as man and wife. The reciprocal love which develops is fully confirmed by a second ceremony at the Church of Saint Nikolaus which coincides with the 'Prague Spring' of 1968.

These revelations concerning Utz's romantic life are, however, cast into shadow by the striking confession of the curator of the Rudolfine museum. She reveals to the narrator that, upon visiting Utz's apartment two days after his funeral, the museum officials were confronted with bare shelves. The porcelains had disappeared:

> The furniture was in place, even the bric-à-brac in the bedroom. But not a single piece of porcelain could be found: only dust-marks where the porcelains had been, and marks on the carpet where the animals from the Japanese Palace had stood. (105)

In George Sluizer's film of the novel, the fate of the porcelains is undisguised; Utz has Marta destroy the collection piece by piece as he lies watching from his bed. It is a scene which has an undeniably erotic charge, and which echoes the early connections established in the novel between collection and sex; Utz's childhood doctor refers to his obsession with Meissen as a 'perversion', whilst his adult compulsion to collect is partly driven, as has been seen, by sexual insecurity. This connection is also reaffirmed by a detail omitted from the work as published, but which is included in the typescript held at the Bodleian: 'I do, however, have one further insight, based on a snippet from Ada Krasova: that an archaeologist, excavating Utz's grave in the Vinohrady Cemetery, would find, clasped to the pelvic region of the skeleton, a Meissen figure of Harlequin with a grinning orange mask' (Box 17 184).

In the novel as published, however, little is certain. The narrator proposes that the porcelain has been destroyed and disposed of as rubbish. This belief is complicated, however, not only by the noted unreliability of the narrator (who himself admits towards the end of the novel that 'Once I took it into my head that the Utz Collection could have vanished down the maw of a garbage truck, my temptation was to twist every scrap of evidence in that direction' (124)), but also by the connection drawn between the dustmen and that symbol of trickery and deceit in the novel, Harlequin: 'He was an energetic young man with laughing eyes and a mop of curly hair', Chatwin writes. 'He performed his task with an air of cheerful bravado. The light lit his face into an orange mask' (122).[5] One cannot help but recall the narrator's admission early in the novel that his work was originally to concern the psychopathology of the collector – sparking the suspicion that this intention has led him to manipulate the facts to this end.

Ultimately, the true fate of the collection – like that of the Golem – remains a mystery.[6] However, the facts of the disappearance of the porcelain and the second marriage do appear to imply that the love between Utz and Marta has successfully negated the collecting impulse – wherever the porcelain ended up. In the light of their love, the collection became, in the narrator's version of events, 'bits of old crockery that simply had to go' (126). Such a conclusion mirrors that of The Songlines, of course; in both of these last two works the central characters are saved from their restless isolation by the emotional power of human affection. Arkady renounces his dusty, book-lined bachelor pad in Alice Springs for Marian, whilst Utz appears to forsake the companionship of his porcelains for the real love of Marta, his true Columbine; a conclusion which appropriately posits Utz, who keeps both the narrator and the reader guessing beyond the end of the novel, as Harlequin: 'And Harlequin ... The Harlequin ... the arch-improviser, the zany, trickster, master of the volte-face' (94).

As well as shielding him from the real world, Utz's figures offered a consolatory defence against mortality. The formula for porcelain, Utz informs the narrator, emerged from the work of the alchemists of Augustus the Strong. In Augustus's court, alchemy was not undertaken as an avaricious pursuit, Utz asserts, but rather was motivated by the promise of discovering the 'substance of immortality' (90). Utz believes that 'the manufacture of porcelain was an approach to the Philosopher's Stone' (92); his collection is thus a means of shoring up against the future.

Such belief in the power of the collection to transcend death can be seen evidenced in Bruce Chatwin's final months. In June of 1988, he wrote to Gertrude Chanler, Elizabeth's mother, that:

> I have been buying your daughter the beginnings of an art collection which I hope will be wonderful.
>
> In New York we bought the wax model for Giovanni da Bologna's Neptune which has to be one of the most beautiful small sculptures in existence. We are making arrangements to give it to the Bargello in Florence with the use of it in our life times. We also bought an incredible German drawing of the mid fifteenth century. (US 512)

Chatwin engaged upon the establishment of this collection – to be titled the 'Homer Collection' after Homer End, the Chatwins' home in the Chilterns – with great zeal; accounts record him racing along the pavements of Central London from dealer to dealer, making money-no-object purchases which, later, had to be returned by family and friends. In an eerie instance of art becoming life, Chatwin had adopted the characteristics of his most recent protagonist.

He was suffering from hypomania, brought on by his illness; a condition which has the tendency to exacerbate traits of personality, as well as inducing frantic enthusiasm and energy. Michael Ignatieff, after visiting Chatwin at Homer End at this time, wrote to him of his impression of the effects of his friend's mental state:

> [Y]ou are in the grips of something, mastered by something, a fever, a conversion, an intoxication, I don't know what to call it, that is forcing its pace on you, forcing you to accelerate, to struggle breathlessly behind it, chucking away your life behind you as you pursue it. Over everything you said there was the image of Time running, running, and you at your wit's end to catch up. ...
>
> I'm not sure it is among the offices of friendship to convey my sense of foreboding & disquiet at how I saw you. I may just be expressing a friend's regret at losing you to a great wave of conviction, to some gust of certainty, that leaves me here, rooted to the spot,and you carried far away. In which case, I can only wave you onto your journey. (qtd. in US 513–14)

Yet, despite – or perhaps as a result of – the pernicious physical and psychological effects of his illness, Chatwin's literary ambitions were unchecked. Astonishingly, given that he had first become seriously ill during the completion of *The Songlines*, he managed to complete work on one further book after *Utz*; the collection of writings, *What Am I Doing Here* (the question mark omitted for – what else – aesthetic reasons).

In addition, he had begun to plan his next novel; it was to be an expansive work, split between three countries, focussing on an emigré artist. The title was to be *Lydia Livingstone*. Chatwin related his plans for this long novel – which Redmond O'Hanlon has called his 'real dream' (104) – in detail to Tom Maschler, and to his wife Elizabeth, who recalls some of the details:

> He had this plan for a Russian novel which was based partly on an artist he met in New York who had used an American woman to get to New York. I knew it was based on this French-American family, and the father wanted to take them out of France as the war was about to begin – the Germans were about to invade. And that was the very beginning of it and they didn't go – he perhaps went, but they didn't go – and he then never lived with the mother again … I don't know where the artist came in – I just know that it had that beginning when the Germans were about to roll in to Paris. (2007)

O'Hanlon recalls a conversation – his last with his friend – which testified to Chatwin's eagerness to begin, his ambition for Tolstoyan narrative plainness, and his intact sense of humor:

> 'Just for now, Redders, I can't hold a pen. It would be ridiculous to start yet, and I hate dictation. But the moment I'm better I'll begin that Russian novel. It's going to work. I can see almost all of it. No tricks!'
>
> His grin gave out in a burst of coughing. As I left, the sun bright on the walls, I took his hands in both of mine. A thought struck him, and he gave a snort of laughter.
>
> 'Redders! Your hands – they're so soft I don't believe you ever go anywhere. You just lie in bed and make it up.' (106–7)

The enticing, scant details of *Lydia Livingstone* suggest that the work was perhaps to mark a move away from Chatwin's previous preoccupations. Such an inference is encouraged by Chatwin's last notebook, where one finds jottings for another possible project – to be called *The Sons of Thunder* – which seems similarly to mark an engagement with new subjects. The title[7] is taken from Mark 3:17 and relates to the name bestowed by Jesus upon the disciples James and John. 'That's it', Chatwin wrote. 'Now I know where to start. The title can be everything' (Box 34). Chatwin noted with certainty: 'It's decided then. I will if I get the strength, write about healing' (Box 34). The subject of *The Sons of Thunder* was seemingly to be of that power bestowed upon the disciples to drive out illness:

3: 14 And he ordained twelve, that they should be with him, and that he might send them forth to preach,
3: 15 And to have power to heal sicknesses, and to cast out devils. (Mark 3: 14–15)

It was a project which had found its inspiration in Chatwin's recent conversion to Greek Orthodoxy. In 1985, he had realised a long-held ambition to travel to Mount Athos, the mountainous peninsula which is one of the seats of orthodoxy. It was a journey undertaken in the footsteps of his hero, Robert Byron, who had written of his 1926 trip to the holy mountain in *The Station*. Whilst there, Chatwin experienced an epiphany apparently inspired by the sight of a rusted metal cross on a small outcrop. Elizabeth comments of his conversion: 'I suppose because he was a researcher, and because he always went to the ends of everything else, he found you'd go back to the beginning; you'd go back to the Greek Orthodox church. He couldn't even talk about it, really ... He said "I had no idea"' ('Chatwinesque').

In 1988, Chatwin made plans to return to Athos for reception into the Orthodox faith. He was, however, too unwell to undertake the journey, though his religious belief remained a powerful internal conviction until the end of his life. It is perhaps unsurprising that Chatwin had, as his life drew towards its end, experienced a conclusive religious conversion. For, as he wrote in *What Am I Doing Here*: 'My whole life has been a search for the miraculous' (282).

NOTES

1 A dichotomy manifest in the different accounts which exist of Chatwin's time in the Sudan. Depending on audience, the stated effect of his journey oscillated between wholesale renunciation of materialism and, as shall be seen later, an aestheticised version of the nomadic model.
2 The idea of the *Wunderkammer* will recur, of course, in *Utz* itself, both in the original example owned by Rudolf II and the mirror-backed glass cabinets which line Utz's apartment, which can themselves be seen as an extrapolation of Chatwin's own reconstructions.
3 It is also reminiscent of the work and life of Ernst Jünger; one of its key themes is the aestheticism of the far right.

4 *Tod* is the German word for 'death'.

5 At the village where the narrator goes to meet the dustmen, two of his friends are also portrayed in the model of the Harlequin: 'He took me to the bar where his friends, in overalls of orange and blue, were knocking back tankards of Pilsen beer' (123).

6 Rudolph Just's collection also went missing after his death in 1972; Chatwin believed at the time of writing *Utz* that the collection had been destroyed. However, two Sotheby's dealers, Sebastian Kuhn and Filip Marco, managed to track down the pieces, which, since Just's death, had become a true burden to the family, even leading to the murder of Just's grandson by criminals intent on stealing the collection. In the 17 October 2001 edition of the *New York Times*, the paper's correspondent, Alan Riding, reported that the collection had been found, more or less intact, in a fifteenth-floor apartment on a Bratislavan housing estate. The pieces were to be auctioned at Sotheby's that December, and the whole collection was expected to fetch $1.45 million for the family.

7 The title is a translation of the biblical *Boanerges* which, in a strange point of connection, was also the name given by T.E. Lawrence to his Brough Superior SS100 motorcycle.

Conclusion
A mythology for every man

You may paddle all day long; but it is when you come back at nightfall, and look in at the familiar room, that you find Love or Death awaiting you beside the stove; and the most beautiful adventures are not those we go to seek. (92)
Robert Louis Stevenson, *An Inland Voyage*

[E]very poet has his private mythology, his own spectroscopic band or peculiar formation of symbols, of much of which he is quite unconscious. (11)
Northrop Frye, "The Archetypes of Literature" in *Fables of Identity*

Bruce Chatwin died on 18 January 1989 in a hospital in Nice. He had reached the point in his own life that had so frequently formed the subject of his elusive and grand theories, returning from a career of wandering to die at his appointed time. He was young – only forty-eight – but, as he wrote in *The Nomadic Alternative*, one's quality of life is not strictly determined by the number of years lived: 'The aim is to live out each stage to the full, and it is immaterial whether the life journey takes fifty or a hundred years to complete' (224).

Chatwin became one of the first high-profile victims of Aids, though, ever the aesthete, he preferred to attribute his illness to a rare fungus of the bone marrow picked up, he variously argued, either from Chinese peasants, a 1,000-year-old egg, or the carcass of a dead whale. Whilst this was not pure invention, as some have claimed – Chatwin had indeed become the victim of a rare fungus – he was only susceptible to its onslaughts as a result of the underlying immunodeficiency that ultimately killed him.

It was only after his death that the true cause of his illness became widely known;[1] for a time it became, in Elizabeth Chatwin's words, 'the only thing he was known for' (*Footsteps*). Some criticised his reticence in confessing to his illness, whilst Duncan Fallowell went so far as to suggest he should have addressed the subject in his writing: 'Aids and the prowling death gave Chatwin the opportunity to write an extraordinary book', he wrote in an article for the *Guardian*. Chatwin's sexuality and illness became the last of a long list of subjects which he was chastised for disregarding in his work. As Elizabeth observes, however, for anindividual as personally reticent as Chatwin, such revelation was hard: '[T]his was a denouement, and he didn't like it' (*Footsteps*).

His death at forty-eight ensured that the books which remain to be read and studied are those of a writer who was still developing. He did not survive to embark upon the second act of his writing life. His peers – including Salman Rushdie, Ian McEwan, Julian Barnes, Martin Amis and Paul Theroux – have gone on to become leading figures in the literary world; whether Chatwin would have matched – or even exceeded – them is just one of many questions his death left unanswered. Tom Maschler is in little doubt: 'Of what I call "my lot" – Ian McEwan, Martin Amis, Julian Barnes, Salman Rushdie – Bruce was the one I was most anxious to know where he was going to go. I think had he lived he would have been ahead of all of them' (qtd. in *US* 7), he told Nicholas Shakespeare.

In recent years, however, there has been some commentary concerning a perceived falling-off in Chatwin's reputation and popularity; William Dalrymple, in an admiring review of *Under the Sun* in the *Times Literary Supplement* commented that 'the pendulum of fashion has swung against Chatwin, and it is now decidedly unhip to admire his work', whilst Blake Morrison asked in the *Guardian*: 'Does anyone read Bruce Chatwin these days?'

In many ways, a slide into unfashionability would have appealed to Chatwin, whose own admiration always gravitated to the forgotten and obscure; many of his favourite twentieth-century writers – such as Mary Webb, Ernst Jünger and Sybille Bedford – experienced a critical and popular diminution subsequent to their deaths. Yet, outside of the literary commentariat, there seems scant hard evidence to back up any claim that his popularity has diminished abnormally for an author who has been dead for nearly a quarter of a century. His work remains well read, particularly in continental Europe, where his popularity exceeds that of the majority of his contemporaries and where, in Italy, a festival is organised each year in his honour. His books continue to be regularly reissued, the initial publication run of *Under the Sun* sold out within weeks of its publication, whilst *In Patagonia* has even been accorded the honour of being published in the United States as a Penguin Classic.

His work has also become profoundly influential. A new generation of writers cite Chatwin as an inspiration, amongst them Robert Macfarlane, Rory Stewart, Richard Grant, Andrew Harvey and William Dalrymple. Robert Macfarlane, author of *Mountains of the Mind* and *The Wild Places*, comments: 'Chatwin was certainly an influence on me. The discovery of my grandfather's book in the opening pages of my first book [*Mountains of the Mind*], which sets me off (via a Narnian wardrobe) on a quest of a kind, through landscapes imagined, historical and real, was designed in part as a nod to Uncle Charlie's scrap of skin.'

That his literature continues to be both influential and well read is, of course, a primary consequence of the inherent formal qualities of his work. His prose style was inimitable and atypical of the period, its brevity contrasting the prolixity of many of his contemporaries. His short sentences compressed detail and time, paring away irrelevancies to preserve an essential meaning. Similarly striking, in an age of confession and self-reflection, was his depersonalised approach to his subject and himself; he remained, throughout his life, a disciple of the Flaubertian school of self-abnegation.

However, perhaps most significant amongst his literary qualities was his alchemical ability to transform and inhabit the form in which he worked, be it the novel, the newspaper article, the biography or the travelogue. Of course, Chatwin's work was not *sui generis*; his method and style were influenced by many writers: Flaubert was an eternal touchstone, as was Hemingway. Chatwin himself wrote in *What Am I Doing Here* of D.H. Lawrence's influence and, for 'bleak passages', that of Henrik Ibsen (*WAIDH* 366). In the same essay, however, Chatwin mentions the advice given to him by Noel Coward at a dinner party held by Anne Fleming: 'Never let anything artistic stand in your way' (366), he told the young author. Chatwin's work clearly conveys the influence of this gnomic statement; he was never a writer whose art was corralled by the strictures of literary form, fashion or period. Chatwin wrote the books he wished to write; one need only glance at the *From the Notebooks* section in *The Songlines* to perceive the iconoclasm of his literary approach. The novel and unusual aspects of his writing were never self-conscious, however. Some have perceived the qualities of postmodernism in his writing; if present, their inclusion is unconscious. Chatwin was simply interested in the form which would most appropriately suit the story he wished to tell: 'He was a great, great storyteller', Werner Herzog has observed, 'like no one else I've ever seen' (*Footsteps*).

However, the specific qualities of Chatwin's literary style are at the very least matched in contemporary appeal by his association with the affliction of restlessness and the possible solutions inherent in the travelling life.[2] His connection with these ideas has become definitive of his wider public image, and has been widely referenced in popular culture from the world music magazine entitled *Songlines* to the pop group Everything but the Girl, who wrote, in their song 'One Place':

> And you know that I have found
> That I'm happiest weaving from town to town
> And you know Bruce said
> we should keep moving 'round.

However, the connection between Chatwin's public image and his preoccupation with the topic of restlessness is most strongly evidenced by the phenomenon of the Moleskine notebook. Chatwin used these notebooks for much of his life – the bulk of those found in the Bodleian are the Moleskine style.[3] His fondness for them was expressed in *The Songlines*:

> In France, these notebooks are known as *carnets moleskines*: 'moleskine', in this case, being its black oilcloth binding. Each time I went to Paris, I would buy a fresh supply from a *papeterie* in the Rue de l'Ancienne Comédie. The pages were squared and the end-papers held in place with an elastic band. I had numbered them in series. I wrote my name and address on the front page, offering a reward to the finder. To lose a passport was the least of one's worries: to lose a notebook was a catastrophe. (160)

However, in an aside which resonates with the general sense of conclusion attendant upon *The Songlines*, he recounts that he had become unable to source them from his usual stationers: 'The manufacturer had died', Chatwin wrote. 'His heirs had sold the business. She removed her spectacles and, almost with an air of mourning, said, "Le vrai moleskine n'est plus"' (161).

The brand was resuscitated in 1998 by an Italian company who fashioned their version after Chatwin's description. The firm now sells millions every year. Chatwin is employed in the promotion of the notebooks – they are sold as the pad of choice for Hemingway, Picasso and Chatwin – and trade on his reputation as a restless creative nomad:

> Following in Chatwin's footsteps, Moleskine notebooks have resumed their travels ... Capturing reality in movement, glimpsing and recording details, inscribing the unique nature of experience on paper: Moleskine

notebook is a battery that stores ideas and feelings, releasing its energy over time. ...
They represent, around the world, a symbol of contemporary nomadism.
('History – Moleskine.co.uk')

The image these cultural phenomena reference undoubtedly emerged in part from the extrinsic material of Chatwin's career: the publicity, the photographs, the biography, the memoirs. However, as has become clear from the preceding study, the theme of restlessness pervades Chatwin's oeuvre – and it is as a result of his consistent engagement with the subject that the myth has sustained and thrived.

The preceding chapters of this work have detailed the specifics of Chatwin's diverse manner of approach to the subject of restlessness. It is, however, appropriate at this juncture to return to the articulation of a more holistic view of his treatment of the theme.

The overall significance and importance of Chatwin's work is not that it offers a premeditated and clearly explicated theory of restlessness. Rather, it builds a sense of the concept through repeated invocation, in both a descriptive and explanatory manner, setting up what has been succinctly defined by John Verlenden as 'a lyrical mythos. This mythos combines anti-materialism with the idea of wandering to produce a potent metaphor for the better life.' The great value and appeal of this construction is found in the sense of inclusiveness it conveys, suggesting to the reader that their individual struggles and frustrations are part of some grander scheme. This idea relates to both the author's theoretical dealings with the topic of restlessness, and his character-based depictions. In Chatwin's characters, the reader sees their own frustrations and anxieties reflected back, providing the solace of communion with a more romantic literary version of the self, whilst the author's theoretical vision presents the argument that the individual feeling of malaise with domestic and sedentary life is not, as it may seem, some prosaic and minor side-effect of settlement, but rather results from a genetic impulse derived from our evolution as a species. Chatwin dresses up our most prosaic dissatisfactions and offers them as proof of our humanity.

The wider cultural impact of this 'lyrical mythos' has been profound. The arguments of Chatwin's work propose peripatetic existence as a main solution to the anxieties and frustrations of life, and have correspondingly contributed to the prevailing internationalist spirit of contemporary Western culture. As Richard Taylor has observed, Chatwin's work prompted a generation to 'break loose and roam the planet. The Chatwin nomadic itch has inspired many to take-off, despite the fierce umbilical pull of "shuttered rooms" in houses filled with stress-filled belongings that tie people down' (61). Chatwin has become an emblem of a certain means of existence, a high priest of restlessness: 'The whole of Chatwin', writes John Verlenden, 'is a How-to book for disgruntled, would-be money culture dropouts'.

Such influence would have almost certainly displeased the author. In a letter to Elizabeth from Afghanistan in 1969, Chatwin wrote: 'I am fed to the back teeth by the happy hippie hashishish culture, (jail is the answer)' (*US* 145). Chatwin's work, as has been seen, treats restlessness as an 'affliction', despite the noted ambivalence of the definition. This affliction is cured by the profound spiritual effect of travel, which he saw in terms close to its etymological source in the French 'travail': 'It means hard work, penance and finally a journey', he told Michael Ignatieff. 'There was an idea, particularly in the Middle Ages, that by going on pilgrimage, as Muslim pilgrims do, you were reinstating the original condition of man. The act of walking through a wilderness was thought to bring you back to God' (1987: 27). Travel for Chatwin has a profound and metaphysical aspect that is absent from modern, hedonistic journeys. Yet, irrespective of Chatwin's reservations – or the identified limitations and idiosyncrasies of his theories – his work offers the reader something of profound value. His writing cathartically articulates a simple desire, oft expressed, yet rarely acted upon – to be elsewhere.

NOTES

1 It was revealed shortly before his death by the newspaper *Today*, though most obituaries referred solely to the fungus.
2 This influence is manifest in the list of authors presented above; all of those who cite Chatwin as important to their work are writers whose primary preoccupation is with the topic of travel.
3 Chatwin's notebooks were, however, substantially less plush than those now manufactured in his name, with far shinier, less robust covers and thinner sheets of paper. The development can be seen to reflect the change in usage – from a writer's tool to a mark of status.

Appendix 1

BRUCE CHATWIN

Papers of Bruce Chatwin

N.B. The box/item numbers in the following list are *temporary* numbers. Reference to individual items should be made in the form 'Bodleian Library, Oxford, Bruce Chatwin papers, *temporary* box no. ·', together with a description of the item (e.g. letter from J.R. Smith to A.N. Other, with the date).

The papers consist of 40 boxes, mainly notes, drafts, manuscripts and typescripts of literary works. Deposited by Mrs Elisabeth Chatwin, 1990. Some of the papers were formerly stored by Chatwin in Bertram Rota's warehouse - see separate lists, attached.

Not available to readers until 2010.

Boxes 1-37. Literary Papers

Boxes 1-29	are alphabetically arranged by title of book.
Boxes 1-8.	In Patagonia
1.	Working papers (photocopies)
2.	Files: a. 'Idle Days in Punta Arenas'; b. 'Fireland'; c. 'Charlie Milward'; d. 'Charlie the Sailor'; e. 'The Kingdom'
3.	TSS - fragmentary
4.	TS - 'first draft'
5.	TS - printer's copy
6.	Notes, letters, fragmentary TSS
7.	Notes and proofs
8.	Letters, reviews, miscellaneous
Box 9.	On the Black Hill - amended TS
Boxes 10-12.	'Nomads'
10.	Notes - 'Good Nomad Stuff', etc.
11.	TSS (fragmentary) and notes
12.	TS and notes
Poxes 13-16.	Songlines
13-14.	Notes
15.	TS - 'first draft' (photocopy)
16.	TS (photocopy; 1987 note)
Box 17.	Utz

Appendix 2

TSS - two, with photocopy of page proofs

Boxes 18-26. The Viceroy of Ouidah

18.	Notes: a. 'Africa'; b. 'Ouidah'; c. 'Konrad Lorenz'
19.	Notes and working papers; publisher's agreements
20.	TSS - three 'Skin for Skin' versions
21.	TSS - two (carbon and top)
22.	TS (S) - pp. 1-92, 92-186
23.	TSS - partial, fragmentary, and an outline of the book
24.	TSS - partial, fragmentary, and a photocopy of an article concerning the slave trade
25.	TS - from blue binder
26.	TS - complete (printer's copy) and page proofs

Boxes 27-9. What Am I Doing Here?

27.	MSS and TSS
28.	Text made up from MSS, TSS, photocopies of printed essays
29.	TSS - two, with MS fragments and photocopies of MS fragments
Box 30.	'Miscellaneous Writings'

Boxes 31-5. Notebooks

Note: Boxes 34-5 contain the black (later) notebooks

Boxes 36-7. Index cards

Boxes 38-40. Miscellaneous Papers

Box 38.	Correspondence concerning the 1989 Sotheby sale of Chatwin papers; and miscellaneous oddments
Box 39.	Miscellaneous papers: a. four magazines (2 *New Yorker*, 1980; *New York Review of Books*, 24 Sept. 1987; *Sunday Times* magazine, 27 Aug. 1978); b. financial correspondence (mainly tax); c. two letters [one imperfect]
Box 40.	China figurine: 'I am starting on a long journey'
Boxes 41-2.	Material purchased from Sotheby sale, 1991 41 = #s 1-15; 42 = #s 16-28. (Each item is listed within each box).

A Bruce Chatwin bibliography

It may seem obvious to the point of banality to observe that Bruce Chatwin was a voracious reader, yet there have been few significant writers of the last century whose breadth and diversity of reference could match Chatwin's. He was referred to by John Updike as the 'demon researcher' (128) for good reason; Elizabeth Chatwin recalls once finding 50 books by his bedside whilst tidying, all of which were being read simultaneously: '[H]e could never go past a book store', she comments. 'It was just a total fascination' (2010). His wide-ranging reading habits bred a seemingly inexhaustible knowledge base; Salman Rushdie has referred to him as 'probably the most knowledgable person amongst my contemporaries that I ever met' (*Footsteps*). His references sometimes eluded his friends, however; Redmond O'Hanlon recalled an early morning conversation with Bruce in which Bunin[1] was mentioned; after Chatwin had rung off, O'Hanlon began 'wondering who or what Bunin was: with Bruce you could never be sure. The new Stravinksy from Albania? The nickname of the last slave in Central Mali? A lighthouse-keeper from Patagonia? Scroll 238B from a cave in the Negev? Or just the émigré King of Tomsk who'd dropped in for tea?' (103).

Bruce's library remains more or less intact at his home in Oxfordshire, though some significant volumes were given away to friends. It is a sizable collection; taking up two long walls of floor-to-ceiling shelving in his study, as well as various bookcases dotted around the house. The most common writers are European, particularly Russian: Turgenev, Pushkin, Tolstoy, Dostoevsky, Bunin, Gogol and, of course, Osip Mandelstam. The French are also well represented, often in the original language (Chatwin had intended to learn Russian in the period of remission ultimately given over to the writing of *Utz*); the works of Balzac, Proust, Maupassant (whose short stories are particularly well thumbed), Racine and Flaubert are all in evidence. There is relatively little modern fiction on the shelves (though Borges and Italo Calvino are both strong presences), and very little from the United Kingdom – D.H. Lawrence being the obvious exception. There is also a substantial amount of poetry; Ezra Pound's *Cantos* appear in various editions, as do the poems of the Alexandrian poet C.P. Cavafy. Also evident on the shelves are T.S. Eliot and, a perpetual favourite, Matsuo Basho.

What follows, however, is not intended as a definitive record of Chatwin's reading – which would constitute a monumental task. Nor is it intended as a record of his favourite works; Nicholas Shakespeare's 'A Chatwin Reading List' (2000: 579–80) in his biography is an excellent starting point for those interested in his preferences. Rather, this bibliography is intended to provide a guide to some of the books which directly influenced Chatwin's literary output, either on the level of style or subject. It is, by its nature, selective, though the section relating to *The Nomadic Alternative* is intended as more extensive, given that work's lack of public availability, and its influence upon Chatwin's later output.

The Nomadic Alternative

An Account of the Kingdom of Caubul, Mountstuart Elphinstone
The Anarchists, James Joll
The Anatomy of Melancholy, Robert Burton
Anima Poetae: From the unpublished notebooks of Samuel Taylor Coleridge, Samuel Taylor Coleridge
Aranda Traditions, Theodor Strehlow
The Art of War, Sun Tzu
Beowulf
The Buddha's Philosophy, George Francis Allen
Buddhist Monks and Monasteries of India: Their History and Their Contribution to Indian Culture, Sukumar Dutt
Bushmen and other non-Bantu peoples of Angola, António de Almeida
Che Guevara: A Biography, Daniel James
Clouds, Aristophanes
Collected Poems, C.P. Cavafy
The Dhammapada
A Discourse on Inequality, Jean-Jacques Rousseau
The Divine Comedy, Dante Alighieri
Essay on the Inequality of Human Races, Joseph Arthur Comte de Gobineau
Ethnological Studies among the north-west-central Queensland aborigines, Walter Edmund Roth
The Evolution of Man and Society, C.D. Darlington
The Flowers of Evil, Charles Baudelaire
Germania, Cornelius Tacitus
The Ghost-Dance Religion and the Sioux Outbreak of 1890, James Mooney
The Ghost in the Machine, Arthur Koestler
The Ghost of Abel: A Revelation in the Visions of Jehovah, William Blake
Gilgamesh
Inner Asian Frontiers of China, Owen Lattimore

In Search of Lost Time, Marcel Proust
Intimate Journals, Charles Baudelaire
Ishi in Two Worlds: A Biography of the Last Wild Indian in North America, Theodora
  Kroeber
*Journals of Two Expeditions of Discovery in North-West and Western Australia during the
  years 1837, 38, and 39*, Sir George Grey
Journal Up the Straits, October 11, 1856 – May 5, 1857, Herman Melville
Ladder of Paradise, Saint John Climacus
Leaves of Grass, Walt Whitman
Leviathan, Thomas Hobbes
Man the Hunter, ed. Richard B. Lee and Irven Devore
Moses: The Revelation and the Covenant, Martin Buber
Muqaddimah, Ibn Khaldun
Mutual Aid: A Factor of Evolution, Petr Kropotkin
Pensées, Blaise Pascal
Personal Narrative of a Year's Journey Through Central and Eastern Arabia (1862–63),
  William Palgrave
The Phenomenon of Man, Pierre Teilhard de Chardin
The Pilgrim's Progress, John Bunyan
The Poems of St John of the Cross, St John of the Cross
Poetic Essay on Living in the Mountains, Hsieh Ling-yün
Politics, Aristotle
Primitivism and Related Ideas in Antiquity, Arthur O. Lovejoy and George Boas
*The Pursuit Of The Millennium: Revolutionary Millenarians and Mystical Anarchists of
  the Middle Ages*, Norman Cohn
The Road, Jack London
Le Roman de la Rose, Guillaume de Lorris and Jean de Meun
The Savage Mind, Claude Lévi-Strauss
Seven Pillars of Wisdom: A Triumph, T.E. Lawrence
The Spiritual Meadow, John Moschos
Statism and Anarchy, Mikhail Bakunin
Tao Te Ching, Lao Tzu
A Thousand Years of the Tartars, Edward Harper Parker
Travels in Arabia Deserta, Charles Montagu Doughty
Urne Burial, Thomas Browne
Walden, Henry David Thoreau
The Wandering Scholars of the Middle Ages, Helen Waddell
Wayward Servants: The Two Worlds of the African Pygmies, Colin Turnbull
Wonders of the Invisible World, Cotton Mather
Works and Days, Hesiod
The Wretched of the Earth, Frantz Fanon

In Patagonia

Idle Days in Patagonia, W.H. Hudson
In Our Time, Ernest Hemingway
Journey to Armenia, Osip Mandelstam
Magellan's Voyage: A Narrative Account of the First Circumnavigation, Antonio Pigafetta
The Narrative of Arthur Gordon Pym of Nantucket, Edgar Allen Poe
Uttermost Part of the Earth, E. Lucas Bridges
The Voyage of the Beagle, Charles Darwin
The Wilds of Patagonia: A Narrative of the Swedish Expedition to Patagonia, Tierra del Fuego and the Falkland Islands in 1907–1909, Carl Skottsberg

The Viceroy of Ouidah

Almayer's Folly, Joseph Conrad
Bahia and the West African Trade 1549–1851, Pierre Verger
Bajazet, Jean Racine
Dahomey as It Is: Being a Narrative of Eight Months' Residence in That Country, J.A. Skertchly
Eugénie Grandet, Honoré de Balzac
A Mission to Gelele, King of Dahome, Richard Burton
Salambo, Gustave Flaubert

On the Black Hill

Collected Poems, Dylan Thomas
The Double: A St Petersburg Poem, Fyodor Dostoyevsky
The Fox in the Attic, Richard Hughes
Gone to Earth, Mary Webb
Kilvert's Diary, 1870–1879: Selections from the Diary of the Rev. Francis Kilvert, Francis Kilvert
Madame Bovary, Gustave Flaubert
The Nose, Nikolai Gogol
Poems, Dafydd ap Gwilym
A Shropshire Lad, A.E. Housman
The Strange Case of Dr Jekyll and Mr Hyde, Robert Louis Stevenson
Studies in Early Celtic Nature Poetry, Kenneth Jackson
Tess of the d'Urbervilles, Thomas Hardy
Welsh Rural Life in Photographs, Elfyn Scourfield

The Songlines

Being and Time, Martin Heidegger
Dialogues, Plato
The Hunters or the Hunted?, Charles Kimberlin Brain
Jacques the Fatalist, Denis Diderot
Kangaroo, D.H. Lawrence
Metamorphoses, Ovid
On Aggression, Konrad Lorenz
Songs of Central Australia, Theodor Strehlow

Utz

Fictions, Jorge Luis Borges
The Golem, Gustav Meyrink
Illuminations, Walter Benjamin
The Magic Mountain, Thomas Mann
Metamorphosis, Franz Kafka
Prague Tales, Jan Neruda

NOTE

1 Ivan Bunin, 1870–1953, was a Nobel Prize-winning Russian writer of poems, short stories and novellas. His story collection *Dark Avenues* was a particular favourite of Chatwin's.

Bibliography

Citations containing a box number refer to the Bruce Chatwin archive cited in primary sources below. In 2011, Nicholas Shakespeare and Matthew Neely completed the cataloguing of Chatwin's archive. My research obviously predates this catalogue, and hence relies upon the – extremely in-authoritative – temporary system which was established when the archive was first handed over to the Bodleian Library in 1990. This catalogue is included as an appendix. For those readers wishing to explore the archive further, the newly completed catalogue can be found at: www.bodley.ox.ac.uk/dept/scwmss/wmss/online/modern/chatwin/chatwin.html#chatwin.H.1.

PRIMARY SOURCES

Chatwin, Bruce. *Anatomy of Restlessness*. Ed. Jan Borm and Matthew Graves. 1996. London: Picador, 1997.

———. *In Patagonia*. 1977. London: Vintage, 1998.

———. Introduction. *A Visit to Don Otavio*. By Sybille Bedford. London: Folio Society, 1986. 11–12.

———. *The Nomadic Alternative*. 1972. TS. Papers of (Charles) Bruce Chatwin, 1963–89. Bodleian Library, University of Oxford.

———. *On the Black Hill*. 1982. London: Vintage, 1998.

———. *Photographs and Notebooks*. Ed. Francis Wyndham and David King. Introd. Francis Wyndham. London: Jonathan Cape, 1993.

———. *The Songlines*. 1987. New York: Penguin, 1988.

———. 'The Songlines Quartet'. *The New York Review of Books*. 19 January 1989: 50–1.

———. Temporary Boxes 1–42. Papers of (Charles) Bruce Chatwin, 1963–89. Bodleian Library, University of Oxford.

———. *Under the Sun: The Letters of Bruce Chatwin*. Ed. Elizabeth Chatwin and Nicholas Shakespeare. London: Jonathan Cape, 2010.

———. *Utz*. 1988. London: Vintage, 1998.

——. *The Viceroy of Ouidah*. London: Jonathan Cape, 1980.

——. *What Am I Doing Here*. 1989. London: Picador, 1990.

——. *Winding Paths: Photographs by Bruce Chatwin*. Introd. Roberto Calasso. London: Jonathan Cape, 1999.

Chatwin, Bruce and Paul Theroux. *Patagonia Revisited*. 1985. London: Jonathan Cape, 1992.

SECONDARY SOURCES

Asher, Michael. *Lawrence: The Uncrowned King of Arabia*. London: Viking, 1998.

——. *Thesiger: A Biography*. London: Penguin, 1994.

Balzac, Honoré de. *Eugénie Grandet*. Ed. Christopher Predergast. Trans. Sylvia Raphael. Oxford: Oxford University Press, 2009.

Bamborough, J.B. 'Burton, Robert (1577–1640)'. *Oxford Dictionary of National Biography*. Oxford University Press, October 2009. Web. 13 October 2010.

Barley, Nigel. 'The Fake with the Pert Rump'. *Times Higher Education*. 4 June 1999. Web. 15 March 2008.

Baudelaire, Charles. *Baudelaire: The Complete Verse*. Ed. and trans. Francis Scarfe. Vol. 2. London: Anvil, 1986.

Berger, Lee. R. 'Brief Communication: Predatory Bird Damage to the Taung Type-skull of *Australopithecus africanus* Dart 1925'. *American Journal of Physical Anthropology* 131.2 (2006): 166–8.

Bergman, Charles. *Orion's Legacy: A Cultural History of Man as Hunter*. New York: Plume, 1997.

The Bible. Introd. and notes by Robert Carroll and Stephen Prickett. Oxford: Oxford University Press, 2008. Authorised King James Version.

Blanton, Casey. *Travel Writing: The Self and the World*. New York: Routledge, 2002.

Borm, Jan. 'Defining Travel: On the Travel Book, Travel Writing and Terminology'. In *Perspectives in Travel Writing*. Ed. Glenn Hooper and Tim Youngs. Aldershot: Ashgate, 2004. 13–26.

Brain, Charles Kimberlin. *The Hunters or the Hunted?* Chicago: University of Chicago Press, 1981.

Bridges, E. Lucas. *Uttermost Part of the Earth*. London: Hodder and Stoughton, 1951.

Bunker, Emma, C. Bruce Chatwin and Ann R. Farkas. *'Animal Style' Art from East to West*. New York: The Asia Society, 1970.

Burton, Richard. *A Mission to Gelele, King of Dahome*. London, 1864.

——. 'The Present State of Dahome'. *Transactions of the Ethnological Society of London* 3 (1865): 400–8.

Burton, Robert. *The Anatomy of Melancholy: A Selection*. Ed. Kevin Jackson. Manchester: Carcanet Press, 2004.

Chatwin, Bruce. 'Bruce Chatwin Collects only Facts Now – and the Odd Sloth Hair'. *Sydney Morning Herald*. 15 January 1983: 32.

Chatwin, Elizabeth. Personal interview. 9 March 2007.
——. Personal interview. 18 March 2010.
Chatwin, Hugh. Personal interview. 14 July 2011.
——. 'Re: Monday – BC Literary legacy et al.' Message to Jonathan Chatwin. 30 March 2009. E-mail.
Chatwin, Jonathan. '"Anywhere Out of the World": Restlessness in the Work of Bruce Chatwin'. Dissertation, University of Exeter, 2008.
Chatwin, Jonathan, Hugh Chatwin, Katherine Maclean and Nicholas Murray. *Bruce Chatwin Remembered*. Bodleian Library, 30 March 2010. Web. 4 November 2010. www.bodleian.ox.ac.uk/__data/assets/file/0011/46982/Bruce_ Chatwin. mp3.
Clapp, Susannah. *With Chatwin: Portrait of a Writer*. London: Vintage, 1998.
——. Telephone interview. 12 February 2007.
Clarke, Robert. 'Star Traveller: Celebrity, Aboriginality and Bruce Chatwin's *The Songlines*'. *Postcolonial Studies* 12.2 (2009): 229–46.
Conrad, Joseph. *Almayer's Folly*. Harmondsworth: Penguin, 1984.
Dalrymple, William. *City of Djinns: A Year in Delhi*. London: HarperCollins, 1993.
——. *From the Holy Mountain: A Journey in the Shadow of Byzantium*. London: HarperCollins, 1997.
——. 'Letters from Bruce Chatwin'. Review of *Under the Sun: The Letters of Bruce Chatwin*, ed. Elizabeth Chatwin and Nicholas Shakespeare. *The Times*. 27 October 2010. Web. 4 April 2011.
Dalzel, Archibald. *The History of Dahomy, an Inland Kingdom of Africa*. London, 1793.
Darwin, Charles. *The Life and Letters of Charles Darwin*. Ed. Francis Darwin. Vol. 1. New York, 1897.
——. *Voyage of the Beagle: Charles Darwin's Journal of Researches*. Ed. Janet Browne and Michael Neve. London: Penguin, 1989.
Deleuze, Gilles and Félix Guattari. *A Thousand Plateaus*. Trans. Brian Massumi. London: Continuum, 2004.
Diderot, Denis. *Jacques the Fatalist*. Trans. Michael Henry. London: Penguin, 1986.
Dixie, Lady Florence. *Across Patagonia*. London, 1880.
Doughty, Charles. *Travels in Arabia Deserta: Selected Passages*. Ed. Edward Garnett. Mineola: Courier Dover, 2003.
Fallowell, Duncan. 'When Sex becomes Sin'. *Guardian*. 1 December 1989: 36.
Featherstone, Kerry. '"Everything Fitted in a Suitcase": Possessions and Nomadism in Chatwin's *The Songlines*'. *Studies in Travel Writing* 5 (2001): 83–105.
——. 'Not Just Travel Writing: An Interdisciplinary Reading of the Work of Bruce Chatwin'. Dissertation, University of Nottingham Trent, 2000.
Fitzgerald, F. Scott. *The Diamond as Big as the Ritz*. London: Penguin, 1998.
Flaubert, Gustave. *Madame Bovary*. Ed. and trans. Geoffrey Wall. London: Penguin, 2002.

——. *Salambo*. Trans. Powys Mathers. Intro. Gerard Hopkins. London: Folio Society, 1940.

Forbes, Frederick Edwyn. *Dahomey and the Dahomans*. London, 1851.

Fox, Ruth A. *The Tangled Chain: The Structure of Disorder in the* Anatomy of Melancholy. Berkeley and Los Angeles: University of California Press, 1976.

Frazer, James George. *The Golden Bough: A Study in Magic and Religion*. London: Macmillan, 1923.

Frye, Northrop. *Fables of Identity: Studies in Poetic Mythology*. New York: Harcourt, Brace and World, 1963.

Fussell, Paul. *Abroad: British Literary Traveling Between the Wars*. New York: Oxford University Press, 1980.

Gibbons, Stella. *Cold Comfort Farm*. London: Penguin, 1994.

Goldsmith, Oliver. *Poems and Essays*. New York, 1824.

Grant, Richard. *Ghost Riders: Travels with American Nomads*. London: Abacus, 2003.

Harvey, Andrew. 'Footprints of the Ancestors'. Review of *The Songlines*, by Bruce Chatwin. *New York Times Book Review*. 2 August 1987: 1+.

Hemingway, Ernest. *In Our Time*. New York: Scribner, 1958.

Hensher, Philip. 'Young Man on the Make'. Review of *Under the Sun: The Letters of Bruce Chatwin*, ed. Elizabeth Chatwin and Nicholas Shakespeare. *Spectator Magazine*. 28 August 2010. Web. 20 March 2011.

'History – Moleskine.co.uk'. Moleskine.co.uk. N.p., n.d. Web. 4 August 2011.

Holland, Patrick and Graham Huggan. *Tourists with Typewriters: Critical Reflections on Contemporary Travel Writing*. Ann Arbor: University of Michigan Press, 2000.

Hood, Stuart. 'On Translating *On the Marble Cliffs* and his visit to Kirchhorst in 1945'. *Ernst Jünger in Cyberspace iv*. John King, n.d. Web. 4 April 2011.

Hope, Mary. Review of *The Viceroy of Ouidah*, by Bruce Chatwin. *The Spectator*. 15 November 1980: 21.

Hough, Graham. Review of *The Viceroy of Ouidah*, by Bruce Chatwin. *London Review of Books*. 6 November 1980: 20.

Hudson, W.H. *Idle Days in Patagonia*. Stroud: Nonsuch, 2005.

Ignatieff, Michael. 'An Interview with Bruce Chatwin'. *Granta 21: The Storyteller*. Spring 1987: 23–37.

——. 'On Bruce Chatwin'. *The New York Review of Books*. 2 March 1989: 4.

Jacobs, Michael. *Andes*. London: Granta, 2010.

Jettmar, Karl. Review of *'Animal Style' Art from East to West*, by Emma Bunker, et al. *Artibus Asiae 34.2/3* (1972): 256–8.

Jünger, Ernst. *On the Marble Cliffs*. Trans. Stuart Hood. Harmondsworth: Penguin, 1970.

Kilvert, Francis. *Kilvert's Diary, 1870–1879: Selections from the Diary of the Rev. Francis Kilvert*. Ed. William Plomer. New York: Macmillan, 1947.

King Guezo of Dahomey, 1850–52: The Abolition of the Slave Trade on the West Coast of Africa. London: The Stationery Office, 2001.

Korte, Barbara. *English Travel Writing: From Pilgrimages to Postcolonial Explorations*. Basingstoke: Macmillan, 2000.

Lacey, Robert. *Sotheby's: Bidding for Class*. London: Time Warner, 1999.

Levi, Peter. *The Light Garden of the Angel King: Journeys to Afghanistan*. London: Collins, 1972.

Macfarlane, Robert. Message to the author. 24 September 2010. E-mail.

Maschler, Tom. *Publisher*. London: Picador, 2005.

Meanor, Patrick. *Bruce Chatwin*. New York: Twayne, 1997.

Melly, Diana. *Take a Girl Like Me: Life with George*. London: Vintage, 2006.

Meyrink, Gustav. *The Golem*. Trans. Mike Mitchell. Sawtry: Dedalus, 1995.

Miller, Karl. *Doubles: Studies in Literary History*. Oxford: Oxford University Press, 1987.

Moore, George. *The Brook Kerith: A Syrian Story*. London: T. Werner Laurie, 1916.

Morphy, Howard. 'Behind the Songlines'. *Anthropology Today* 4.5 (1988): 19–20.

Morris, Desmond. *The Naked Ape*. London: Jonathan Cape, 1967.

Morris, Jan. *The Matter of Wales: Epic Views of a Small Country*. Oxford: Oxford University Press, 1984.

Morrison, Blake. Review of *Under the Sun: The Letters of Bruce Chatwin*, ed. Elizabeth Chatwin and Nicholas Shakespeare. *Guardian.co.uk*. 4 September 2010. Web. 4 April 2011.

Moss, Chris. *Patagonia: A Cultural History*. Oxford: Signal Books, 2008.

Muensterberger, Werner. *Collecting: An Unruly Passion*. Princeton: Princeton University Press, 1994.

Murray, Nicholas. *Bruce Chatwin*. Bridgend: Seren Books, 1993.

——. 'The Wanderer Contained: Bruce Chatwin's *On the Black Hill* and Human Restlessness'. *Bruce Chatwin: His Work and Life*. New College, Oxford. 19 July 2008. Keynote speech.

Musters, George C. *At Home with the Patagonians*. Stroud: Nonsuch, 2005.

Newby, Eric. *A Short Walk in the Hindu Kush*. London: Picador, 1974.

O'Hanlon, Redmond. 'Bruce Chatwin: Congo Journey'. In *Telling Lives: From W.B. Yeats to Bruce Chatwin*. Ed. Alistair Horne. London: Macmillan, 2000.

Ovid. *Metamorphoses*. Trans. David Raeburn. London: Penguin, 2004.

Palmer, Andrew. 'Bruce Chatwin: A Critical Study'. Dissertation, University of Sussex, 1995.

Pascal, Blaise. *Pensées and Other Writings*. Trans. Honor Levi. Oxford: Oxford University Press, 1995.

Pfister, Manfred. 'Bruce Chatwin and the Postmodernization of the Travelogue'. *Lit: Literature, Interpretation, History* 7.2 (1996): 253–67.

Pilkington, John. *An Englishman in Patagonia*. London: Century, 1991.

Plato. *Five Dialogues*. Trans. G.M.A. Grub. Indianapolis: Hackett, 2002.

Proust, Marcel. *The Way by Swann's*. Trans. Lydia Davis. London: Penguin, 2002.

Racine, Jean. *Bajazet*. Paris: Flammarion, 1995.

Raglan, Fitzroy Richard Somerset. *The Hero: A Study in Tradition, Myth, and Drama*. New York: Vintage, 1956.

Riding, Alan. 'ARTS ABROAD: Stranger Than Chatwin's Fiction'. *New York Times*. 17 October 2001. Web. 24 August 2011.

Riera, Pilar Escriche. 'New Ways of Seeing and Storytelling: Narration and Visualisation in the Work of Bruce Chatwin'. Dissertation, Universitat Autònoma de Barcelona, 1995.

Rimbaud, Arthur. *A Season in Hell and Other Works/Une Saison en Enfer et Oeuvres Diverses: A Dual-Language Book*. Trans. and Ed. Stanley Appelbaum. Mineola: Courier Dover, 2003.

Rousseau, Jean-Jacques. *A Discourse on Inequality*. Trans. Maurice Cranston. Harmondsworth: Penguin, 1984.

Rushdie, Salman. *Imaginary Homelands: Essays and Criticism 1981–1991*. London: Granta, 1991.

Ryle, John. 'Nomad'. Review of *With Chatwin*, by Susannah Clapp, and *Anatomy of Restlessness*, by Bruce Chatwin. *The New York Review of Books*. 4 December 1997: 6–7.

Said, Edward. *Orientalism*. 1978. London: Routledge and Kegan Paul, 1980.

Sebald, W.G. *Campo Santo*. Ed. Sven Meyer. Trans. Anthea Bell. London: Hamish Hamilton, 2005.

Shakespeare, Nicholas. *Bruce Chatwin*. London: Vintage, 2000.

——. 'Bruce Chatwin's Journey to Mount Athos'. *The Telegraph*. 16 August 2010. Web. 20 March 2011.

——. Introduction. *In Patagonia*. By Bruce Chatwin. New York: Penguin, 2003.

——. Personal interview. 4 August 2010.

Sitwell, Edith, ed. *Planet and Glow-worm: A Book for the Sleepless*. London: Macmillan, 1944.

Skertchly, J.A. *Dahomey as It Is: Being a Narrative of Eight Months' Residence in That Country*. London, 1874.

Skottsberg, Carl. *The Wilds of Patagonia: A Narrative of the Swedish Expedition to Patagonia, Tierra del Fuego and the Falkland Islands in 1907–1909*. London: Edward Arnold, 1911.

Solnit, Rebecca. *Wanderlust: A History of Walking*. London: Verso, 2001.

Steinbeck, John. *Travels with Charley: In Search of America*. London: Heinemann, 1962.

Steiner, George. Introduction. *On the Marble Cliffs*. By Ernst Jünger. Trans. Stuart Hood. Harmondsworth: Penguin, 1970.

Stevenson, Robert Louis. *An Inland Voyage, Travels with a Donkey, The Silverado Squatters*. London: J.M. Dent & Sons, 1925.

Stewart, Iain. 'The Sincerest Form of Flattery: A Note on Bruce Chatwin's "The Estate of Maximilian Tod" as an Imitation of Borges'. *The Modern Language Review*. 96.3 (2001): 723–31.

Strehlow, T.G.H. *Aranda Traditions*. Melbourne: Melbourne University Press, 1947.

——. *Songs of Central Australia*. Sydney: Angus and Robertson, 1971.

Sugnet, Charles. 'Vile Bodies, Vile Places: Travelling with Granta'. *Transition* 51 (1991): 70–85.

Taylor, David. 'Bruce Chatwin: Connoisseur of Exile, Exile as Connoisseur'. *Travel Writing and Empire: Postcolonial Theory in Transit*. Ed. Steve Clark. London: Zed Books, 1999. 195–211.

Taylor, Richard. 'Bruce Chatwin: Walkabout in Australia'. In *Literary Trips: Following in the Footsteps of Fame*. Ed. Victoria Brooks. Vancouver: GreatestEscapes.com, 2000. 52–67.

Theroux, Paul. *Fresh Air Fiend*. London: Hamish Hamilton, 2000.

——. *The Old Patagonian Express*. London: Penguin, 1980.

Thompson, John. 'The Hero was a Slaver'. Review of *The Viceroy of Ouidah*, by Bruce Chatwin. *New York Times*. 14 December 1980: 28.

Thubron, Colin. 'Born Under a Wandering Star'. *Daily Telegraph* 27 June 1987, weekend section: 1.

Towers, Robert. 'A Novel of Pastoral Vision'. Review of *On the Black Hill*, by Bruce Chatwin. *New York Times Book Review*. 2 January 1983: 27.

Updike, John. 'The Jones Boys'. Review of *On the Black Hill*, by Bruce Chatwin. *The New Yorker*. 21 March 1983: 126–30.

Ure, John. *In Search of Nomads: An English Obsession from Hester Stanhope to Bruce Chatwin*. London: Constable, 2003.

Verger, Pierre. *Bahia and the West African Trade 1549–1851*. Ibadan: Ibadan University Press, 1964.

Verlenden, John. 'New Lyric Messiah for Money Culture Dropouts'. *Corpse.org*. Exquisite Corpse, n.d. Web. 4 April 2011.

Washburn, Gordon. Foreword. *'Animal Style' Art from East to West*. By Emma Bunker, et al. New York: The Asia Society, 1970.

Webb, Mary. *Gone to Earth*. London: Virago, 1999.

Williams, Glyn. *The Desert and the Dream: A Study of Welsh Colonization in Chubut 1865–1915*. Cardiff: University of Wales Press, 1975.

——. *The Welsh in Patagonia: The State and the Ethnic Community*. Cardiff: University of Wales Press, 1991.

Williams, Hugo. 'Freelance'. *Times Literary Supplement*. 29 November 1991: 18.

Williams, Marie. 'A Dystopian Modernity: Bruce Chatwin and the Subject in the Modern World'. Dissertation, University of Salford, 2004.

Winwood Reade, W. *Savage Africa*. New York, 1864.

Wright, Rachel. 'Literature by Foot: Travel Writing and Reportage by Novelists Graham Swift, Colin Thubron, Bruce Chatwin, V.S. Naipaul and Poet James Fenton'. Dissertation, University of Oxford, 1995.

'Yarn Spinner'. *Guardian.co.uk*. 10 April 1999. Web. 28 February 2011.

Youngs, Tim. 'Punctuating Travel: Paul Theroux and Bruce Chatwin'. *Literature and History* 3rd series 6.2 (1997): 73–88.

FILM, TELEVISION AND RADIO

'Chatwinesque'. Narr. Robyn Ravlich. *Sunday Night*. ABC. 8 February 2004. Radio.

Cobra Verde. Dir. Werner Herzog. 1987. Anchor Bay, 2004. Film.

In the Footsteps of Bruce Chatwin. Dir. Paul Yule. Berwick Universal Pictures. 1999. Television.

On the Black Hill. Dir. Andrew Grieve. British Film Institute, 1987. Film.

The South Bank Show. Dir. Nigel Wattis. London Weekend Television, 7 November 1982. Television.

Utz. Dir. George Sluizer. Viva Pictures, 1992. Film.

Index

Literary works can be found under author's names, with the exception of works by Bruce Chatwin, which can be found under their title.
Note: '*n.*' after a page number indicates the number of a note on that page.

Acheson, Nigel 77, 78
Afghanistan 27-8, 160
Africa *see* Dahomey, Mauretania, Niger, South Africa, Sudan
Aids 128
   BC's death from 155-6
Amis, Martin 156
Anatomy of Restlessness 12
'Animal Style' *Art from East to West* 21-4, 25, 30*n*.5
anti-primitivism 32-3, 41
archetype of the journey 35-6, 47, 50*n*.1, 62-4
archive *see* Bodleian archive
Asher, Michael 10-11
Asia House *see* 'Animal Style' *Art from East to West*
Australia 72*n*.2, 89, 114-17 *passim*, 125-6 *passim*, 128-31 *passim*

Bail, Murray 11, 133*n*.1
Balzac, Honoré de 147
   Eugénie Grandet 85
Barnes, Julian 156
Baslow 104
Baudelaire, Charles 4, 7, 127

'Anywhere Out of the World' 20, 141
Bedford, Sybille 156
Benin *see* Dahomey
Berger, Lee 133*n*.3
Bergman, Charles 118
Betjeman, Penelope 106-7, 109, 132
Birmingham 105-6, 111*n*.5
Bodleian archive 3, 4, 12, 31, 68, 128, 150, 158
Borges, Jorge Luis 139
Bragg, Melvyn *see* South Bank Show, The
Brain, Charles Kimberlin
   Hunters or the Hunted?, The 117-20
Brazil 5, 75, 77, 81-2, 85, 86
   erotic appeal of 77-9
Broad and Narrow Way, The 101-2
Bunin, Ivan 163, 167*n*.1
Bunker, Emma 23
Burton, Richard 10, 75, 77
Burton, Robert 7, 24-5, 127
Byron, Robert 10, 26, 27, 29-30*n*.4, 153

'Cabinet of Curiosities' 62, 136–7, 153*n*.2

Cartier-Bresson, Henri 20

Cassidy, Butch 60, 67, 73*n*.5

Chanler, Gertrude 151

Chatwin, Charles (BC's father) 10, 15, 103, 105, 124, 136

Chatwin, Elizabeth 52, 90*n*.5, 107, 122, 142, 153, 163
  on BC at Edinburgh 18–19
  on BC's illness 128, 132, 155–6
  on BC's influences 79
  on *In Patagonia* 51, 72*n*.1
  on BC's literary persona 123
  on *Lydia Livingstone* 152
  and marriage to BC 77, 106, 132–3
  on *On the Black Hill* 96, 103
  on BC's personality 49
  on BC's restlessness 8–9
  on Sotheby's 20
  on BC's taste 141
  on *The Viceroy of Ouidah* 72, 79
  on BC's writing 1, 46
  on BC's writing process 70–2 *passim*, 128

Chatwin, Hugh, 3, 13, 122
  and *On the Black Hill* 95, 105, 111*n*.5, 112*n*.8

Chatwin, Margharita 3–4, 111*n*.6, 136

Chaworth Musters, George 55

Clapp, Susannah 13, 15–16, 48, 60, 67, 71, 78, 87–8, 100, 129, 135, 137, 138
  editing *In Patagonia see In Patagonia*, editing of

Cobra Verde 89–90

collection
  Bruce Chatwin's enthusiasm for 136–8
  influence of childhood upon 143–4
  and mortality 150–1
  negative effects of 135–6

and nomadism 39, 135–6, 138

Conrad, Joseph 80, 88
  Almayer's Folly 82–3
  'A Coup' 76–7

Coward, Noel 157

Dahomey 72, 82, 86, 90*n*.1
  Chatwin's detention in 76–7, 79
  eroticism and 77, 84
  historical associations of 75–6

Dalrymple, William 156, 157
  From the Holy Mountain 128

Dart, Raymond 117–18

Darwin, Charles 41, 53, 72*n*.4

Davidson, Robyn 11

Deleuze, Gilles and Guattari, Félix 22

Diderot, Denis
  Jacques the Fatalist 122–3

Diogenes 6, 29

Dixie, Lady Florence 53

Doughty, Charles 10, 40

Eagle Stone 104

Edinburgh 18–19, 106
  influence of 20–2, 24, 142

'The Estate of Maximilian Tod' 139–42

Fallowell, Duncan 155–6

Featherstone, Kerry 147

Flaubert, Gustave
  general influence of 157
  influence on *The Viceroy of Ouidah* 79–80, 87, 91*n*.9
  Madame Bovary 79–80
  Salambo 72, 79–80

Forbes, Frederick 75

Foster, Kate 142, 148

Frazer, Sir James 50*n*.1

Frye, Northrop 155

Fussell, Paul 25–6

Gibbons, Stella
  Cold Comfort Farm 110
Golem, myth of 146, 150
Goni, Uki 50
Grant, Richard 31, 133n.6, 157
Granta 76
Gray, Eileen 51–2

Hardy, Thomas 110
Harvey, Andrew 2, 157
Hemingway, Ernest 9, 26, 78, 157, 158
Herzog, Werner 89–90, 157
Hodgkin, Howard
  The Japanese Screen 9, 138
Holland, Patrick and Huggan,
  Graham 7, 14n.3
'Homer Collection' 151
homosexuality 77
  in *On the Black Hill see On the Black
  Hill*, homosexuality in
Hope, Jonathan 100
Hope, Mary 88
Hough, Graham 88
Howells, Jonathan and George 93–4,
  99, 107, 111
Hudson, W.H. 51, 53, 55, 64, 72n.4

'I Always Wanted To Go To Patagonia' 22, 103
Ibsen, Henrik 157
Ignatieff, Michael 1, 120–3 *passim*, 131,
  132, 135, 151
In Patagonia 2, 7, 10, 14n.1, 20, 51–3,
  72, 73n.6, 73n.10, 91n.10, 113,
  137, 140, 156
  characters of 5, 49, 56–60, 125, 129
  editing of 71
  employment of quest form in 47,
  62–4
  narrative unreliability of 64–8
  narrator of 60–2, 65–6
  and *The Viceroy of Ouidah* 74, 79

writing of 68–70
Ivory, James 24, 48

Jacobs, Michael 68
Jettmar, Karl 24
Joe and Jean the Barn 109–11
Jonathan Cape 3, 25–6, 31, 51, 52, 68,
  72, 94
Jünger, Ernst 49, 153n.3, 156
  On the Marble Cliffs 94–6
Just, Rudolph 142–3, 148, 154n.6

Keneally, Thomas 130, 131
Kilvert, Francis 108
Kinski, Klaus 89–90
Korte, Barbara 14n.3

Lacey, Robert 15, 16
Lawrence, D.H. 110, 157
Lawrence, T.E. 10–11, 77, 154n.7
Lees-Milne, James 76
Leigh Fermor, Joan 46
Leigh Fermor, Patrick 21, 47, 68, 71–2
Levi, Peter 27–9
Lorenz, Konrad 33
Lydia Livingstone 152

McEwan, Ian 156
Macfarlane, Robert 12, 157
Maclean, Katherine 15–17 *passim*, 137
Mandelstam, Osip 9, 28
Marlborough 9, 15, 18, 122, 136
Maschler, Tom 25–7, 30n.8, 45–6, 72,
  152, 156
Mauretania 77
Meanor, Patrick 52
Melly, Diana 106–7, 120
Meyrink, Gustav
  The Golem 146
'Milk' 50n.6, 78–9
Miller, Karl 88, 106
Milward, Charles 62, 68, 124, 143

Moore, George 92
'The Morality of Things' 135, 139, 145
Morphy, Howard 129, 131
Morris, Desmond
    The Naked Ape 25, 27
Morris, Jan 108
Morrison, Blake 156
Muensterberger, Werner
    Collecting: An Unruly Passion 143–4
Murray, Nicholas 3, 47, 74, 75, 94,
    110

Newby, Eric 52, 124–5
Niger 48, 79
noble savage 33, 41–2
Nomadic Alternative, The 6–8, 15, 22,
    28–9, 49, 50nn.1–6, 52, 60, 63,
    74, 104, 111, 113, 120, 123, 127,
    135, 155, 164
    argument of 32–45
    bibliography for 164
    commissioning of 25–7
    existence of 3–4, 31
    influence upon later work of 47–8,
        53, 83, 102
    influence upon *The Songlines* of 48,
        114–15, 121
    proposal for 25–6
    rejection of 45–6
'The Nomadic Alternative' (essay)
    21–4
notebooks 65, 68–70
    Moleskine 12, 158–9, 160n.3

O'Hanlon, Redmond 152, 163
On the Black Hill 2, 5, 48, 49,
    85, 87, 91n.10, 92, 108–11,
    111–12nn.1–9, 113, 121, 126
    biographical influences on 100,
        103–7
    division between England and
        Wales in 100–3, 107–8

    dualism of 93
    homosexuality in 91n.6, 98–9
    and *On the Marble Cliffs* 94–6
    twins in 93–4, 96–100
    Whitbread award and 88
Ortiz, George 8, 137
Ovid
    Metamorphoses 113, 116–17

Palmer, Andrew 67, 72, 110, 121, 137
Pascal, Blaise 4, 7, 24
Patagonia
    attraction to immigrants of 53–4
    Bruce Chatwin's journey to 51–2
    emptiness of 53–4
    Welsh emigration to 54–5
Pawson, John 138, 141
Petrarch 4, 32
Pfister, Manfred 14n.3, 65
Photographs and Notebooks 12
Piggott, Stuart 18, 28
Pilkington, John 59, 64–5
Plato 25
    The Apology 122
    The Symposium 122
Prague
    Bruce Chatwin's visit to 142
    For Golem *see* Golem, myth of
Proust, Marcel
    The Way by Swann's 104

Racine, Jean 91n.9
    Bajazet 86–7
Raglan, Fitzroy Richard Somerset
    (Lord) 50n.1
Ravlich, Robyn 20
Rimbaud, Arthur 12, 127
    Une Saison en Enfer 142, 147
Rogers, Deborah 25, 45, 51
Rousseau, Jean-Jacques 33, 42
Rushdie, Salman 59, 126, 130, 132,
    156, 163

Russell, John 94
Ryder Haggard, Henry 88
Ryle, John 77, 129

Said, Edward 84
Sawenko, Toly 124
Scott Fitzgerald, F. 140
Sebald, W.G. 10, 136–7
Sethi, Sunil 87, 91n.9, 106
Shakespeare, Nicholas 1, 7, 13, 31, 48,
        52, 56, 62, 71, 73n.7, 90n.5, 117,
        124, 164
Sifton, Elizabeth 89, 127
Sitwell, Edith 127
Skottsberg, Carl 64
Solnit, Rebecca 50n.4
Songlines, The 2, 3, 6–8, 11, 91n.6,
        91n.10, 111, 113–14, 117, 131–3,
        134n.9, 137, 150, 152, 158
    characters of 125–7
    controversy and 129–131
    dialogue in 121–3
    From the Notebooks section 127–9,
        157
    narrator of 123–5
    and Nomadic Alternative, The see
        Nomadic Alternative, The, influ-
        ence upon The Songlines of
        thesis of 116, 119–20
'The Songlines Quartet' 116, 128
Sons of Thunder, The 152–3, 154n.7
Sotheby's 15–19, 29n.3, 142, 154n.6
    Chatwin's departure from 16–18,
        124
    Goldschmidt sale 16
    influence of 20–1, 137–8
    South Africa 118–19
South Bank Show, The 8, 62, 67, 103,
        111
Souza, Francisco Felix de 72, 79
Steinbeck, John 4, 8, 32
Steiner, George 95, 96

Stevenson, Robert Louis 18, 106, 155
Stewart, Iain 139
Stewart, Rory 157
Strehlow, Theodor 7, 120
    Aranda Traditions 114
    biography of 114, 130, 133n.7
    Songs of Central Australia 115–17
Sudan 16–17, 19, 136, 138, 153n.1
Sugnet, Charles 88
Sunday Times 2, 20, 48, 49, 51, 94
    Chatwin's telegram to 52, 72n.1

Talbot Rice, David 19, 29–30n.4
Tanworth-in-Arden 105
Taung Child see Dart, Raymond
Taylor, David 14n.3, 29n.1, 66
Taylor, Richard 159
Theroux, Paul 14n.7, 65–6, 70, 87,
        156
Thesiger, Wilfred 10, 66, 124–5
Thompson, John 80, 88
Thubron, Colin 20, 29n.2, 129
Toyne, Philip 129

Under the Sun 12, 156
Updike, John 99, 163
Ure, John 30n.9
Utz 2, 5, 7, 47, 49, 85, 87, 91n.10,
        126, 133, 135, 139, 143–7, 151–2
        passim, 153n.2, 154nn.5–6, 163
    inspiration for 142–3
    structure of 147–50
Utz (film) 143, 149

Verlenden, John 159, 160
Viceroy of Ouidah, The 2, 37, 48, 72,
        81–5, 89, 90nn.4–5, 91n.7, 91n.8,
        91n.10, 113
    characters of 5
    contrast to In Patagonia of 74–5
    critical reception of 88
    film of see Cobra Verde

influences on 79–80, 86–7
structure of 85–8
writing of 87–8
Vogue 83

Wales 54–5, 58, 101–4 *passim*, 106–8
    passim
Washburn, Gordon Bailey 21, 23
Webb, Mary 110, 112*n*.7, 156
Welch, Cary 9, 21
What Am I Doing Here 2, 12, 67, 89,
    152, 153, 157

Whitbread prize 2, 88
Williams, Marie 14*n*.3
Wilson, Peter 16, 18, 28, 29*n*.3
Winding Paths 12
Wyndham, Francis 49
Wunderkammer see 'Cabinet of
    Curiosities'

Yaghan Indians 41–2
Youngs, Tim 14*n*.3

Zavaleta, Jorge Ramon-Torres 49

CPSIA information can be obtained at www.ICGtesting.com
Printed in the USA
BVOW04s1743121015

421814BV00005B/27/P